Make It So

First Steps Toward The Future Federation, Today

Dave Ascoli

ISBN-13: 978-1974418381
ISBN-10: 1974418383

daveascoli@yahoo.com

*This book is dedicated to
Gene Roddenberry's vision of the future…
…and the hope it offers!*

Contents

Introduction

"Space, the final frontier. These are the voyages of the starship Enterprise. Its five-year mission: To explore strange, new worlds, to seek out new life and new civilizations, to boldly go where no man has gone before."

Ah, I remember making sure I was in front of the TV on Thursday nights to watch *Star Trek*. A whole new universe opened up for me and millions of others through the years. For me it wasn't about any of the social issues of the day, it wasn't about breaking ground by having a black woman on the bridge, or a Russian, or an Asian. It was about one thing: Imagination. I would watch an episode, usually with two or three of my brothers and my little sister, and then afterward we would play *Star Trek*. We would go out in the yard and boldly go where we had never gone before. It was a blast! A blast to watch and a blast to play.

As I look back now, I know I was definitely not alone. The concept of *Star Trek* generated several series: *Star Trek: The Original Series* (*TOS*; 1966-1969), *Star Trek: The Next Generation* (*TNG*; 1987-1994), *Star Trek: Deep Space Nine* (*DS9*; 1993-1999), *Star Trek: Voyager* (*Voyager*; 1995-2001), *Star Trek: Enterprise* (*Enterprise*; 2001-2005) and *Star Trek: Discovery* (2017 - ?), and at least ten full-length movies, not to mention an animated series, *Star Trek: The Animated Series* (1973-1974), and hundreds of books, official and unofficial—all this on the vision of Gene Roddenberry and the imaginations of those who followed in his footsteps. Why has this series and its spin-offs been so wildly popular? Perhaps because it addresses a need all humans share, a need to be important in the scheme of things, to have purpose, to be validated. In *Star Trek* we see a future that not only empowers humans, but also displays a goodness to which many of us aspire.

In most of the movies in the science-fiction genre, earth is invaded by evil aliens possessed of advanced technology and driven by a desire to annihilate us. But in *Star Trek*, the universe is not brimming with maniacal species wanting to feed on us. Furthermore, as a member of the United Federation of Planets, earthlings are even in a position of leadership, and humans have something real to offer the universe. The strength of the human race as depicted in *Star Trek* isn't in our technology or our military. It is not based on economics. The human race is defined by our unique qualities of hope and compassion and our unquenchable desire to explore and to learn. Captain Kirk and company never gave up. They always found a way to get through each week's challenge. Not by killing, not by over-powering or threatening, but by understanding, by listening, by refusing to give up. When violence occurs, it is always in self-defense, always the only choice left. And when the mission is over and the final entry of the Captain's Log is made, they continue to the next adventure. They continue to explore.

Throughout the decades of *Star Trek*, there were always glimpses of our past mistakes: pollution, hunger, poverty, and war. *Star Trek* references a World War III that pushed us to near extinction. Mr. Roddenberry portrays it as a turning point in terms of the incessant killing and warring we seem to accept today. And, of course, as a member of the Federation, Earth no longer has the petty rivalries we are living with today. In the future, we recognize that we are a part of a bigger universe and, as such we see how similar all humans are, not how different we are. The human race finally begins to get it right.

As I got older, my fascination with this future world as depicted in *Star Trek* continued, and even now I dream of that future and I believe we can get there. In fact I believe we can get there without a world war. In my mind the question is not whether such a future could happen, but how we can make it happen? This book is an exploration of that question and I would suggest that we can look to *Star Trek* as not just a possible future, but as a blueprint for how to achieve that future. What if there were no poverty, no hunger, no war, and a respectful balance with nature? Harmony! What if that was not just a dream, but also a pathway? What if we explored strange new possibilities, sought out a new way for our civilization to exist, and what if we boldly challenged how things are being done now in a way they have never been challenged before?

In order to explore this possibility, we need to know two things: where we are, and where we want to go. In part I, the first four chapters of the book, the question of where we are now is explored. Specifically, our political system, poverty, education, big business, big government, and the media are examined in some depth. The discussion in this book is exclusive to the United States. However, that is not to say it could not be adapted to extend beyond our borders.

The next question, *Where do we want to go?*, is covered in part II. No poverty, no hunger, no war, and living in harmony with our planet. What if that was our goal? What would America look like in the *Star Trek* universe? How could we use what we see in *Star Trek* to help solve our current problems and help us realize this future? The first hurdle we need to get over is to remember we are "boldly going where we haven't gone before." By definition that means we need to embrace change. What are we willing to do? What are we willing to sacrifice to get there? It will not be achieved without effort.

Throughout the different series, the challenge for our future counterparts is self-improvement. Whether that means exploring the stars, or developing new types of energy, or mastering the piano, each individual decides for himself and through his choice the community is enriched. Without the distractions of need or want, humans spend their time learning and growing. Each individual is empowered and thereby valued; growth for the sake of growth. The fundamental difference in the future is the society is driven by each individual, rather than each individual being driven by the society.

To get there will require changing our current paradigm. This change must be made individually. There is no one, no entity, no government that can make these changes for us. But we are not completely on our own. There are many specific scenes, plots and events that occur throughout the *Star Trek* universe that can provide insight into what that change might look like and offer guidance for solving the problems we face today.

As I asked earlier, what are we willing to sacrifice to get to a future of no poverty, no hunger, no war? If our goal is harmony, with civilization and nature, if the challenge of life is self-improvement, then we have to make the changes on an individual basis. This book seeks to translate what we see in the United Federation of Planets to our current situation to help us decide how to make better choices and actually solve the problems we face everyday. It's all about individual choice. In that regard we have three options: We can do nothing, we can do what we have always done, or we can boldly change and go where we have never gone before.

Part I

Chapter 1

Rediscovering the Family

The entire colony on Omicron Ceti III is happy and healthy. They seem to live in complete harmony with each other and the planet. As they welcome the landing party from the Enterprise, Mr. Spock meets an old friend who had fallen in love with him years before. Her name is Leila and she welcomes Spock. The landing party can't understand how the colonists are in such great condition and their colony is thriving, especially since the planet is being bombarded with Berthold rays, a dangerous form of radiation.

Leila offers to show them how they have survived and invites Spock to join her. Spock is taken to an unusual flower and as he leans in to take a closer look, spores are shot from the flower and Spock inhales them. The impact is immediate. No longer able to use his Vulcan training to control his emotions, he turns to Leila and begins to return her affections. He also now understands how important the spores are to the colony and the planet.

He brings some of the flowers with him as they rejoin the landing party and exposes all the members. The mission is forgotten, replaced by the overwhelming sense of pleasure and peace brought on by the spores. They infect the whole crew until only Kirk is left. Kirk is finally infected and they all agree to abandon the Enterprise and join the colony permanently. Kirk beams up one last time to get some things. In his cabin he resists the spores and displays a violent anger, which has the effect of removing their influence, and Kirk is himself again.

He devises a plan to get Spock back to normal and the two of them then work together to remove the influence of the spores on everyone. One of the final members of the colony to come to his senses was Elias Sondoval, the leader of the colony. Elias was telling Dr. McCoy how wonderful the planet was just before they both regained their senses. As soon as the effect of the spores wore off though, the discussion changed. Elias looked around and said, "We've done nothing here. No accomplishments, no progress. Three years wasted. We wanted to make this planet a garden." McCoy told him he couldn't stay on the planet. The spores were the only way to survive the Berthold rays. He told Elias that once they were cleared at the Star base, they could be relocated, depending upon what Elias wanted. Elias responded, "I think we'd like to get some work done. The work we started out to do." All the colonists were beamed up and, once again, Captain Kirk had saved the day ("This Side of Paradise," *Star Trek*; S1, E24).

The spores solved the immediate threat of the Berthold rays, allowing the colonists to begin settlement on a beautiful planet with plenty of resources. They built roads and homes. They raised crops and developed a peaceful community, taking only what they needed and respecting the environment. All the colonists seemed happy and satisfied. The landing party's first response was admiration, and rightly so. By all appearances it was a perfect society.

However, from Elias's perspective they had "wasted" their time. They went through each day completing tasks and going through routines that sustained them, but did not challenge them. Moreover, it was not a lifestyle of their choosing. The spores bestowed it upon them. That is the fundamental difference between us and our future counterparts. They are driven from within to strive for more, to continually challenge themselves. Our future counterparts need self-fulfillment and are unwilling to settle for anything less.

In psychological terms this is referred to as self-actualization.

Humans who are self-actualized seek to fulfill their full potential. They seek to integrate the "real self" with the "ideal self" to become a fully functioning human being in control of their own destiny. This notion has been developed by a psychologist named Abraham Maslow. According to Maslow's theory, self-actualization cannot be reached until other, more basic needs are met. He places them in a priority in which physical needs are first: food, water, shelter, and clothing. Then, safety needs: personal and financial security/stability. Love/belonging needs: family and friends. Esteem: self-esteem/respect. Lastly, self-actualization: internal motivation to strive to achieve one's potential. These different needs are referred to as Maslow's Hierarchy. (Refer to the following figure.)

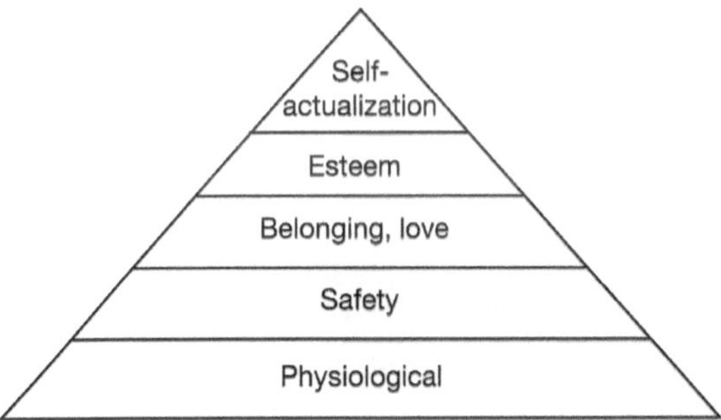

In the world of *Star Trek* each individual is self-actualized. This means they cannot be happy living a life that prevents them from reaching their full potential, or from making their own choices. That is why Elias said his colleagues' time was wasted. It is not that the colony was without merit, but that it was not of their own choice. In a society of self-actualized citizens all that is required is the ability for each citizen to have the liberty to make choices. Under these conditions, each individual will strive to improve and, thus the community at large will thrive. This has huge implications for how a government would be structured and practiced.

Applying Maslow's Hierarchy to a self-actualized society would mean, by definition that everyone's need for safety, shelter, housing, food, stability, and belonging has been satisfied. Everyone has financial security. Everyone has a positive self-image. The government of those people would be vastly different from the government we are familiar with today. If we want to build a society like that, we must address these lower-level needs first.

Perhaps our biggest barrier, and biggest challenge, to reaching this goal is poverty. Poverty is the opposite of opportunity and it can lock people out of a society, giving them little chance to achieve. Even worse, it removes the ability of those individuals to make choices for themselves. Unlike our society today where we create poverty and then expect our government to structure policies to help support those in poverty, the society of the future incorporates the old adage, "An ounce of prevention is worth a pound of cure," into its planning and creates a society that doesn't breed poverty.

While we may not be deliberately breeding poverty, like the spores our short-term approach to poverty is causing a long-term side effect that prevents our society from evolving into one in which the citizens are self-actualizing. We have learned to accept our society's notion that the best way to help those in poverty is to give them material support. However, while this may help in the short-term, it does nothing to address the causes of poverty. As a result, poverty has become institutionalized.

In an effort to help, we keep repeating the same practices that perpetuate the problem. And, like the colony on Omicron Ceti III under the influence of the spores, we see no other way. We don't even think about it. We don't see a problem and until we do we will do nothing to fix it. We have created a poverty class who are destined to feel useless, unable to be in control of their own destiny.

Our education system is one of the root causes of poverty. I will address this in the next chapter. This discussion will focus on how we might change policies to help break the cycle of poverty using what we see in *Star Trek* as a guide. Like the example with the spores, removing challenge and free choice from individuals is central to this discussion. It prevents individual growth, and can result in societal atrophy.

In "The Caretaker" (*Voyager*, S1, E1), when Captain Janeway is talking to the Caretaker about the people on the planet, she tells him, "It's the challenge of surviving on their own that helps them evolve." In that episode we also learn that the OKampa (the name of one of the races of beings on the planet), actually lost abilities they once had because the Caretaker started taking care of them.

The message from both of these episodes is very clear: empowerment is of vital importance to human beings. Individual challenge and individual participation is essential for a society to progress. Using this message as a guide, how might we find a way to help those in poverty who are currently locked out of the system, without causing the long-term effect of societal atrophy?

Obviously, the individual who is stuck in poverty struggles with lower self-esteem and often a loss of dignity. Being faced every day with a sense of uselessness is a tough, painful way to go through life. Not having a job or a sense of purpose encompasses a lot more than not having income. It can eat a person up from the inside, leading to depression, a sense of helplessness, alienation and even anger. These are strong emotions that can scar a person for her entire life. Moreover, in terms of Maslow's Hierarchy these people are the furthest from self-actualization because they are struggling to meet their most basic needs.

It is important to recognize that poverty is not just about money, it is about human dignity. Prolonged poverty can lead to disenfranchisement from the society at large. This places a burden on everyone. Any society risks implosion when it is unable to provide a culture of participation and a sense of belonging for all its members. First there is the issue of helping those who can't participate. Then there is the issue of combatting the fallout from those members who feel they don't belong. Sometimes this fallout leads to violence.

The need to help those who can't participate impacts economic policies, and the need to create a sense of belonging impacts social polices. To the extent a society spends time and resources on these issues, social growth is necessarily limited, and the culture may begin to fracture.

In today's America we are debating this issue every day. While average Americans deal with the reality of poverty, politicians fight over who controls policy, and they differ in their ideas about the causes of the problem and about what the solutions should be. Solutions are usually narrowly defined by specific conservative and progressive agendas, which, because they are often ideologically opposed, result in little being done. Unfortunately, as they debate the issue, we are stuck living with the reality. One of the central components of that debate and of our reality is the notion of social safety nets. While everyone agrees the notion of a safety net is important, there is great disagreement concerning how it should be defined, how it should function, and who it should serve. I am going to take a look at America's safety net and view it as our future counterparts might see it. From the future's perspective of self-actualization, the concept of a safety net would be to help those who slip to get back up and return to what they were doing. In practice, if a safety net were widely used it would suggest that something is seriously wrong.

The term "safety net" comes from the way high-wire acts use a net to prevent death. Simply looking at how, and for whom, the safety net works in a circus can offer insight on how this idea can be applied to a society. First, the high wire performer has to be trained on the ground with basic skills and an understanding of what she will be doing once she is on the wire. Then a safety net is placed under the area where the performer will practice. When she is ready, she climbs the ladder and practices. When she falls, she lands in the safety net, hops off and goes back up the ladder to try again. This cycle repeats itself. In the case of a good performer, she would be climbing the ladder fewer and fewer times while remaining on the high wire for longer periods of time. In the best case scenario, she stops needing to use the safety net altogether and a star is born.

In that same sense, a social safety net is exactly the correct approach. We train citizens—this would be called school—with the basic skills needed, and an understanding of what they will be required to do as adults in the "real world." This preparation includes skills like learning tasks and completing them successfully, being punctual, being clean, working with others, taking directions, etc.

However, everything you need to prepare for your first job, or "high-wire performance," doesn't come from school. Like our high-wire performer, to become a star you need to show improvement over time. In the real world this translates into showing initiative, having reasoning skills to solve problems, having confidence, over coming obstacles, being responsible and accountable. These traits may be addressed in the academic world, but they are born and developed initially in the home environment. Indeed, a strong family not only provides these traits, it can also provide the physiological, safety and belonging needs that Dr. Maslow talked about. A strong family plays an important role in preparing us for the "high-wire" while bringing us closer to the goal of self-actualization.

I was fortunate as a child. I had two parents and neither one of them was addicted to drugs or alcohol. They never beat or abused me. They never spent a minute in jail. They were faithful to each other and believed strongly in the family. They were involved in the community and worked hard. They taught me that I can do whatever I choose to do if I am willing to put in the time and effort. That is as true today as it was back then.

Add a strong family to a good education and young folks are ready to start "performing." More importantly, they will also have the skills necessary to overcome failures and actually improve. Long before needing to use the safety net provided by society, they will have used the safety net provided by a strong family. They will have learned how to get back up and try again. This practice of trying again develops a confidence that remains intact as the child becomes an adult and enters the world.

Once in the real world our new "performer" may slip and need help from the society at large. In that event, like our high-wire performers in training, when the social safety net is needed it is used briefly and then the individual hops off the net, climbs back up the ladder and does it again. Over time the net is never used. The performer becomes a "star." The young adult becomes successful in the work place and begins her own life.

Building a young person into a contributing community member is more likely to occur when the institutions of family and education are effective, supportive and consistent. In terms of education, there is no research that does not include a strong home-study environment and supportive parenting as vital components of a student's success. Henderson and Berla (1994) analyzed 85 studies that documented the comprehensive benefits of parent involvement in their children's education: Education is not exclusive of family and home environment.

In a sense I lived like a 24th century child. I had a strong family and a good education. I worked hard, was encouraged and my parents taught me how to move through failures (I had several) and come out stronger. As a result I have been able to have opportunities for employment as well as enjoyment.

As our family institution has weakened over the past half-century, the need for a safety net has increased. However, our policies over the past fifty years seem to have twisted the use of the term "safety net." Politicians have created policies that have no specific end-date. That is to say, they have accepted there will always be poverty and people who need help. Rather than fixing that problem, they have chosen to create a permanent "net." As such, a more accurate description of our policies would be a safety hammock, not a net. Our policies seem to be built on the notion that some people are destined for poverty, so why bother trying to climb back up the ladder? We simply provide relief to those that need it and like the colony on Omicron Ceti III we believe life is good.

Now, the comfort of a hammock is nice for a while, but there will come a time when you just want to get up and do something different. Getting relief might be helpful, but sooner or later, like those affected by the spores, there comes a time when most people want to feel good about themselves by being efficacious.

While putting food in someone's mouth today helps that individual, it does nothing to prevent future generations from being born into poverty. By ignoring the problem we now have millions of Americans without the basic skills to care for themselves and their children. Climbing the ladder just to get on the high wire is impossible, let alone actually performing on the high wire. These people are locked on the ground with nowhere to go, and they are passing their low sense of self-worth to their children and grandchildren.

I am not suggesting that out-of-work, or under-employed adults are relaxing in hammocks. But our policies over the years have resulted in relaxing our standards of what is expected from the institutions of family and education. Although we may intend to take care of those in need, like the OKampa, as a society we lose many abilities essential for growth by continuing these kinds of policies. Decade after decade, generations of failing these people have contributed to an increasing demand to meet their needs from a policy standpoint, as well as a downward spiraling of self-worth, with no end in sight for those affected. Our policies have built poverty into our culture. Our safety net is huge and we are constantly struggling to find ways to make it bigger.

Unfortunately, as the safety net expands, we are making little progress with poverty. For instance, according to the Office of Management and Budget, expenses that collectively make up what many think of as the safety net (Social Security, Income Security, Medicare/Medicaid, Health and the VA) have increased by more than 40% from 2003-2013. Moreover, these expenses (referred to as mandatory spending) are projected on a trend-line to go from 25% of the Federal budget in 1965 to 63% by 2024. According to the U.S. Bureau of the Census, the poverty rate in 1965 was 17.3% and in 2010 it was 15.1%. It doesn't seem like we are making much progress.

These kinds of results and policies would set off alarms in the society portrayed in *Star Trek*. Constant expansion of the net means something is wrong. The logical conclusion would be that these policies are not moving us closer to a self-actualized society. However, because "the spores" tell us this is the best way to express our compassion and address the issue, we think we are being helpful.

The result is we have two groups of Americans needing help: those currently locked out, and those yet to be born who are destined to be locked out unless we do something different. Any solution needs to address the short-term needs of those locked out now as well as the long-term need of changing the paradigm so that future generations will not have to suffer through this. Our future counterparts would undoubtedly build a society that prevents poverty from occurring, rather than accepting poverty as inevitable and focusing on helping those stuck there.

A basic common sense approach for solving any problem would be to identify the problem, quantify what can be quantified, define the result you're looking for, discuss and implement a solution, measure its progress, and be ready to change if you don't see those desired results. Moreover, it is important to stay focused on the problem and not personalize it. Allowing personal bias and emotions to interfere can affect the whole process.

This was a consistent approach in the world of *Star Trek*. If you're a fan or even a casual observer, you know who Mr. Spock is. He's the Vulcan science officer, the guy that doesn't do a lot of smiling, but knows all kinds of stuff. *Star Trek's* The Next Generation had Mr. Data, an android. Both of these characters provided an objective approach to problem solving. That meant they could look exclusively at the data and not be distracted by anger, fear, greed, distrust or other emotions that could influence a solution to any problem. It is this need for objectivity that is the greatest challenge to solving problems in today's America.

Progressive and conservative ideology/ideologues filter messages through their own bias, which often causes them to judge the messenger. If they don't like the messenger, the message can be lost. Because of this animosity, objectively solving problems is beyond their capabilities. To make matters worse, each passing year widens the gap between both sides thus making it more difficult to get anything done. Unfortunately, neither the progressives nor conservatives have Mr. Spock or Mr. Data.

It is also important to remember that in the 24th Century, solutions could span decades, perhaps generations. From the challenge of raising the sea floor discussed in "Family" (*Star Trek: TNG*; S4, E2), to terraforming a planet in "Home Soil" (*Star Trek: TNG*; S1, E17) we see endeavors taking well beyond the two, four, or six-year terms our elected officials have. This means that problem solving is done on a long-term basis and not influenced by re-elections. In the future, solutions to problems are determined more objectively and are not restricted by political election cycles. Although there are international efforts today that address some global problems that extend beyond election cycles, they are often influenced by the wealthy nations and are only effective to the extent those wealthy nations continue their support. This support is subject to change. In some cases very quickly.

In *Star Trek: First Contact* (1996), Commander Riker and Counselor Troi tell Dr. Zefram Cochrane that after the Vulcans made first contact, Earth began to unite in a way it never had before, and within fifty years, poverty, war and hunger were eradicated from earth. We have not had an open visit from an alien world to help unite us yet, so fifty years to solve our problems might not be enough time. We need to recognize that to fix some of the problems we see today, many who are alive today may not see the end results. This presents a challenge; we have become accustomed to instant gratification. As an electorate we seek candidates who will provide short-term solutions. This will need to change if we truly want to eradicate hunger, poverty and war.

In the future, the challenge for individuals is self-improvement, not material wealth. Since poverty, war, hunger and want no longer exist in the future, it would be logical to assume that the self-improvement we're talking about would fall under two categories: Doing less harm, or doing more good. This could apply to the individual and/or the society.

Using *Star Trek's* universe as a model our solutions should protect civil liberties and have a clearly defined notion of "due process." They should provide objective goals and means to measure those goals. They should address long-term solutions targeting the problem rather than the symptoms of the problem. Lastly, they should seek to do less harm or more good concerning the specific issue. Furthermore, if money is not required, the role of government would be quite different.

For our purposes there are two general trends that need to begin: scale down government services and taxes, and increase individual participation and empowerment efforts. To the extent that we develop a society of self-actualized, motivated and responsible citizens, success in these areas can be achieved. As our society becomes self-actualized, poverty will evolve away and be replaced by citizens with more choice and more opportunity. However, we must remember that this begins with empowering the individual, not by empowering our government.

If it is done correctly, both the services and expenses related to the safety net will be greatly reduced. It's hard to imagine that anyone is on food stamps in the 24th century, not to mention other means-tested aid. They are in control of their lives. This means the government will no longer be tied to micro-managing citizens' lives, and can more readily focus on supporting specific global projects like the Atlantis project in "Family" (*Star Trek: TNG;* S4, E2), in which they are trying to create a new continent in the

Atlantic ocean. The question becomes, what would be a logical strategy to help move us to our future?

As mentioned earlier, in terms of poverty there are two groups who need help: those currently without the skills necessary to climb out of poverty (or onto the metaphorical high-wire), and those yet to be born. Obviously, two distinct components need to be addressed: Short-term and long-term. I will address the short-term first.

Currently, we have multiple generations of unskilled citizens who define life by what they can't do. Generation after generation of children grow up knowing they will never be successful. Generation after generation of children are raised in homes where success can only be watched on TV. Miraculously, some have made it out. This, however, is not the case for most. According to the Center for Poverty Research, for every one hundred children that live in poverty through elementary school, only thirteen will make it out of poverty as an adult. The longer a child is in poverty the more likely he will stay in poverty.

There are currently adults and their children who can't speak, read or write Standard English. (For the purpose of this book, Standard English would be the spoken English that is heard on any of the franchises of *Star Trek*.) Standard English is the first necessary skill needed for most people to find a career, not a minimum wage job, a career. Slang, cursing, insults and general disrespect will have no place in the future.

In *Star Trek IV: The Voyage Home* (1986) Spock and Kirk are on a bus in 20th century San Francisco and some young guy (dressed as kind of a cross between Goth and Punk) is blasting his boom box. After being asked to turn it down by Kirk, the guy turns the radio up. The lyrics of the song at that moment are, "And I say screw you." Spock does the old Vulcan nerve pinch and puts the guy out, as well as the music. This receives cheers from the other passengers.

In other scenes Kirk describes the culture as "primitive" and "paranoid." Spock asks Kirk about Kirk's new use of swear words.

Kirk explains that in the 20th century no one listens to you if you don't use them. You can watch any version of *Star Trek* and you will see very little cussing, and virtually no name calling outside of humorous references to Mr. Spock and his pointy ears. Disagreements or arguments are not personalized and voices are not raised. Pejoratives are simply not used. There is a basic respect and genuine concern, almost to a fault.

When the Enterprise, for example, is taken over by a young human, Charlie, with incredible psychic power in "Charlie X" (*Star Trek;* S1, E3), Captain Kirk tries to keep the Thasians from taking young Charlie back to their planet, even though keeping Charlie with humans might have been dangerous and even cost lives. Kirk is genuinely concerned for Charlie's well being. As a member of today's society, I would have gotten rid of Charlie in an instant. Human interaction in the future is much different from today.

Let's try to be logical in our approach. First, if we want those who need help to be able to take part in a successful interview, there need to be jobs for which to interview. Currently jobs fall under two general categories: government and private. At the writing of this book there are about seven million unemployed adults. However, this number only reflects the numbers of people seeking employment. (This is referred to as the "participation rate.") There are another ninety million adults who have stopped looking for jobs for a variety of reasons. That brings the total to about ninety-seven million people.

To be clear, this number does not translate into the number of people suffering because they have no job, nor are they all living in poverty. This number includes younger folks living with their parents, full-time students, older folks living a semi-retired lifestyle, part-time employees, people on disability, incarcerated, or otherwise unable to work. A detailed analysis of unemployment in America is beyond the scope of this book. Suffice it to say, millions of people need help.

The number of jobs needed cannot be supported within the

government. We currently have about four million people employed by our government. (The United States government is the largest single employer on the planet.) In any case, we are looking to reduce the size of government. In the 24th century there will not be a tax system like we have today since there is no money to collect. Without a so-called "revenue stream," the size and scope of our government would drastically change. Also, with poverty gone, the need for many of the government programs we currently have (and their costly bureaucracies) will disappear. The private sector would be the logical choice for growth, but with this weak economy, opening millions of new jobs to help people today is unrealistic, especially when you consider so many jobs evolving out of existence as technology advances.

At first glance, solving the problem of employment sounds like a tall order. However, this situation could present us with a unique opportunity to address our short-term need while beginning the transition to a 24th century society where money is no longer needed and self-improvement is the challenge. Employing a strategy of empowering individuals could actually help solve current issues of poverty as well as future needs for employment at the same time.

As mentioned, the short-term group of people currently in need span several generations, from newborn to octogenarian, or older. Therefore, the solution for this group needs to be tailored for each generation. Knowing the benefits of a strong family, it would be logical to start there. Perhaps it would be easier to address the problems by looking at a fictional family.

Let me introduce you to the Smiths. Red is the oldest generation. He is seventy years old. His son, Blue is forty-seven years old. Blue has a daughter, Orange, who is twenty-two and she has just had a baby girl named Purple. The Smiths have lived in poverty, or just above poverty all of Red's life. Red did not finish high school, but found a good blue-collar job and worked hard for forty years. He is now retired. Red receives a little pension money and lives alone in a small house. Between his pension, Medicare, and social security, Red gets by. However, he doesn't see his family a lot since Blue moved to a different state years ago in search of a job.

Blue was married for a while but his wife died and he raised Orange alone since she was three. Blue finished high school but did not go to college. When his wife died, he lost his job due to depression. He's doing better now, but for the past twenty years he has drifted between jobs and is currently unemployed. He hasn't seen his daughter for a few years. She had a tough time growing up. With her father moving around from job to job, she found herself alone a lot. She fell in with the wrong group of kids at school, got into drugs and dropped out. She has also had problems with the law and spent time in juvenile detention as well as one year in prison for shoplifting. She just got released from prison and is currently unemployed. She lives in a halfway home for women. She receives housing assistance and food stamps; however, it is not enough to support her drug habit so she prostitutes herself to get by. She is looking for a permanent place to live and raise her new child.

Purple is the child of one of Orange's customers, and she has no idea who the father is. Purple was born with some congenital health issues as a result of her mother's drug habit and needs care. Although Orange does receive some care for her daughter through local non-profit clinics, this doesn't include the kind of preventive and diagnostic care that would mitigate the daily challenges Purple faces and allow her to have a more normal childhood. In short, Purple is destined for failure if something doesn't change.

The Smiths are not representative of all the millions of people in poverty and needing jobs, but they do present similarities found in many families in need of help. Under our current system of government assistance, the safety net provides individual assistance for Red, Blue and Orange…and soon Purple will qualify. There are federal formulas that are applied to each member of the family to determine what form of assistance they will be given and how much each member will receive. Unfortunately, this formula approach, while it is intended to be fair, serves to weaken the family structure.

For instance, if Orange moved in with her father, she would receive less money/fewer benefits, which could have a negative impact on Purple. The formula, well intended, becomes a one-size-fits-all approach and restricts choices that could be beneficial to some recipients. Moreover, the formula is not designed to improve anyone's situation, just accommodate it—presumably forever. When Purple comes of age and has a child, Pink, the formula will be applied to her as well.

With no specific information to cite from *Star Trek*, I am going to nonetheless make a generalization: Any Trekker, or Trekkie would tell you that problems in the future are solved, not perpetuated. With that in mind, we will look at 24th century life and use it as a model to help end the problems currently impacting millions of people today. We know the institutions of family and education are important and that empowering individuals is commonplace. In that context, let's take a look at the Smiths.

Red doesn't need a job, nor does Purple, but Blue and Orange do (at least our current system would see things that way). However, because of the age difference (forty-seven and twenty-two) the type of jobs could be very different. We would hope for a more career-oriented job for Orange. Blue probably doesn't need the same type of training/education as Orange does. Blue has had some experience, whereas Orange didn't even finish school. She also is suffering from an addiction.

What if, to begin helping the Smiths, we started with the need for a strong family? If a strong family is important, then families living together shouldn't be punished, and helping others shouldn't be defined exclusively by the amount of money they receive. Indeed, in the future there will be no money. And, if money is not involved we should design a system based on the principle of, whatever is taken, something is given in return. This is much like the Aldeans, who explain in "When the Bough Breaks" (*Star Trek: TNG;* S1, E17) that what has helped their society evolve away from jobs and money was the notion that those who take must give equally. This notion allows everyone an opportunity to participate and be valued. We need to solve the Smith's problems without spending more money.

What if the government encouraged Blue to move back with his father without either one of them losing any of their current benefits? Taking it a step further, what if Orange, and her new daughter, could also move into Red's home and not lose any of the financial assistance she is currently receiving? Immediately, a family is born, or re-born. That one single step provides significant new hope for Purple.

Now the family can begin to work together to solve their own problems. In the future people are responsible for their lives. To the extent possible our solutions to any problem need to move us in that direction as well. The question now is how can we best support the Smiths in their own efforts to improve, as well as get us closer to the kind of society we want in the future without spending any more money? The current individual assistance each member is receiving would stay in place with a condition: The Smiths need to meet monthly goals.

Orange would be the logical choice to focus on for getting a career job. She has the greatest potential for higher earnings in a career position that could span several decades. However, she needs education, counseling and training. She also needs help kicking her drug habit. If she is busy with her education, Purple will be left at home alone. If Blue gets a job, then Purple's only supervision will be her grandfather who is seventy years old. Here is one possibility of how the family can work together to solve their problems and earn credits to insure there is no interruption of money coming into the household.

First, Blue would build his own job. He would become the Family Support Agent and homemaker. He would be required to work with local drug-rehab programs and become Orange's personal support to help her kick her habit. For each month she is off drugs, points are earned. He would also receive whatever training he might need to take care of his granddaughter, Purple, while Orange gets the education/training needed to pursue a career. As Orange advances in her training/education, she receives points. Blue would also be there to help his father when needed.

Family goals would be established and shared with a local resource center. Each member would have something to strive for, some way to improve himself or herself. The goals might look like this:

- Get Orange clean and able to stay clean.

- Orange will stop prostituting herself immediately.

- Orange will complete her GED and, with help from the resource center, identify and pursue a career and the education/training needed for that career.

- Orange will complete the education/training program.

- Orange will find gainful employment (not minimum wage).

- Blue will care for Purple and prepare her for pre-school. He will get support for this from his local resource center.

- Blue will care for Red. He will get support for this from his local resource center.

- Blue will learn about healthy eating habits and how to prepare meals.

- Red will volunteer one hour a week to share parts of his history/culture at a local school.

- Red and Blue will volunteer two hours a week to work at the local resource center.

Each goal would have monthly measurements built in. These goals would be reviewed as a family with the local resource center each month to insure progress was made. All goals must show progress in order for enough points to be earned to maintain all current financial assistance. Additionally, if points are earned, Purple qualifies for the health care she needs, rather than the basic care she gets now; again, everyone gives in equal proportion to what they take.

The cost from the government would not increase, but it would not be reduced either, as it might under our current system. That could be considered a negative; however, the family is being encouraged to help each other. The main resources are being focused on the individual with the most potential to pull out of poverty in the near term. A member of the family is, in effect, working as the social worker to coordinate the efforts of the family. Blue would have much higher interest in helping his own family, than some social worker who stops by from time to time.

Purple has a grandfather and great-grandfather right in the home. Culture, tradition, and guidance become more personal and have a greater value. Supervision increases and having role models in the home will build Purple's sense of self worth. This will help build confidence for Purple as she begins her life.

In this model, one job is created immediately, and one individual is being targeted for a career position in the near term. The oldest generation of the Smith family is sharing his experiences at a local school facilitated by a teacher. All members of the Smith family participate in each member's success. This would help to build self-esteem for everyone. The final goal would be to have Purple's future child never experience poverty. All of this effort on the part of the Smith family helps provide the assistance they need now, and also focuses on eliminating the need for assistance for future generations of Smiths. This solution requires effort and sacrifice. It places family responsibility above individual rights and interests.

This solution does leave questions. It does not address possible changes in family dynamics. Orange or Blue might find a partner. It also leaves open the question of future children. It is not a perfect solution, nor is it meant to be. It is meant merely as a possible approach, an idea with which a new discussion can begin. It strives to empower, rather than merely support, those having difficulties.

Each successful month would result in growth in the family's confidence and sense of worth. This would help to change the home environment for Purple. Rather than seeing failure, she would experience success. Her family would be passing down a positive message of encouragement and self-determination, rather than despair and hopelessness.

The local resource center would simply be an organized and coordinated effort on the part of current programs such as Big Brothers/Sisters, the Salvation Army, city libraries, Americorps, Ameri-I-Can, My Brother's Keeper, etc. This collaborative effort to organize and provide resources would become very important in communities, and, as part of earning their credits, community members would volunteer for general staffing needs so that few additional costs would be incurred.

This approach obviously would require local support to define and administer formulas. Also, it needs to be flexible and capable of quick response, which means it could not be effectively handled by a federal bureaucracy. Transferring the decision making from the federal government to the local government would result in a smaller federal government. This is an added benefit of this approach, since reducing the cost of government is another goal to reach our 24th century America.

Certainly not all people who need help today would fit into a family like the Smiths. However, the notion of individuals helping each other could transfer to any type of group: friends, family, co-workers. By allowing those in need to help each other without losing their current assistance, different roles within a group could be worked out whereby each member is contributing something.

The group could be nothing more than a couple of friends moving in together, pooling their current financial assistance and helping each other. Every group would have goals, every member would have roles, and they would be responsible to each other. In effect, the national safety net would become localized to communities and families.

This is an approach rooted in the belief that everyone wants dignity and would be happy to participate in society if given an opportunity. This is what the future might look like as reflected in *Star Trek*. This is one of the reasons I love *Star Trek* so much: It's not about what is, it's about what could be.

Poverty is gone in this future. It's not gone because money is given to everyone. It's not gone because the government is supporting everyone. It's not gone because everyone is an entrepreneur. It's gone because individuals, ALL individuals, have control over their lives. They believe, each of them, that they control their own destiny. Their dreams are possible. They gladly accept the challenge of improving themselves and contribute their efforts, not for gain, but for satisfaction. Just take a look at some of the lyrics from the theme to Enterprise, by Russell Watson.

It opens with:

> It's been a long road,
> To get from there to here.
> It's been a long time,
> but my time is finally here.
> And I can feel a change
> in the wind right now.
> Nothing's in my way.
> And they're not gonna
> hold me down no more.
> No they're not gonna hold me down.

That is not the message of someone who is living day-to-day at minimum wage, or someone relying exclusively on others. This is someone who sees the future as a challenge to be conquered, not a weight to be carried, someone in control and confident.

The song continues:

> It's been a long night,
> Trying to find my way.
> Been thru the darkness,
> Now I finally have my day.
> And I will see my dream
> come alive at last.
> I will touch the sky.
> And they're not gonna hold
> me down no more.
> No they're not gonna change
> my mind.

In the future we recognize that there have been difficult times in the past, but we got through them. Dreams are no longer defined by a politician, a political party or anyone else. The individual takes responsibility for his own dream. Here is part of the chorus of the song:

> 'Cause I've got faith of the heart.
> I'm going where my heart will take me.
> I've got faith to believe.
> I can do anything.
> I've got strength of the soul.
> And no one's going to bend or break me.
> I can reach any star.

How many people living in poverty today would love to follow their hearts? How many people who currently cannot live without the government's help believe they "can reach any star"? Is it na-ive to believe we can change what we are doing today in order to help Purple's children have "strength of the soul" and "faith of the heart"; to believe they can "do anything?" Are the children living in poverty today being told how wonderful they are? Are they being encouraged every day to do their best? Are they told how important they can be to the future, or how dreams belong to them? Do they have the confidence not to let anyone, or any-thing hold them down? Are they looking forward to making their mark? By all means, there are some. But the sad fact is, children of poverty living in broken families have a very difficult time getting out. Many simply look to get through the day.

We have children having babies, we have children killing each other, we have children running away only to find themselves caught in human trafficking and becoming sex slaves. We have children growing up without fathers in homes with very little su-pervision. We have children full of doubt and fear. More often than not, these children's parents, perhaps even their grandparents, grew up the same way. We cannot waste another generation. We cannot continue to treat children as part of an equation to determine how much money the family (often a single-parent family) will receive, and then tell ourselves we're working on solving poverty.

As Captain Kirk helped the colony of Omicron Ceti III shake the influence of the spores, we must "shake" ourselves from the influence of current practices we have come to accept as rational. We owe it to the future. We owe it to the children.

Consider what we are currently doing. There are people in need in our own communities. Our current system's solution is for us to give our money to strangers in D.C., have them build offices, hire staff and develop a procedure to take our money and give it right back to our neighbors. These strangers have never met our neighbors, or us and probably never will. Their only clue as to how to help our neighbor is to read an application form our neighbor filled out and submitted.

Further understand that this application is then compared to other applications completed by needy people living in entirely different communities and, quite possibly having entirely different circumstances to deal with. Consider all the money that is being spent on building offices and hiring staff that could go directly to those in need. Mr. Spock would laugh out loud (and he is a Vulcan that controls his emotions well) at how illogical it all is. It is time to stop using our past to pave the way for our future. The past may be useful to tell us what we shouldn't do, but it should not restrict us from seeking new paths for the future.

Chapter 2

Unlearning our Education System

A young boy sits under a night sky full of stars. His parents are watching him through a window. His mother softly tells her husband that it is getting late and he should come in. Her husband agrees it is getting late but says to wait. He says to let him dream a little while longer. The boy's name is Rene and he is Picard's nephew. He is dreaming of joining Star Fleet when he gets older and traveling the stars. His father is old-fashioned. He didn't approve of his brother, Jean-Luc leaving home and joining Star Fleet many years earlier. He is not particularly happy with his son's current dreams because it would mean he would leave home for who knows how long. Nonetheless, he wants him to dream.

This final scene from "Family" (*Star Trek: TNG*; S4, E2) speaks to what we should aspire to achieve within our school system: Children should grow up with dreams of their future, dreams of their own. They should not have to worry about their safety, their health, or their next meal. They should not have to wonder if they will ever "make it out" of their current situation. They should always see the future as a place that welcomes them, not something to be feared, a place to run toward, not from which to hide.

Star Trek portrays a future of endless possibilities. There are countless references to a future of no poverty, no hunger, no want and no war. In, "The Neutral Zone" (*Star Trek: TNG*; S1, E25) three people from the 20th Century are found and later revived on the Enterprise. We discover through Captain Picard that in the future the human race has stopped obsessing over owning things; poverty and want have been eliminated. One of the individuals from the 20th Century asks what he is supposed to do, what is the challenge. Picard tells him that the challenge for people is to improve themselves, learn how they can best be a part of their world.

This is a future where people pursue self-improvement rather than possessions, where people want to learn simply for the sake of growing. They are not trying to get something from someone; they are trying to better themselves and, in turn, contribute to the greater community. Even crime would appear to be all but erased. In *Star Trek: Voyager,* two crew members, Mr. Paris and Mr. Kim, are reminiscing. Mr. Paris tells Mr. Kim about a time he was pick-pocketed in Paris, France during his academy days. Mr. Kim responds with a very surprised, "Really!" Mr. Paris explains that it was a bit of a show done just for tourists and the money was returned. He humorously adds, "Most of the time." ("The Cloud," *Voyager;* S1, E5).

This kind of society is built on a culture of education. While it would be logical to assume that school plays an important part in this learning, it would not stop there. Within a culture of education, learning would include the necessary support for learners outside of the learning environment. Whether students are in a formal classroom, or doing some kind of independent study, or research, they need support. In most cases this would come from the home. In the event that was not possible, others would fill that role.

When Wesley Crusher decides to stay on the Enterprise and not join his mother, who was transferred to Star Fleet Medical, Picard agrees, but then identifies three staff members to help support his growth ("The Child," *Star Trek: TNG;* S2, E1). That is a natural response within a culture of education. It is one thing to celebrate and encourage students' dreams, but to empower students to achieve those dreams requires a society that is willing to support the process of learning whenever needed. This kind of society is built on the principle that if each citizen is focused on self-actualization and challenges him or herself to grow, then society will grow. Those who help others grow, also grow.

It may seem that we would need to change a lot of our thinking to get there. However, that is not the case. Many public schools existing today have mission statements that would fit nicely in the 24th Century. I worked in four different districts in Arizona, all of which had mission statements that spoke of developing "lifelong learners" who contribute and participate in the community. I did a quick search of public school mission statements online. I chose the first five that were listed.

1. "Challenge the minds, challenge the bodies, and challenge the dreams of all students while focusing on excellence." (Portsmouth Public School, VA).

2. "Provide a safe teaching and learning environment which will insure, with the support of the students, parents and community, that all students, upon graduation, will have the academic and social skills to be successful, lifelong learners in a global society." (Rockford Public School, MI).

3. "As we move towards the future, our vision is to foster a community of 21st Century learners who actively seek knowledge and demonstrate global awareness." (Rockland High School, MA).

4. "Every public school student will graduate ready for post secondary education and work, prepared to be a globally engaged and productive citizen." (Hanover Public School District, PA).

5. The district, "is committed to excellence in education by nurturing, challenging, and inspiring all students to achieve their full potential and to become productive citizens in a global community." (University Elementary School, LA).

I am sure these five are representative of most districts throughout the country. As you can see, if our graduates possessed the skills and abilities that our schools openly state as their missions, we might already be as advanced as the 24th Century. Our districts have wonderful goals for our children. Unfortunately, a great many children do not achieve these goals. Something is broken.

A discussion of what is broken could include many different topics such as nutrition, parental support and encouragement, socio-economics, race, gender, home environment, teacher training, past experiences, inherent biases, curriculum, self-esteem issues, teaching methods, cognitive deficits, behavioral deficits. And the list goes on and on. Unfortunately, with such diverse topics, not everyone will agree on solutions. Like-minded adults tend to gravitate toward each other and this can result in groups only pushing specific agendas to repair what they see as broken with the system, rather than approaching the problem more holistically. Additionally, it is not uncommon for these separate efforts to find themselves competing for limited funds or worse, conflicted philosophically.

Groups pushing specific agendas often need political support to begin implementing these agendas. Garnering political support requires finding common interests between a politician and a group's agenda. Politicians need votes. Votes come from adults, not children. Because adults who are members of large groups can provide more votes, politicians will seek out those groups, or voting blocks. Boom! Special interest groups are born.

These special interest groups organize and use their numbers to influence elections. Candidates, whose goal it is to be elected, listen to the special interest groups…Boom! Educational policies come to reflect what the special interest groups want. Education gets caught in a tug-of-war between special interest groups. Classrooms and curriculum become the purview of politicians.

These groups can disagree quite a bit on the problems facing education. For instance, teachers unions will talk about discipline in the home and teacher salaries. Civil rights groups will talk about a biased curriculum, racism, and the system in general. Charter school advocates will talk about giving children and parent's choices. The business community will talk about the need for developing a new work force. Child advocacy groups will talk about nutrition, nurturing, and after-school programming.

Every special interest group has valid points. However, they also have their own agendas and will work with other groups only to the extent that it doesn't detract from implementing their agendas. As a result, sometimes special interest groups come into conflict. The group with greater numbers and better organization helps elect a politician who supports their agenda. New agendas often affect classroom instruction. New strategies or new approaches are brought onto a campus and last only as long as the agenda is supported, or until the next new agenda comes along.

The problem is simple: education is now controlled by politicians. A politician's interest may not reflect educational values or processes, but rather popular support. These debates over what we should do to fix education get muddied by the political interests of different groups and the needs of the children get lost. In contrast to Spock's famous dictum—"The needs of the many outweigh the needs of the few"—in this case, the needs of the politicians seem to outweigh the needs of the children.

There is one thing that unites all these special interest groups: They are all comprised of adults. Until the adults start changing their approach, we will see no real reform in education. In 1995 I attended a seminar where I heard Dr. Willard Daggot, founder and president of the International Center for Leadership in Education, talk about education reform. He made a comment that has stuck with me for twenty years.

He said we have been pushing education reform for a generation (that takes it back to the 1970's), without any significant improvement in terms of student success. He suggested that most of the reforms targeted student changes, from curriculum to class size to length of class period. Then he made his memorable comment. He said until reform efforts affect change on the part of the adults, true reform will never occur. Changing how a student sits, what kind of book she reads, how long his class period is, how many tests she takes or how often he gets a pat on the back won't reform the system. It will simply satisfy special interest groups. Adults—teachers, parents, administrators and politicians—need to change what they are doing and how they are supporting education before we can see real reform.

One example of this is school integration. Integrating the schools became a symbolic effort of race integration as a nation. It was the right thing to do. However, the adults (politicians, civil rights and other special interest groups) pushed hard to make it happen quickly. As a result, we simply started bussing young children from their homes and putting them in strange schools and, in some cases, a hostile environment. The adults took some pictures and took some credit, and that was it.

We integrated schools on a policy level, not culturally; certainly not on a level where the kids felt comfortable. Adults may have had to change pick up times and locations, or talk to different administrators or teachers when they had a question, but compared to the children, their lives didn't change. The children's lives, the folks who can most easily have their confidence destroyed and who would most need that confidence more than ever, were literally and figuratively uprooted. Confidence for any young student can be a challenge. Throw into that challenge a new campus, new kids, new teachers and generations of a race paradigm the law was trying to change overnight, and good-bye confidence, hello anxiety. Once a student loses confidence, it is very difficult getting it back. You can't just tell a child, "You need to find more confidence."

There is a conversation between Captain Picard and ship's counselor Deanna Troi concerning a famous negotiator who lost his confidence after the death of his "chorus" (three people who used telepathy to express not just the words, but the emotions of the negotiator who was deaf). The negotiator, named Riva, did not want to continue negotiations on Solais. Picard asks Troi if anything can be done and she responds by saying, "Confidence is based on oneself. It is not easily given." ("Loud as a Whisper" *Star Trek: TNG*; S2, E5). Captain Picard and Troi were talking about a seasoned, professional adult negotiator. Imagine Troi's response if the issue had involved a vulnerable child.

What could school integration have looked like if the adults focused on doing what is best for children? Here is one suggestion. Consider two schools: one is black, one is white.

Year one: Superintendents and school boards from both districts meet, discuss resources, current curricula and current class sizes, target numbers for the change and all other pertinent issues. Throughout the year all of them meet weekly to plan, discuss, organize and share. A couple of months before the end of the year, a few teachers and one administrator from both districts are identified as the "test classrooms."

Year two: The selected teachers and administrator work at the schools to which they will be assigned as resource and planning consultants. Throughout the year they meet weekly with the superintendents and school boards and discuss how to begin implementation. They also meet with the staffs of the schools. By the fourth quarter of the second year, the transition teachers are partnered with teachers in the targeted classrooms. They work together in the classroom with one white and one black teacher in each room. Teachers meet daily to discuss delivery and classroom management styles and expectations. Parents of targeted students are introduced to each other and begin meeting monthly.

Year three: The targeted students hold an assembly at the beginning of the year. The assembly includes the targeted students who will change schools as well as the students of the classrooms they will join. They spend a couple of days breaking the ice and developing strategies for learning in the "new integrated classroom." Throughout the first and second quarter, through pen pals and field trips, the targeted students communicate regularly with the school they will attend and visit the classrooms to which they will be assigned. Students are assigned partners and work on a semester project together. During this year, parents are working with their children to understand what they are going through, what they are thinking, and what concerns they might have.

During the 3rd quarter a two-week "test" is run with all targeted students attending their new schools and new classrooms. At the end of the two-week test, they return to their original schools and are assigned another project with their counterparts. The project? Answer the following questions: What went right? What went wrong? How would you change it? During this quarter, parents of all targeted students visit each other's homes for dinner, or community barbecues, and they deepen their relationships.

During the fourth quarter, they review and share their projects with the school boards and administrators. The last week of the school year, all students (those targeted to move, and those in the classrooms that will receive bussed students) and their parents meet every two weeks (alternating schools) with administrators and teachers involved in the project to go over final planning for the next year.

Year four: Bussing begins. There are several series of regular meetings and discussion forums with parents, students, teachers, administrators and whoever else is involved, reviewing, critiquing and changing the implementation as needed throughout the year. At year's end, a general review of classroom academic performance, student behavior, campus challenges/logistics, student feedback, teacher feedback, parent feedback and administrator feedback is made in an open forum for the communities at large.

This is just an example. These specifics might be adjusted. The point is that beyond phone calls, some teacher meetings and a handshake, we did very little planning. Then we simply threw the kids into classrooms. Adult lives were changed very little. While busing may have had a positive overall affect on segregation practices of the time, this was short-lived.

A detailed analysis of the impact poverty and race had and continue to have on desegregation is very complex. Moreover, the relationship between poverty and race makes it difficult to make clear distinctions. Suffice it to say, the policy of desegregation never filtered down to a cultural level. It was more cosmetic and, as a result, because root causes of segregation were never addressed, communities remained segregated.

Had the process been closer to the one outlined above, it might have taken longer, but children would have fared better, confidence would have been higher, and children would not have been forced to do the heavy lifting of school desegregation. Parents and teachers would have played a more substantive role, and perhaps even bonded more. Indeed, it is possible that parents, and to some extent their communities, would have integrated on a cultural level.

In the spirit of our future counterparts, let's take a look at how education could change. Perhaps the best way to start is to heed Dr. Daggot's input and place children first. For our purposes it would be like pretending they all can vote. I want to reiterate that the approach to this issue, like all issues in the future, will be driven by logic and reason. Let's pretend Mr. Spock is one of our consultants.

First, let's get rid of a huge myth about our public education system: Learning takes place in the classroom. This is false. *Some* learning may occur in the classroom, but that depends on the teacher, the student, and the parent. *Teaching* takes place in the classroom. Whether or not the child learns is a different matter. There are many factors involved. Most of which will fall into three general categories: academic environment, home environment, and student readiness. Teaching and learning are two different things. One does not guarantee the other.

There are people who believe teachers should be held accountable for student learning. That is a valid belief within the context of the academic environment of the student. Teachers can be held accountable for teaching. However, if there is deficiency in the other two areas over which the teachers have very little control, then they cannot be held accountable for student learning. Parents, students, teachers, administrators, school boards and the community should all be held accountable for learning. This accountability should begin before a child—a future student—is born.

Here are some facts:

- Children born to mothers who are chemically addicted are at greater risk for health issues, some of which directly affect cognition. Sometimes the risk is very high.

- Two loving, caring parents in the home are better for a child than one loving, caring parent.

- Children whose parents recognize the need for, and value of, education are more likely to achieve in school than those whose parents don't.

- Children whose parents provide the hierarchy of needs outlined by Maslow (physiological, safety, love/belonging and esteem) are more likely to be successful in school.

These are facts cited in hundreds, possibly thousands of educational books, journals, and research papers. Study after study, (Brown, 2004; Carlson & Corcoran, 2001; McLanahan & Sandefur, 1994) has found that children raised in traditional family homes—two married parents—fare better than those who are not. Indeed, a study by a team of researchers at the University of Calgary's Hotchkiss Brain Institute (HBI) suggests that benefits might even include increased adult brain cell production.

Using these facts we can begin to see what we can do to help improve learning in the classroom. (And remember, this process begins before the child is born.) The first point concerning chemically addicted mothers involves current policies and debates as to how we deal with drugs in America. On a personal note, I have supported the legalization of marijuana since my first joint back in 1972. I mention this because I want to assure you I am not approaching this issue from my personal beliefs, just facts.

In the future, our counterparts seem to have avoided the issue of drugs altogether. They appear to have gotten rid of drugs, both illegal and prescription. This is mentioned in "The Neutral Zone" (*Star Trek: TNG*; S1, E25). Also, Mr. Paris says that humans "gave up smoking centuries ago." ("Ex Post Facto," *Voyager*; S1, E8). We also know that all of society no longer chases money, but focuses on self-improvement. Surely, a society that has reached that level understands the importance of not being chemically addicted when pregnant.

We know that free choice is valued in the future as evidenced throughout all the different series and movies. It would be logical to assume that our future counterparts hold themselves responsible and accountable for making their own decisions about having children. There is nothing in any of the productions that suggest there are "pregnancy" police.

We also know that people practice sex regularly. I didn't do a count, but if I did, Captain Kirk might have come up the winner. Casual sex doesn't seem to take a hit in our future's approach to this issue. In "The Outrageous Okona" (*Star Trek: TNG*; S2, E4), Okona is staying on the Enterprise while his ship is being fixed and has sex with at least one crew person. When he is called to see the Captain he assumes he is in trouble for his behavior. Picard makes it plain that he is free "to socialize" with any of the crew members. The important thing is that these "socialization" sessions do not seem to end up in unwanted pregnancies. In the *Star Trek* world, it would appear that effective contraception is accessible to everyone and/or our decision-making skills concerning sex have improved.

Regarding the next issue that two loving, caring parents are better for a child than one, I am not trying to suggest a single parent is bad for a child, but merely that two loving parents are better than one. I know some single parents (all mothers) who are wonderful parents. On the occasions when that topic comes up they all, to a person say it presents challenges for them that can be stressful. There is also a secondary issue: wealth. A single mother with financial means can hire live-in nannies, or other help. A lot of single mothers don't have this option.

Our future counterparts offer a few examples. We know that Captain Kirk fathered a child who was raised by Dr. Marcus, his mother, and became a scientist himself (*Star Trek II: The Wrath of Khan*, 1982). Dr. Crusher (*Star Trek: TNG*) and Commander Cisco (*Star Trek: Deep Space 9*) were single parents. However, they started as traditional families and the spouses died. Also, they lived where they worked, making supervision much easier. In the case of Wesley Crusher, he worked with his mother.

In all three cases they lived in a society where money did not matter as much as it does in our society. Dr. Marcus, Dr. Crusher and Commander Cisco may have had choices unavailable to single parents in today's world. And, of course, in all three cases the parent was well educated and probably placed a high value on education.

We do know that poverty doesn't exist in the future. We do know that it does exist today. We know that poverty rates for children of single parent homes are greater than those of children with two parents. To the extent that single-parent homes must cope with poverty, future policies and society at-large would more logically support and encourage two-parent homes as being in the best interest of children. It is from these homes that children stand the best chance of reaching the level of self-actualization that is commonplace in the 24th century.

In today's society there are a plethora of reasons why we have so many single-parent homes. While the government can adopt policies and programs that assist these single parents, they must also work to provide policies and programs in support of building a strong family and reducing the number of single-parent homes in the future. These policies and practices may include anything from Public Service Announcements to community education centers, to public school presentations. Planned Parenthood could be a great example of this. Currently their website has links to birth control options. Perhaps they could also have a link directing visitors to the importance of having two married parents as being in the best interest of children and their education and the need to think of these things *before* pregnancy.

However, we cannot depend on government or sponsored programs alone. Every adult must accept responsibility for his or her role in building a society that recognizes the importance of education. A young child's environment is critical. According to a report from The National Scientific Council of the Developing Child, "Because children's experiences are limited by their surroundings, the environment we provide for them has a crucial impact on the way the child's brain develops (Strong-Wilson & Ellis, 2007, p. 43). What a child sees and hears at home, on TV, and in the community has a strong impact.

A two-parent home in which both parents value education provides the best environment for the child. Furthermore, if society at large also recognizes the plasticity and vulnerability of the child's developing brain and the importance of children as the adults of the future, it becomes easier for parents to walk the walk (not just talk the talk). Before adopting any policy or practice, before publishing a song or producing a movie, before developing a new advertising campaign, before we do anything as a society we should simply ask ourselves, "Will this be good for our children?" That is how people living in a culture of education would behave.

In the United States education is considered to be a right. As a result, some parents take education for granted. This can lessen the importance they place on education, reducing the likelihood of student success. I currently live in China. My nephew's parents who live here had to pay quite a lot of money for their child to get through Middle School. He is testing for High School now and once his scores are known, the list of available high schools will be presented to him. That will also be a pretty large expense. During his parents' discussion, the topic of his not attending high school at all came up.

Children in China are not compelled to go to school. This may increase a parent's support for the child's success in the classroom because they value education more. The point is, education is not taken for granted here as much as I've seen it taken for granted by some in the United States. Parents supervise their children to insure that homework is done before they allow them to play. I know students who aren't allowed to watch TV or use their computers during the week.

When I taught at a private English school here I observed a very different attitude toward me than I found from many parents in the United States. As a teacher in the United States, I knew before school started which children were not going to be behavior problems; who were going to work hard and do their best. These were the children of parents I had met at open houses. These parents expressed the kind of concern I later got from almost all the parents I met here in China. I would add that I taught in Japan for five years and at Ho Chi Minh University in Viet Nam one summer and I observed the same concern for their children's education.

In my experience in these three countries, parents want their child to be successful in school. They rely on and listen to the teacher for guidance. They provide a space and supervise their children to do their homework daily. Whenever I needed to meet with a parent, it happened. Any behavior issue I brought up was acknowledged by the parent and followed up on. That is not to say there are no problems for teachers, but rather they can count on the support of the parents to deal with all of the problems in the classroom that are brought to their attention. The priority for children is education, and the go-to person is the teacher.

This kind of support is not seen from all parents in the

United States. Regardless of where we live, we as parents need to care about our children's education, and we need to work closely with their teachers. We need to join PTA's, attend board meetings, volunteer in the classroom, supervise our children, follow-up on homework, attend all conferences, understand curricula and the goals of and for our children. We also need to prioritize our children's activities to support their education: turn off TV's and video games, open books, stop going shopping and go to museums instead, stop texting friends and write in journals instead.

As you read this, it becomes readily apparent why children with two loving, caring parents stand a better chance. A second adult can increase household income, provide greater supervision for children, and possibly allow more time for parents to participate at the school. I met parents like this when I was a school principal. I always appreciated them and had great respect for all they did, but I always felt regret…that they were so few in number and that they did so much.

The last issue that I raised is meeting the needs outlined in Maslow's hierarchy. For Maslow, "Education is learning to grow, learning what to grow toward, learning what is good and bad, learning what is desirable and undesirable, learning what to choose and what not to choose." (Maslow, Abraham, *The Farther Reaches of Human Nature* [1971]).

According to Maslow's theory, a person cannot self-actualize until other, more basic needs are met. Here is another, expanded presentation of that hierarchy. Dr. William Huitt, an educational psychologist summarizes them this way:

- physiological: food, water, shelter, clothing.
- safety/security needs: out of danger.
- love/belonging needs: be accepted by family and friends.
- esteem: to achieve, be competent, gain recognition.
- cognitive: to understand and explore.

- aesthetic: order and beauty.
- self-actualization: find self-fulfillment, realize one's potential.
- self-transcendence: to help others find self-fulfillment.

For children, the likelihood of meeting these needs increases when there are two loving, caring parents in the home. While a two-parent home which is financially, emotionally, and developmentally prepared for children, will not guarantee educational success for the child, such a home will definitely improve the likelihood that the child will achieve success.

If we want to ensure that every child is on the path to self-actualization, we need to do everything we can to support that goal. Our future counterparts are already there, so each individual has already learned, "what to choose and what not to choose" as Maslow put it. In today's society we will need public policy to help support the right choices. In terms of education, public policy should support and encourage dual-parent homes and discourage single-parent homes.

Good education policy is often measured on the surface. We talk about state-of-the-art technology, a computer for every child, a safe, clean building in good repair, and excellent teachers. All of these things support teaching, but they don't ensure learning. Without a strong home environment that supports the importance of school, loving and caring parents who work with and encourage the child, and the finances needed to meet Maslow's hierarchy, learning will be compromised.

We will have to stop doing what we are currently doing and do what is best for the child. We need to stop allowing the needs of the politicians and special interest groups to outweigh the needs of children. I will talk a little about what a school in the future might look like as revealed by *Star Trek*, but the importance of thinking about what a child needs *before* her first day of school (*even before conception*) cannot be overstated. Using the Smiths from the example in chapter one, if we want young Purple to grow up in a better world, one that breaks the cycle of poverty, we need to give her our full attention and support. Not merely a new tablet.

There are few examples of school classrooms in *Star Trek*. Keiko O'Brien sets up a school on Deep Space 9 ("A Man Alone," *Deep Space 9;* S1, E4), but it is a makeshift, first-day look. Captain Picard visits an art class to give an award to a student, but that was more a formal presentation and may not represent a typical classroom on any given day ("Disaster," *Star Trek: TNG;* S5, E5). So, to build a classroom of the future we will have to do some conjecture by working with what we know of academic requirements and assessments and assuming that, in the future, these types of decisions and policies are research-based and measured by results, not votes.

What we know for sure is that adults in the 24th Century live in a culture in which the standard for everyone is to become self-actualized. Their lives are focused on self-improvement. To do this, one must have basic skills to navigate the community, specific skills that support their interests, and learned behaviors to continue their improvement and support their efforts. It is likely that schools support this in the classroom. Students are not just taught subjects, they are taught specific skills and behaviors as well. Indeed, it could be that these skills and knowledge are the means to develop behaviors supporting self-actualization.

Currently, the education system in public schools in America is implemented as follows. The federal government helps fund and support states' efforts to develop general goals or standards assigned to each grade level for K-12 schools. Then the states are held accountable for student success. Generally speaking there are three reasons for this approach. First, we want to insure a 6th grader from Oregon who moves to Kentucky will be relatively prepared for his new 6th-grade classroom. Second, as a nation, we want to compare results across the country to determine deficiencies and then correct them so that no state, or student is left behind. Lastly, we want to be able to produce data that can be used to compare us with the rest of the world's students to insure we are globally competitive for jobs.

Using our current paradigm, all of this is perfectly logical. However, if we want to create an education system that encourages self-actualization, there are two current practices that need to be modified: Content/grade-level structure, and curriculum-driven classrooms.

Our current system compartmentalizes student growth by content and grade. In education this is referred to as scaffolding: using prior information to act as a foundation for learning new information. Establish a target and assist students in reaching it, then establish a new target, help students reach that one, and so on. With the advent of Common Core, we have actually defined it by specific targets at specific ages for all students across the country. Many of these targets are not a result of the student's ability, but rather his age. It is an assembly-line approach, which requires each student to adapt to the system rather than the system adapting to the student.

For the most part students who suffer from this system are offered two remedies: grade retention and grade advancement. Whether initiated by the school or home, the result is that a student repeats or skips a grade. Typically, this process is driven by a student's scores and classroom performance, both of which could be impacted by other factors and may not be indicative of the student's actual ability. In either case these remedies simply place a child at a different point in the assembly line.

Classroom instruction is driven by curriculum and defined by textbooks. While there are creative and energetic teachers who build very positive learning environments in classrooms, the textbook must be taught. This is partly due to the push for 'high-stakes' testing with billions of dollars at stake! State standards are tied to the tests, and textbooks are designed around the standards. This is referred to as "alignment." The principle is simple: Teach the text and kids will perform better on high stakes tests. In many cases there are efforts to actually teach to the test as the "test season" draws near.

This approach does little to help students become self-actualized. Those who are able to pursue personal growth, probably do so as a result of their home environment (those homes which meet Maslow's basic needs) rather than as a result of the education system. Unfortunately, for a growing number of students our current system encourages dependent behaviors rather than independent behaviors. Students learn early just to do what they are told. Those who can't may lose interest and eventually, usually after behavior issues and/or poor attendance, drop out of school. Those who can do what they are told are comfortable just getting to the goal. When they get there they simply wait for the next goal to be presented and then they go after it.

While this approach may create a good work force, it teaches students behaviors that are the exact opposite of the behaviors needed for self-actualization. When speaking about self-actualization, Maslow said, "What a man can be, he must be." Determining what someone can be is specific to each individual and can differ greatly among students. In speaking about the Cognitive Needs level, Maslow says that we truly need to explore who we are and only through this journey can we learn and grow.

This may be unique to our species. Commander Riker and Q have a discussion about this need that humans have to learn and grow. In fact, Q expresses concern that humans might even surpass the Q Continuum at some point in the future (The Q continuum are a species of omnipotent beings.) Q even offers Riker the chance to join the Continuum so that he can better understand how this thirst for knowledge drives the human race ("Hide and Q," *Star Trek: TNG*; S1, E9).

The grade level standards are so specific, the curriculum so structured, many students are forced to learn things that have no bearing on who they are and what they can become. Students can quickly lose interest. As lack of interest turns to boredom and, eventually frustration, many students see education as a necessary evil and can't wait to get out into the "real world." Unfortunately, they never reach their full potential. Most of them become good "worker bees" for business. They have learned those skills well: do what you're told, do not question, and learn to live with it.

We don't know the curriculum of a 24th Century classroom, but we do know that students in the future need to learn to identify specific personal goals, develop strategies to meet those goals, and continue to raise the bar on their own in order to develop independent behaviors for self-improvement. Indeed, learning the 'A-B-C's' would just be the first step. The important part of the curriculum would be teaching the student to apply what he learns to his own life in his efforts to become self-actualized.

This cannot be done on an assembly line. It cannot be done by requiring students to conform and do as they are told. We will need to reconsider everything we know about curriculum, classrooms, homework and assessments. To do this we really need to drop our current mind-set and focus on our goal of each student realizing his potential. So let's begin.

If teaching students to have initiative and to have the ability to acquire and apply new information so they can measure self-improvement and continue to grow becomes the driving force in the classroom, the curriculum would no longer be driven by text books, or possibly even content standards, but rather by the student's ability to demonstrate growth and/or natural talents. This demonstration of growth might be a tangible product (much like the project-based learning that has strong research-based evidence of student learning), a presentation to others, or a successful collaboration with others. A student's natural talents might be anything: art, music, math, creative writing, carpentry, mechanics, coding, speaking, etc. Each student presents a new possibility.

In addition to a student's ability to demonstrate growth and natural talents, what we know about cognition and student readiness would also need to be considered to create an effective educational experience for each student. Generally accepted concepts that have significant impact on student learning include multiple intelligence, learning style, student readiness, social skills, and content relevance to the student's life and interests. Looking at education from this perspective it quickly becomes apparent that the "curriculum" of the future would be significantly different from what we see in the classroom today.

For our purposes, ability will be used to define student skills. Capability will be used to define student potential. For example the skill of reading is an ability; whereas, being able to read a novel and interpret its meaning into one's own life is a capability. Critical thinking is a skill. Being able to read a newspaper and pull out the subjective, analyze the objective, then put it into the context of one's life is a capability. A classroom focused on teaching ability might look very different from a classroom teaching capability. In terms of student readiness and cognitive development, learning skills would occur at the earlier ages. Reaching potential would occur at later ages.

It could be argued that in general terms our current system does address both needs. Our current system does distinguish between ability and capability. K-12 is used to teach ability, and universities or colleges are charged with helping students reach potential. However, I would argue that by the 24th Century we discover that not all humans need to wait to reach a specific age to start realizing their potential. Moreover, one can realize his potential without a university degree.

At the age of fourteen, David Karp left high school and opted for home schooling. David's real passion lay in building his own microblogging platform and public schools did not teach that. Many universities did not at the time either. You may be wondering who this guy is. David is the founder of Tumblr. Although he sold his company for more than one billion dollars after only six years, David's satisfaction comes from what he has done. In an interview with Josh Halliday, of "The Guardian," Karp said, "There are a lot of rich people in the world. There are very few people who have the privilege of getting to invent things that billions of people use." This is self-actualizing behavior.

We have examples of such behavior in the future. There is a seventeen-year-old at the helm of the Enterprise. While there is no specific information concerning Chekov's education, it is obvious he learned his skills well and seems to be realizing his potential. And he is not alone. Wesley was a middle-teen when he first arrived on the Enterprise. Soon after he was an acting Ensign.

In "When the Bough Breaks" (*Star Trek: TNG*; S1, E16), A young boy named Harry runs away from calculus class. He gets kidnapped from the Enterprise. The boy's age is never mentioned, but he is about twelve years old…taking calculus. Twelve years old is somewhere around 6th grade in our current system. Calculus is not offered in the 6th grade in public schools of today.

There can be no doubt that these future kids got to where they were, not by being held in grade levels, moving on like cattle year by year, and waiting to complete twelve or thirteen years in traditional classrooms. It would appear that the 24th Century has developed an education system that is student centered, rather than curriculum centered; An education system which allows for students to move at a pace not defined by age, but by readiness, ability and demonstration of capability.

Assuming education in the 24th Century would be grounded in research and effectiveness, it would not be surprising if school starts much earlier than it does in our time. According to Patricia Kuhl, co-author and co-director of the Institute for Learning & Brain Sciences, in their last trimester fetuses learn speech rhythms and even some phonetic sounds of their mothers. We know language acquisition starts to be acquired in infancy, and by age two, sentences are being formed and vocabulary expands greatly. Indeed, toddlers and young children's minds are exceptionally absorbent and ready to learn. With this knowledge it is logical to assume that listening and speaking skills would be taught at relatively early ages. As fine-motor skills develop, letters and numbers could be introduced and taught at a much earlier age than they are today in public schools.

Formal education would start at an earlier age for our 24th Century counterparts. Scaffolding is an effective strategy to help children learn skills. When the child demonstrates success (capability), he or she moves to the next "level." This would be the fundamental difference between early education today and in the 24th Century. In our current system, grade levels are defined by ages. In the future, ability levels might replace grade levels. For example, let's say it takes an average of three years to learn how to read—going from awareness to exploration and finally to fluency. Our current system defines the stages of reading and incorporates them into grade-level curricula so that a student goes through three grade levels (ages) to complete all the stages: first, second, and third grades.

In the 24th Century, schools might have ability bands—in this case first grade through third grade would be a band—within which certain abilities must be learned, but students would move at their own pace. We might see reading labs where children of different ages who are at the same stage of reading are working together to master that stage. Students would move in and out of groups depending upon how quickly or slowly they learn the specific skill. Students who learned quickly would move out of that reading ability band and into the next band, perhaps a capability band.

In this approach, students are the drivers of what they are learning and how fast they learn it. This is referred to as student-centered learning. This approach could be used in other disciplines: arithmetic, writing, speaking and listening. When the student demonstrates the needed proficiency, he moves into a different class environment, one in which his potential is addressed.

As a student attains a functional level of reading, writing, arithmetic, speaking and listening, she would then begin to learn how to use those skills to develop her unique potential. (Of course, "functional" is the key word here. The definition of this word could be a book in itself. Suffice it to say, a functional level would mean that the student has demonstrated measurable competence and readiness to begin the next stage of learning.) This classroom might look much different from the earlier classroom.

Before moving on I want to address two research-based concepts that have proven to be effective for learning: Project-based learning, and integrated curriculum. These concepts complement each other. Project-based learning utilizes the student's ability to incorporate many skills into his or her learning. As the concept suggests, students work on a project that incorporates many skills—reading, writing, critical thinking, math and other knowledge—into the production of a project. Project-based learning can be done in a group or individually. The other concept, integrated learning, specifically focuses on helping students make connections between typical 'content' classes, e.g. math, social studies, language, etc.

Classrooms of the future might incorporate these two concepts into an education process that would not have seven periods a day with students moving from one classroom to another. There could be direct-instruction classes where students learn new information, project labs where students work in teams or individually to complete their projects, lecture halls where students present their projects and their findings, and lastly, discussion classrooms where students talk about each project, ask questions, perhaps even defend their projects.

Topics they might be speaking about, or reading and writing about could include nature, history, the arts, government...any topic that was relevant to the student. Their assessments would be based on how well they spoke, wrote and/or presented material to others, how well they could defend their conclusions as well as how well they could lead discussions.

Classrooms would not be confined to a physical space. Students from around the globe (or the universe in the case of *Star*

Trek) could be working on the same project. Using current technology this can be done. Two or three hundred years from now, certainly it would be easy. (*Star Trek* fans know about transporters. Using that technology would actually let students 'beam' to any classroom in the world to physically interact with each other.)

Again, you can see that this approach is student-centered. Students are using skills they learned in early school to explore their interests as well as their potential. Teachers are acting as facilitators and coaches. They provide new information and strategies, but they do not define how students apply them. It's important to remember that students of the future aren't struggling with such basic needs as food, clothing, and housing. Their day-to-day safety is not an issue. They are confident and eager to try. Their parents are involved and supportive. The home environment is stable and nurturing. A culture of self-improvement is the norm. Teachers and schools wouldn't be pushing students through the system. They would be guiding and supporting them as they grew. And in that culture, growth would be celebrated, not test scores.

It appears that schools would still be divided by grade levels. Jordy attended Zephram Cochran High School (*Star Trek: First Contact*, 1996). Also, in *Star Trek: Generations* (1994), Captain Harriman tells Captain Kirk how he learned all about Kirk in grade school. This makes sense since there is no indication that basic child development changes in the future. Elementary school, middle school and high school would be a logical approach to meeting the developmental and social needs of a growing child

There could be several types of teaching roles, or teachers in the system. Since it would be possible for students to move through content and possibly grade levels based on how quickly they master the targeted skill, the system would require specific support for each student. One way to achieve this is to have academic advisors for each school: elementary, middle, and high school. Every student would be assigned an advisor.

The advisor's role would be to track the progress of the student through school and to communicate with the parents. The elementary school would be a period of six or seven years in which the only skills, or "subjects" would be reading, writing, speaking, listening and math. These skills would have teachers who would be responsible for direct instruction of new information to students. These teachers would focus on presenting new material and assessing a student's ability level as it relates to the new material.

Certainly there would be a need to establish what the requirement for advancement is, but generally the speaking, reading, writing and listening levels would be that which you hear on any of the *Star Trek* franchises. Specific lexicons would come in the later grades. However, the level necessary to participate in most of the casual conversations you hear on the Enterprise could be taught at the elementary level. Required math in elementary school would likely include arithmetic, algebra and geometry. Even higher levels of math would be available for those students who were ready.

This would not be much different from a traditional classroom today. However, how long a student stays in that classroom would be determined by how quickly she gains the ability necessary to move on. Advisors would track the student's growth and work with the direct-instruction teachers and parents to insure the student meets all requirements of the elementary school.

To see how this might operate, let's look at Purple Smith, the young girl from Chapter One. Let's say she is very good with numbers, speaking and listening. She is average with reading and her writing is weakest. Students enter elementary school at age three or four and exit at age nine or ten.

As Purple's strengths are identified, she moves quickly through her math, listening and speaking classes. She moves at an average pace through her reading classes, but struggles in her writing classes. All students must meet certain requirements before they exit elementary school. Because of her abilities, Purple meets the math, listening and speaking requirements around age six and is no longer required to attend these classes. Through her advisor, she is working with an academic coach to start applying those skills to small projects that will help prepare her for middle school. She is right on track for reading so her classes continue throughout elementary school.

The system then focuses on her writing. Her advisor, together with her direct-instruction teacher, set up a plan with her parents and Purple herself. This would be much like an IEP (Individual Education Plan) currently used in special education programs. During her last two years in elementary school there is an increase in her writing support until she achieves the required level.

Purple's first three years in elementary school would have similarities with our current elementary school. Of course, she would be attending advanced math, listening and speaking class, or working on projects. For her last three years her direct-instruction time would be increased for writing, stay the same for reading, and be replaced with project learning for math and speaking.

Every student would have a variation of this experience. The only thing for certain would be that each student would be required to meet the established level of proficiency for each discipline before entering middle school. Younger students who require more structure would have an experience similar to what we see in schools today. As they get older that experience could differ greatly.

Middle school would be the place for students to start exploring their abilities and discovering capabilities. The five basic skills would no longer be taught in classrooms. Those skills would be applied to projects and exploratory classes. In addition to academic advisors and direct-instruction teachers, middle school would have project facilitators. These teachers would work with students as they completed projects throughout middle school.

There would be a project selection list from which each student can choose a project. A set of guiding questions for each project would be supplied. Students would do the research, organize the material, address the questions and present their findings to the class. Class discussions comparing findings would be facilitated, and their project findings would be archived and accessible to future students. This approach changes the current paradigm in public schools. Rather than being taught what to think, they would learn and practice how to think.

Advanced math and vocabulary classes would be available to students who wanted them, as well as specialized training classes, but projects would be the basic form of learning. Projects would be designed to integrate social skills and humanities with students around the globe. The project facilitator would work with the students and assist as needed. Completed projects would be presented to other students and the faculty.

Exploratory time would be split between standard offerings: music, physical education, art, technology, family and consumer sciences, etc. and student's individual interests. The internet, chat rooms, blogs, video conferencing and video archives could be used to help each individual student explore his personal interest. For instance, David Karp could have used this time to develop coding skills and discuss with others his interest in building microblogging platforms.

This exploration would not necessarily happen at school. It would happen wherever, and whenever it was the most beneficial for the student. Perhaps, in David's case, others who shared his interest might live in other states, or countries. Maybe a teacher at a high school in Liverpool has developed an online class for microblogging. With the help of his project facilitator, David would explore and develop his interest using all these resources.

High school would be similar to middle school but, again, there would be an addition. High school projects would enlist the membership of professors and professionals around the world. They could include developing new theories, new software, new hardware or new strategies as they relate to global needs. These projects would be presented at conferences. Presentations might also include recommendations for future action.

Rather than teaching students what scientists are discovering, students would be in the "virtual" lab during the discovery process. Rather than reading about scientists' data and their conclusions, they would be collecting their own data and sharing their own conclusions. As students end their high school experience, they would have a much better understanding of who they are, what direction they would like to take in their future, and which university best fits their needs.

This is not to suggest that all students would go to a university. In a world of self-actualized people, it would be logical to assume trade schools, apprenticeships, internships and other less formal opportunities would be available. Once a student has learned how to learn, where he choses to continue to learn is his decision.

Not all projects would be related to the sciences. Students in high school would have the opportunity to begin exploring their own personal interests. Perhaps one project is developing a musical score for other students whose project is writing a play. Projects are determined by the students, and school is a place to facilitate the completion of projects.

What I have just outlined is only one possibility. The important thing to remember is that the schools of the future would be much more dynamic and student-centered. There would be less structure around classrooms, schedules, and curriculum, and more structure around helping students learn how to become the persons they are meant to be.

Carl Rogers, who has contributed significantly to the discussion of the importance of student-centered learning said, "The only learning which significantly influences behavior (and education) is self discovered." The process outlined above teaches and encourages self-discovery. This translates into building a citizenry that seeks self-fulfillment, exactly the kind of future we see in *Star Trek*.

It is important to clarify that student-centered instruction is not about students doing whatever they want. It is about students' abilities and capabilities playing a deciding role in the process.

Self-actualization is reaching potential. This requires an honest assessment of one's abilities, establishing strategies and setting goals to improve those abilities, and regularly assessing improvement. This is not taught from a teacher or a textbook. This comes with practice. Student-centered learning provides that practice.

Adults are around to guide and assist, but students do the work, track their own progress, and establish new goals. They are accountable for their improvement. They learn how effort translates to growth. They are allowed to become themselves rather than being pushed into a mold. Carl Rogers puts it all into perspective. He said, "People are just as wonderful as sunsets if you let them be. When I look at a sunset, I don't find myself saying, 'Soften the orange a bit on the right hand corner.' I don't try to control a sunset. I watch with awe as it unfolds." In this new dynamic school system, students would be allowed to unfold and be who they were meant to be.

When Captain Jainway's ship was stranded in the Delta Quadrant, 70,000 light years from home they didn't simply do nothing and hope they could get back. They decided they were going to go back despite the fact that it was going to be a seventy-five year journey. Indeed they recognized that they would probably be dead before they get there. However, they committed themselves and stayed focused. They encountered luck—good and bad—made some bad decisions, got distracted, but they adjusted, tried new things and, most importantly, never lost their focus ("Caretaker," *Voyager*; S1, E1&2).

From the very beginning there were struggles. Janeway had to learn to work together with the Maquis, who were also stranded in the Delta Quadrant. Former adversaries came together for a common goal: Get back to Earth. That entire series is a testament to what self-actualized people can do. When it comes down to it, the whole franchise was about boldly "going." Not boldly "talking," or boldly "expecting," or boldly "getting ready to go"…but, boldly going…boldly doing it.

To the extent our education system is supposed to prevent poverty or prepare students to participate in society, our education system is broken. What we have tried has failed. In the *Star Trek* universe, we would be looking for and trying new ideas. The effort for us will be difficult and risky, potentially dangerous, and we will most certainly hit roadblocks. However, if we trust in ourselves, commit to the goal and stay focused, we will also most certainly get there. It may be seventy-five years away, maybe longer, but we are not taking this journey for us. It is for our children and their children.

If education is truly important, if our children are our biggest resource and our best asset, then we owe it to them not to just do something, but to do everything we can. We have two choices: move toward the future with purpose, or sit back and wait for it to come to us. Just ask yourself, "What would Mr. Spock do?"

Chapter **3**

We the Puppets

On a distant Class M planet, a landing party lead by Captain Pike discovers survivors of a crash seventeen years earlier. They beam down and happily inform them to prepare to return to Earth. The survivors welcome the news and start to prepare to go home. The doctor confides to Captain Pike that he is amazed at the good health of all the survivors. One of them tells the captain and the doctor there is something special on the planet that has helped them stay in such good condition. A beautiful young lady, born just after the crash, offers to show Captain Pike what has helped them all stay healthy. As she escorts the captain away, the other survivors and their makeshift camp suddenly disappear.

The Enterprise crew, stunned, quickly discover their captain wasn't escorted away to be shown anything. He was kidnapped. They track him to a closed gateway in the side of a small mountain. Mr. Spock and the others use their phasers to try to break through, to no avail. They are forced to return to the ship without their captain. On the Enterprise, Mr. Spock and the doctor report to the First Officer in the briefing room. Spock tells the group everything was an illusion. The doctor confirms that assessment and tells the group that whoever is responsible "had us seeing just what they wanted us to." ("The Cage," *Star Trek;* S1, E1).

There are many examples of reality being masked, altered, or otherwise hidden in *Star Trek*. Whether it is some kind of drug ("The Game," *Star Trek: TNG*; S5, E6), or some powerful being who can control the mind ("The Cage"), or a being who can change matter and create whatever reality he wishes (like Q), or being trapped in a void by an entity called Negilum ("Where Silence has Lease," *Star Trek: TNG*; S2, E2). In all examples, the respective captains and crews seek to break free of the illusion. They would rather have the harsh reality than the pleasant lie. Captains Kirk and Picard both leave the Nexus (a place where they can live their dreams in peace) to return to a reality that results in Kirk's death (*Star Trek: Generations*; 1994). Episode after episode of the various franchises repeats a theme of humans wanting to be in control of their destiny, regardless of the results.

It is important to note that the beings who seek to control humans in the future are not always doing it out of malevolence, or even ill-will. Sometimes it is just a lack of understanding; sometimes there is a genuine belief that they are helping humans; and of course there are those times when it is being done out of malevolence. In all cases, however, the need for humans to be in control of our own destiny triumphs in the end. Misunderstandings are cleared up, or the "bad guys" are defeated, the illusion is eventually overcome, and captains and crews return to reality to continue with their self-determined lives.

Indeed, in "The Menagerie" (*Star Trek*; S1, E11&12), Captain Pike, after suffering a horrible injury that leaves him completely paralyzed, returns to the class M planet he was originally kidnapped on and voluntarily stays to live the illusion that was offered years ago. However, this time it was his choice…and that made the difference.

There are forces at work in America seeking to create illusions for all of us. Two specific illusions that relate to the *Star Trek* universe are important to identify because they represent impediments to building a society of self-actualized and compassionate citizens dedicated to ending war, hunger, money, and want. As we look closely at these illusions, answers to ways we can escape them will emerge to be addressed later in the book.

There are two different notions that have been central components of American society—especially politics—for decades now: the notions of "free market" and "free society." Many Americans believe we have both in the United States. The general interpretation in both cases is that the consumer or citizen is the person to whom the word "free" applies. That is to say, We The People have the freedom to make our own choices when it comes to what we buy, and how we live. Obviously this is intended to be circumscribed by the parameters defined by our Constitution. (Indeed, that very document was written from the perspective that the power of free choice should always be determined by us as opposed to, say, a large, wealthy corporation, or a large bureaucratic government.)

Most Americans think that we can drive markets to provide goods and services that we see as necessary and helpful, and that we can direct our government to enact laws and regulations that we believe are necessary for the greater good. However, the exact opposite is true: Markets are driven by corporations, and our government directs policies. They, the corporations and the government, are the "free ones." We The People are just pawns and as such are manipulated daily. Perhaps that is an overstatement, and in reality corporations and the government can't actually do whatever they want, but most people would agree that they certainly have more freedom to do so than the average *Star Trek* viewer.

In the *Star Trek* universe, people acquire goods using credits. (I will discuss credits in detail in Chapter Six.) From the open market at Farpoint Station ("Encounter at Farpoint," *Star Trek: TNG*; S1, E1-2) to Quark's bar on the Deep Space 9 Station, goods and services are provided and markets exist. Indeed, markets don't just exist, they are being managed. In *Star Trek* (2009), Lieutenant Uhura orders three Bud Classics as well as a Jack Daniels. The fact that there are Bud Classics suggests there is also a newer version of Bud, which could only be explained as a move to satisfy a newer clientele—a new market.

Big-ticket items are also bought and sold: Kirk's farm (*Generations*, 1994), James T. Kirk's presumed step-father's Corvette and his motorcycle that he gives to a worker at the ship-yard in Iowa (*Star Trek*, 2009). Also, in that same movie Dr. McCoy mentions that his ex-wife's lawyer took everything he owned but his bones in the divorce. We know there are restaurants and bars as well. What seems to be missing is marketing and advertising.

In S*tar Trek* (2009) Kirk and Uhura are in a bar. There are no company signs on the walls of the bar. If you have ever been to a bar in America you know of what I speak. There are dozens of eye-squinting, bright neon company signs. This is not so in the future. In *Star Trek, Into the Darkness* (2013) we see a cityscape of the future London: many high-rises, not one billboard, not one sign. Nothing is being advertised.

Later in the movie as Kahn crashes the USS Vengeance into San Francisco we see the same thing. Spock chases Kahn through the city, which contains not one billboard, no advertisements at all. In fact, throughout that sequence of the chase we see many residents of San Francisco and no one is wearing branded items. Most of the clothing is earth tones and plain. There are no team jerseys and no company logos, and that includes hats. We see the same thing on *Deep Space Nine*. The promenade is vacant of advertising. It is full of shops, full of customers, but no advertising. This approach seems to support individuals in making their own choices concerning what they need. This would translate into markets driven by the customer rather than by business itself. It would be logical to assume that word-of-mouth advertising would make or break a business.

We know corporations do exist and markets are managed, but that process is much less aggressive than it is today. We also know there is no TV, which of course means no TV commercials ("The Neutral Zone," *Star Trek: TNG*; S1, E26). There is no evidence from any of the *Star Trek* franchises that people read newspapers or magazines. Paper doesn't seem to be used much at all, which would suggest junk mail doesn't exist. As Mr. Spock might say, "It would seem logical that mailers weren't being thrust upon consumers." Labels and logos are no longer important. In "The Last Outpost'" (*Star Trek: TNG;* S1, E4), humans meet the Ferengi. Data remarks that the worst quality of capitalism—"Let the buyer beware"—is the Ferengi model, which suggests it is no longer the model of 24th century humans.

In that same episode, the Ferengi, in an effort to gain favor with the Portal, speaks of the humans committing crimes by **not** selling weapons and other technology to underdeveloped planets for profit…just the opposite of what we do today. In fact, capitalism itself is satirized in the depiction of the Ferengi throughout many different episodes.

The Ferengi's society is based on the ability to accumulate profit. Profit is the goal. If profit is not involved, then it's not worth the effort. For example, in "A Man Alone," Quark's brother removes his son from the school that Keiko O'Brian opened on the Deep Space 9 Station because there was no profit in it (*Deep Space 9:* S1, E4). There is an exchange between Quark and his mother in "Ferengi Love Songs" (*Deep Space 9:* S5, E20) that illustrates the Ferengi's love of profit. Quark's mother tells him, "You have proven yourself a true Ferengi. You've betrayed friends and family for personal gain." Quark replies, "Sounds good when you say it."

In today's America there are some who believe American capitalism is similar to what the Ferengis practice. We hear a lot about corporate greed and betraying others for personal gain. One could make a reasonable argument that, in general terms, progressives see today's American capitalism as similar to the Ferengi's system.

In the future Earth's economic system is much less aggressive. What we don't know however, is the extent to which the economy is controlled by the private sector vs. the government. We only know that marketing and advertising is not part of the economic system in the future. I believe this to be the central difference in defining to whom "free" refers when we hear "free market." With marketing and advertising, "free" refers to businesses being free to create markets, create needs, and create consumers. Without marketing and advertising, "free" refers to the consumer being free to decide what she wants, when she wants it and from whom to get it.

In the *Star Trek* universe, there are many examples of the importance of individuals making their own choices. The results of the choice do not seem to be as important as the ability to make the choice, which is central to the human condition. Perhaps this is best expressed in "Best of Both Worlds" (*Star Trek: TNG*; S3, E26/S4, E1).

The Borg invade Federation space and attempt to assimilate humans. The Borg ship pronounces they wish to improve themselves and tells Captain Picard that human biological and technological distinctiveness will be added to their own and that human culture will adapt to service the Borg. Captain Picard tells them that is impossible: "Our culture is based on freedom and self-determination."

In America today, there are many who believe that the government is taking away our individual right to freedom and self-determination, similar to what the Borg wanted to do in "Best of Both Worlds." We hear a lot about government overreach and wanting to improve everyone's lives. One could make a reasonable argument that, in general terms, conservatives see today's government as being similar to the Borg.

Certainly there is a government in the future, albeit a little larger. There is a global government ("Up the Long Ladder," *Star Trek: TNG*; S2, E18). It is difficult to guess how that government functions since there is no direct evidence or examples to cite. What we know for certain is there is no money. This is important because all current government programs rely on money. This gives the government the ability to shape society and prioritize needs. I believe this to be the central difference in defining to whom free refers when we hear "free society." With money, "free" refers to the government being free to decide how Americans will live. Without money, "free" would refer to the individual having freedom to choose his or her own path and lifestyle.

Looking at "free market" and "free society" through the lens of *Star Trek*, it becomes easy to see the illusion we live under. In a true free market, individuals are not trained and targeted to consume corporate goods and services. In a free society, individuals are not trained and targeted to consume government goods and services. Simply put, individuals who are self-actualized, responsible, and accountable are in control of their own lives and are free to choose for themselves what they will do and how they will live.

In our country today, like two giant beasts fighting over food, corporations and government fight for control over us. They would each have us believe they can create a wonderful life for us. They maintain that their interest is in our well being, and that may be, but regardless of their motivation whatever they create for us would simply be an illusion. In the *Star Trek* universe, individuals don't need corporations or governments to create a wonderful life for them. Our counterparts in the future seem to be able to do that on their own.

For them, a tough reality is better than a pleasant alternative as long as the individual has the choice. Jordy foregoes real eyes, Wesley Crusher foregoes instantly becoming a man and Riker refuses an opportunity to join the Q Continuum because it was not their reality ("Hide and Q," *Star Trek: TNG*; S1, E10). In the episode cited at the beginning of this chapter, "The Cage," Captain Pike is offered any reality he wants as long as he stays on the planet. He could have spent his life in his childhood memories of green pastures, riding his childhood horse in the countryside. No war, no stress, no demands, just enjoy each day.

In fact prior to beaming down to the planet, Captain Pike was talking with the doctor about leaving Star Fleet. He was tired of making decisions that led to crew members' deaths. The doctor told Captain Pike that a man either faces life head on and licks it, or withers away. That is the nature of our 24th century counterparts: facing reality and moving forward on their own. Having control over their destiny means much more than having someone provide them with a wonderful life.

Unfortunately, as business and government struggle to create this illusion of a wonderful life, our two major political parties have joined the effort on an ideological level. That is to say, people's characters and personal choices are being used as fodder in this political fight to maintain the illusion. Disagreements are now met with personal attacks and real issues are obfuscated by political drama.

In general terms, progressives tend to side with and support the notion of allowing the government to create its idea of a wonderful life. Conversely, conservatives generally tend to side with and support the notion of allowing business to create its idea of a wonderful life. As such, both sides of the equation have been given an extra word: "Big." Big business and big government are how political parties tend to describe the "other" side. The way each side uses these terms suggests the "other" side needs some kind of restraints so that people can be protected.

Transforming the function of business and government into an ideological discussion separates both groups into distinct and even opposing forces—a completely new illusion—rather than two necessary pieces of our society. This seems to be causing greater and greater distress and distrust within our society. Moreover, as the discussion becomes more impassioned, both sides step further away from each other. The discussion has become ugly. Political ideology has placed large groups of people at odds with each other. The more differences that are identified, the more entrenched in their ideology each group becomes. The more entrenched they become, the more those on the "other" side are demonized. It is a spiraling of distrust and intolerance that has grown for decades.

Progressives would have us distrust the 1% of people who fall loosely under the category of very wealthy; a little more than three million people. Our government is made up of about 4 million people. That is about 1.3%. Conservatives would have us distrust that group. To the extent that political parties are supported, these two separate groups of less than 3% of the population own the discussion, and decide the fate for the other 97%. (That's my group.)

Consider the original *Star Trek* series. All the fans of the series know about the guy in the red shirt who accompanied Captain Kirk and Mr. Spock on landing parties. He was the one who always died. Regardless of the threat or danger to Spock or Kirk (or other regulars for that matter), viewers always knew they would survive. However, we also knew that the guy in the red shirt would surely die. Every time. When it comes to being empowered and having control over our choices, we in the 97%, are kind of like the guy in the red shirt. It just doesn't look good.

There is no direct referencing of the relationship between business and government in the 24th Century. However, everything seems to suggest that in the future there is no conflict between the two. As mentioned, one major difference between us and the society of the future is money. Our government and corporate America are full of it! It influences everything they do. In the episode, "Conspiracy" (*Star Trek: TNG*; S1, E25), a parasitical species is trying to infiltrate and take over Star Fleet in preparation for an invasion. Bug-like creatures are introduced into the host and then control what the host does. The only way to destroy them is to destroy the host. Not a pleasant thought. In the end, Picard and Riker kill Commander Remmick who is the host of the leader of the parasites. As a result, all parasites die and the invasion is thwarted. Money is not a life form. However, it does seem to control many people's behavior much like the parasites. In this context, removing money from business and government completely might solve a lot of problems. Indeed, that is what happens in the *Star Trek* universe.

Without the parasite of money our counterparts in the future seem to work well together. Businesses, big and small, from bars and cafes to beer companies and car manufacturers are operating. Government seems to thrive as well—from low crime rates and no poverty to large planetary projects like raising tectonic plates to develop a new continent. What the future has that we don't are self-actualized, responsible individual citizens committed to improving themselves.

In the last chapter I talked about the kinds of sacrifices we need to make in our education system to replace it with something that would get us closer to our counterparts in the future. Until we get there it might be difficult to get rid of money. It might be like the chicken-egg paradox. We can't just kill money like Picard and Riker killed the parasites. We can, however, look at how money has infiltrated our lives and perhaps find ways of reducing its negative effect on our behavior. Maybe we can find ways of removing some of the "tentacles" of money's hold on us.

Before starting this discussion, we must remember that the 24th century does not have currency…at least not on earth. There is currency in the galaxy. Quark tells a customer who's been kicked out of his casino that he will return her currency ("Captive Pursuit," *Deep Space 9:* S1, E5). Also, a man named Mudd was arrested for buying a ship with counterfeit currency ("Mudd's Women," *Star Trek:* S1, E7). On planet earth, however, we have developed a system that no longer requires money. Getting to that point will certainly require rethinking what we are doing today and perhaps even sacrificing some "rights" we practice.

But again the question is, what are we willing to do to get rid of poverty and hunger? It won't just happen by luck. We'll have to figure it out. Currently we do have currency and it is very important in today's America. The goal of this discussion is not to explain how to get rid of money, but rather how the free market has been transformed into a playground for business to create consumers, rather than citizens being free to choose. Thus making currency somewhat like a drug we believe we need in order to survive.

Many Americans believe that we have a free market. The problem is the consumer doesn't go to the market, the market is shoved down his throat: mailers, commercials, advertisements, internet pop-ups, companies working with other companies…buy this car, or rent this room and get frequent flyer miles, etc. We need to put the consumer in charge of the market, not business. As I have demonstrated earlier, in the 24th century the market is not forced into the consumer's daily life.

There is no TV. That's the first step ("The Neutral Zone," *Star Trek: TNG*; S1, E26). And the tone Picard used when explaining this fact suggests that TV was not replaced by a different 'boob tube." (Certainly there is a future version of the Internet, but it would not be "watched" like a TV.) The implication is that the distraction or waste of time for humans to sit and watch something rather than actively pursuing improvement in their lives was gone. I would extend this to video games, DVD's and movies as well. Let me digress a bit to explain why.

In the 24th century there is the holodeck. This is an enclosed space where matter can be manipulated to create any environment for the user. Throughout *Star Trek: The Next Generation*, the holodeck is used for adventure and relaxation. It's important to note that the relaxation is interactive. For instance, in "Elementary Dear Data" (*Star Trek: TNG*; S2, E3), Data creates a Sherlock Holmes mystery in which he is playing Sherlock Holmes and must solve the mystery. He invites Jordy and Dr. Polaski to join in. Although it is used as a distraction, they are the central characters and must navigate the streets of old London to solve a mystery…they're not in a chair watching. The holodeck is also used for training and learning. There is no direct evidence that holodecks exist on earth in the future, but I believe it to be a fair assumption that they do. Quark's bar on Deep Space 9 Station has halo-suites he rents out to customers. Given the choice of holodecks or movies/video games, I am sure most would choose the former. Unlike movies and video games where you are usually sitting and watching (If you're like me, you're eating popcorn when you watch a movie), in holodecks you are moving, running, swimming, climbing, riding a horse, battling a creature, or skydiving. Or, on the other hand you're visiting a distant galaxy, visiting one of the moons of Jupiter, inside a molecule studying it, running a science experiment. There is virtually no limitation.

Add to this the notion that the challenge for people in the future is to improve themselves, it is logical to assume holodecks are a tool to that end. For instance, if you love climbing mountains then you might use it to climb Mt. Everest as practice for the real thing. If you are a creative writer, you might use it to bring your story to life. It would seem logical that for the most part the holodeck is used as a means to an end rather than just entertainment as we think of it today. Our counterparts in the future have dropped habits that interfere with pursuing their dreams. Because they are using technology to further the human experience rather than avoid it, they no longer have a need to live vicariously.

All of this supports the notion that individuals who are self-actualized and work to improve themselves are more likely to do that in a society that doesn't have a corporate model of consuming as much as we can. In the future, the consumer controls her own consumption. She chooses what, how much, what brand and when. She isn't influenced by outside pressures (corporate or peer). In the future it appears that mass consumption is not the goal of capitalism.

In today's America, corporations have done an excellent job of creating consumers. They have also done an excellent job of creating the illusion that consumption is good. Many folks from my generation remember the notion of "keeping up with the Joneses." This idea supports a competition between consumers as to who can consume the most. Whole markets have been created just for the purpose of encouraging consumption. As the markets were created, companies quickly realized that customers could be more easily turned into consumers if they had access to more money.

To this end, businesses and banks have worked together to create and embed credit cards in American society. Indeed, this

is what turned business into Big Business. Credit cards give customers the ability to become consumers. Consumers can easily be
trained to collect more things. Companies take advantage of people's desire to want things. In "Dear Data" (*Star Trek: TNG;* S2,
E3), Jordy talks about the old days when people traveled by ship
and sail. Data doesn't understand why Jordy pines about those days
and Jordy responds, "It's human nature to love what we don't have."

Jordy's comment was not in the context of materialism, but it
can be applied to materialism. Big business has taken advantage
of this "human nature" and has worked hard to get all consumers
to "want' what they sell. And they are subtle and relentless in their
efforts. They do this by invading our homes and personal time.
They interfere with our desire to relax, and they thrust their goods
and services upon us. Whether you like to read, take walks, or just
relax at home, advertisers will seek you out and bombard you with
the message that you need to buy, buy, buy. They continually look
for ways of robbing us of our time. Television has become perhaps
the best example of this.

Using *Star Trek* as an example, I randomly selected Season
1, Episode 4 from different versions of the franchise: *Star Trek*
("Where no Man has Gone Before," 1966), *Star Trek: The Next
Generation* ("The Last Outpost," 1987) and *Star Trek: Enterprise*
("Unexpected," 2001). If you compare the data from these three
examples, you can see how advertising is slowly taking more of our
time to sell us their products. All episodes are one hour long. Here
is how that one hour breaks down:

Year	Program Minutes	Percent	Advertising Minutes	Percent
1966	50:21	83.9%	9:39	16.1%
1987	45:42	75.4%	14:18	24.6%
2001	44:18	73.8%	15:42	26.2%

Over a thirty-five year period they have increased the time they tell us what to buy by more than sixty percent. Conversely, the viewers get less programing. This is how people are converted into consumers. We're told what we need and where to get it. And with cooperation from banks we get credit cards mailed to us and are told we are pre-approved. All we have to do is complete an application form.

Many of us, taught to do as we're told in school, fall into the trap and spend a lifetime consuming. According to Nielsen, seventy-eight billion dollars was spent on TV advertising alone in 2013. Billions more are spent on "branding" items: Movies, clothing, cars, food products, fast food. All of this money is spent by big business to tell us what we should want. That isn't a free market. That's a market that is in your face pushing materialism, just like a drug pusher. Taking advantage of human nature—wanting things we can't have—big business and banks have made it easy for many people to struggle with "keeping up with the Joneses."

This struggle results in creating debt. It is with debt that corporate America gains power, and consumers lose control of their own lives. In the *Star Trek* universe this notion no longer exists. The "free market" is not thrust upon customers. In a society that lacks the drive to collect material wealth, corporations have less control and individuals have more.

In *Star Trek*, "TheWrath of Khan" (1982), Kirk on the Enterprise is hiding in a nebula from Khan who surprised them and badly damaged the Enterprise. The nebula interfered with sensors, essentially blinding Khan who was firing randomly in the general area. Khan's weapons were getting closer and Kirk was trying to determine the next step. Mr. Spock tells Kirk that Khan is intelligent, but because of his limited experience in space he is thinking two-dimensionally. Kirk then orders the Enterprise to drop down below Khan's ship and then come out of the Nebula to surprise Khan from below. It works.

Analogously, we generally think one-dimensionally when we

think of wealth. We think of income or revenue. That is our world. Big business has trained us to think in those terms so that we can continue to consume. But wealth can also be obtained by reducing spending. If we reduce our need to consume, we become wealthier.

In a free market where the consumer has the power, that is what would happen. Consumers would only purchase items that they determined were needed and only when they were needed. The goods and services they consumed would be determined by the quality of the product rather than the corporate logo and the advertising. A small business would have a better shot at competing with larger businesses. This would result in a more competitive market and allow some of the best qualities of capitalism—innovation, hard work, craftsmanship and entrepreneurship—to fill market needs. Individuals could enter the market and control their destiny.

Large corporations would not be able to control whole markets as easily. With greater competition, community-run businesses would stand a better chance. What was referred to as the "mom and pop" stores would resurface. Without the ability to use fancy ads, jingles, and famous spokespeople to create false "needs," consumers would make decisions on their own. In short, they would be driving the market, rather than the market driving the consumer.

Of course this comes with a sacrifice. We would need to rethink many of the habits and customs we practice today. Fashion, entertainment and sports, among other industries, have been targeted by big business. Even holidays have fallen victim to big business. Many large corporations work together to create markets designed to reinforce habits of consumption.

One example of this crossover and cooperation is entertainment. When a blockbuster movie is made, movie studios work with advertising and marketing companies to brand the characters in the movies, let's say a superhero character, as well as particular corporations, let's say McDonalds. Somewhere in the movie you will see a McDonald's, or at least its logo. It's usually in the background, but it will be framed so that it is hard to miss. As soon as the movie comes out, McDonalds will run a series of "specials" that will allow customers to get "collector" glasses featuring the characters from the movie. A particular purchase will provide you with a "free" glass and perhaps a discounted cost for filling it with one of your favorite drinks from McDonald's.

After several weeks you can get a full set of all four, six, or however many glasses. And, if you use your credit card you will receive 2% cash back on your purchase. How cool is that? You can acquire the glasses (and all the food you need to purchase to get the whole set). McDonald's, the movie studio, the glassmaker, the soft-drink company and the bank get your money. Your decision to get the glasses, however, is reinforced every time you watch TV and see a commercial showing the glasses. You can show off your collection to your friends.

This happens all the time with movies and television shows. Depending upon the type of movie, fashion and music can also be brought into the mix. Popularity of movie and television personalities bring in big bucks convincing us how to dress and showing us how we should look. The clothes the actors wear are described in detail. Hairstyles are also important. We tend to treat movie stars as if they are a special class of people. They are just like us. However, they are backed by large corporations. As a result their faces are seen by millions of people and, of course, they are members of the 1% club.

The Academy Awards is a huge moneymaker designed by Hollywood movie studios working with a variety of large corporations and banks. Their goal is to get us into the theater. Once we are at the movie theater the consuming begins and has the potential of increasing exponentially. First the ticket, then the snacks, then, if you like the movie, you can start buying T-shirts, and lunch boxes and action figures and bed-sheets and underwear and....anything that can be sold. And, of course there are the endless sequels. Stars become rich because the big businesses they work for convince us to give them our money.

The same kind of thing happens in professional sports. When an NFL team changes the color of their uniforms they make millions of dollars with the change; at least to the extent it is a popular team. The fans will buy new clothing, hats, accessories and car decorations for "their" team. And, because of their special exclusion from Anti-trust laws (more on that later), sports teams "own" the ability to record and broadcast the game. This allows advertising companies to perpetuate the need to consume and help large corporations make a lot of money. Zachary Seward, Senior Vice President of Quartz news website researched the NFL in this regard. According to his research, the average NFL game broadcast is about three hours and twelve minutes. The game is officially 60 minutes (unless it goes to overtime). Another 60 minutes will be used to air about 100 ads. (The remaining time is accounted for by penalties, injuries and other delays.)

We have been trained to consume, to collect things. Sometimes we don't even know why we collect them. We know we can't take them with us when we die, yet we collect them, and then we give them to our children so they can add them to their collection. In *Deep Space* 9's, "Q-Less" (S1, E7), Odo doesn't understand Quark's endless pursuit of material things. He talks about how pointless it is to collect item after item until one's home is full of stuff only for the owner to die and have everything divided up by relatives who then start all over again. It's not a good sign that our current behavior resembles the Ferengi.

Then there is the absurdity of the whole make-up industry. Corporations convince us to buy stuff to spread over our faces, on our lips, eyes, in our hair and pretty much all over the body so that we can look and smell acceptable. For women especially, it is almost impossible to be natural. They would be risking their careers. If I were a woman I would be really annoyed every morning when I had to slather stuff all over my face.

Large corporations have trained us to believe that the only way to express love, appreciation and to respect tradition is by buying products to give to each other. According to a CNN article, "Valentine's Day, by the Numbers" (Belle Reynoso, 02/14/2013) 18.6 billion dollars was spent for Valentine's Day. I don't mean to challenge tradition and beliefs, but we should at least ask ourselves two questions: Is buying things the only way to express our love for that special someone? How much would we spend on this holiday if there wasn't one word of advertisement anywhere, telling us to do so? This is just one holiday; think of the billions of dollars we spend every year just on holidays. That money leaves our pockets and goes to large corporations. What if that money stayed in our homes and in our communities? There is a good chance that it could have a measurable impact on poverty.

There is a lot of talk currently about the wealthy 1% and income inequality. But it is not only about income. It is also about how we choose to spend our money. We are feeding the system. The rich are getting richer and the poor are getting poorer because the rich invest millions of dollars to convince the poor to spend billions of dollars on things we don't need. Capitalism has been replaced by corporatism and consumerism. Then we are told that America has a free market and we need to keep it free. Corporations have a free market. It is our choice to give them our money, and if we choose to do so the blame rests squarely on our shoulders. However, we are at a disadvantage in the current system. Getting rid of poverty, hunger, war and, the biggie, money, are not easy tasks. They are, however, worthy goals. The free market as it exists today will not aide in that effort. I believe it actually would prevent us from getting there.

Giving individuals the power to make decisions and removing all outside influence and interference from those decisions is a step that our counterparts in the *Star Trek* universe have taken. If we want to take control of our future, we must begin by taking control of our present. We simply need to decide who should have control—big business or the individual? In the *Star Trek* universe, that control lies with the individual.

As mentioned above, the *Star Trek* universe has a world government and it also supports efforts of the planet ("Up the Long Ladder," *Star Trek: TNG;* S2, E18). In, "Family" (*Star Trek: TNG;* S4, E2), Picard is considering leaving Star Fleet, and his friend is trying to recruit him to oversee a government project involving lifting a tectonic plate to create a new continent. Having a means to organize large efforts and prioritize the needs of the governed requires a special effort and that requires government. However, as with big business, many Americans are under an illusion that they are free to decide how they live. We believe that we elect representatives of The People to enact policies that reflect the priorities established by The People. But that is not the case.

I believe the intent of our Constitution can be put into one simple sentence: Mr. Government, you ain't my boss! That's it. Simple. That is what we were supposed to be about. We'll have a government to maintain some basic common needs, but The People are in charge. Of course, the big debate is what are those "common needs?" Over the past couple hundred years our government has gotten very big. It makes decisions today that would have probably precluded the Constitution's ratification had they been discussed during the convention all those years ago.

That is not to say change is bad. However, it is important to know who is dictating the change. While the government has grown throughout its existence, the pace increased dramatically in the 20th century. I believe the accelerated growth of our government rests on one event: The passing of the 16th Amendment to our Constitution (The establishment of an income tax). Basically the 16th Amendment says, people will continue to work, but the government gets a kickback.

Now, of course the sales pitch was that the money was going to be used for the common good. (Can you see a pattern here? "Common" needs and "Common" good. Those words have given politicians a lot of power, and lawyers a lot of money.) They just never said who would decide the common good. And that is the biggest difference between big business and big government: Government mandates, business has to persuade. When big business makes money they do what they can to get more by trying to convince us to do things. As mentioned above, they're pretty good at it. However, when you give government money to do what they wish, they don't need to convince the public, just the politicians. To do this, coercion is not uncommon.

It even happens in the future. In *Deep Space 9* ("Dax," S1, E7), Odo, the Chief of Security at the station, wants to use Quark's bar to hold an extradition hearing. Quark objects because he doesn't want to lose business —"business is business." Odo says fine, and starts talking about having to make some changes in Quark's bar because they violate building codes on the station. The hidden message: "Do what I say, or else." As a member of the "government" on Deep Space 9, Odo coerced a "citizen" of the station into doing something he didn't want to do.

Albeit in this case it was minor, it is significant to note the power government has and the need to be cautious about giving it too much power. I think it is fair to say that many conservatives believe our current government has too much power. While the question of having too much power can be debated, it is a fact that our government is doing much more today than it was in the beginning. That is not necessarily a bad thing, but we should at least consider the following questions:

- Why is it getting bigger?

- Is it efficient?

- Is it effective?

In the context of the *Star Trek* universe the government is big. It is global after all. However, although there is no direct reference to this, as a viewer you get a sense that there is not a lot of tension between The People and the government. I think it is fair to say there is a lot of tension between The People of America and their government today. While it is mostly conservatives who frame the notion of "big government" as a bad thing (much as it is mostly progressives who frame big business as a bad thing), there can be little doubt that our government is big. Big is not necessarily bad, but the question of why is it getting bigger is important.

First, in a future where no money exists, it would seem difficult to support a government that is constantly growing. At least the kind of government we are familiar with. From this perspective, it might be wise to start looking at ways we can solve problems without requiring our government to expand, or requiring more money. As difficult as this may be, it will be more difficult the longer we wait.

The three questions above are difficult to address separately as there are sure to be issues that crossover into all three categories. Therefore, this discussion will move between them from time-to-time. Perhaps our government has gotten big because it is inefficient, or ineffective. Or, perhaps it's inefficient because it is big. Regardless, the government we have has been deliberately structured and built into its current size by politicians and lawyers. It has not been an organic growth.

The architects of our current government are politicians. With, or without the support of The People, they have designed big government. Once the plans are drawn, the "builders" come in. The builders of our big government are lawyers. They look at the plans and then piece things together using the tools of their trade: words. They craft words, mostly specialized words, in documents that only they can understand. Much like a traditional homeowner when a "room" needs to be expanded, you call them back in to take care of it. Politicians then codify these words. Lawyers make a lot of money from government. Lastly, there is a group who keep the house in good repair. They are called "experts" and they bring their tools, statistics and studies, to fix any problems, or make additions. In short, big government is owned by politicians, provides untold dollars for lawyers and uses experts to make sure their "house" is in good repair and validate what they are doing.

The challenge our current big government has is that the architects disagree with the plans. Rather than sit down and map out what our government should be they are building essentially two separate structures four years at a time. Sometimes eight years. When a new project manager comes in, the whole structure is re-designed. This, of course requires more lawyers to come in and piece it together and, in turn, more experts to come in and maintain it.

This may be seen as a cynical analogy, but I think in general terms it is a fair analogy. Certainly, some "project managers" are better than others, but if everything has the possibility of changing so frequently, there is no way to build a solid foundation. Without a solid foundation, any project manager can pretty much do whatever he wants and failure is almost inevitable.

Typically, people think of the Constitution as our foundation. However, with the help of lawyers we have pretty much turned our foundation into mud. Each new project manager uses new experts to redefine our Constitution. What was originally a straightforward document has become a document drowning in a sea of lawyers and experts telling us what each word means, only to have each word redefined by a new set of lawyers and experts. We the People are not in control. That's the bottom line.

We are shut down, shut off and told to shut up. Unfortunately, unlike our counterparts in the future who are self-actualized, we take it and do what we're told. Some of us actually believe that politicians know better than we do and should not be questioned. Others believe the power of the vote keeps The People in control. Unfortunately, I will show you later how big government, with the help of big business has learned how to sell politicians, much like I used to sell appliances years ago.

As the result of this chaos in our government, in my lifetime we have had one president (project manager) assassinated, one resign from office, one who became president without receiving a single vote from The People, one impeached, one convicted of war crimes in a world court, and one who has openly lied in front of The People as well as openly mandated that laws not be followed. I am not making this up. These are all documented facts. If that is not enough to tell you there is a serious problem with big government, throw this book away, go get a latte.

Regarding why we are growing and whether or not we are efficient and effective, let's look at that past fifty years in terms of major government efforts. Our government has openly launched no fewer than three "wars" on big issues: Poverty (1960's), drugs (1980s) and Terrorism (2000's). Today, all three issues are bigger than ever. Today the middle class is falling into poverty. Some would argue it's actually disappearing before our eyes.

Just in the 21st century deaths due to overdose of prescription drugs has more than doubled and illegal drug use has increased. States are openly defying federal laws and passing laws to legalize marijuana. In terms of terror, just turn on your TV. The FBI has active investigations in ALL fifty states trying to keep us safe. The short story is, once our government declares "war" on something, the issue gets bigger. (It kind of makes you wish the government would declare "war" on peace...maybe we would have more of that.)

I did some Internet searches trying to find definitive numbers in terms of how much money has been spent, and there is a lot of variation. Suffice to say, more money has been spent on these three wars than our government has spent on everything else since our nation was created. Trillions and Trillions of dollars that have resulted in the issues getting worse. Our government has been failing for decades. However, to listen to them (conservative and progressive politicians) everything would be wonderful if only their party was in power. From 2008-2016 conservatives blamed the plight of our nation on Obama. Hillary Clinton, when she was the Democratic nominee for president, openly declared Republicans her "enemy" in a debate. It's like two children standing over spilt milk arguing over who did it:

"YOU did it."
"I did not. YOU did."
"Did not."
"Did too."
"Did not."
"Did too."

Of course, sooner or later the adult steps in, tells them to stop arguing and to clean up the mess. Unfortunately, our government has no adult in the room. So conservatives and progressives not only blame each other, but have come to hate each other to the point that now they are calling each other the "enemy." They no longer care about cleaning up the mess. They are fixated on assigning blame. How can we be surprised that our government doesn't work?

Now an average Jane might ask, "How can they get away with this?" It's very simple. They have taken our money to hire professional liars to change reality. They are called "spin doctors" because they can take facts, spin them using "experts" (again, paid for by us) to explain to us how wonderful they have been doing. These spin doctors are paid to tell us what politicians really meant to say when they say something stupid. They use cherry-picked statistics and make up a story that shows how well they are doing. They give money called "grants" to hire experts and/or retain lawyers to make sure nothing gets done.

In the spilt milk example above, progressives and conservatives would hire lawyers to talk about how wonderful each child is and cite previous examples of the other's misdeeds. They would get experts to find finger prints on the milk carton, develop a time-line of events from when the milk was purchased and originally placed in the refrigerator to when the carton wound up on the floor. They would hire investigators to dig up dirt on each other. They would conduct polls, asking their friends what they think, or who they believe. But no one would even think to just clean up the milk and move on. That is our government, and we pay for all of it.

Experts are great at finding facts that support a political agenda. They are equally good at removing, or dismissing facts that tell a different story. That's how they get paid. Both big business and big government use "experts" in this way to convince us that what we see in front of our face isn't real. Many in government refer to common sense legislation, but their common sense is always in the context of their distorted reality (Again, that word, "common"). Progressives and conservatives actively campaign to prove they have nothing in common with each other. So when either side uses, "common sense" to describe what should be done, what they really mean to say is, "You're stupid and I'm not." Much like the "I'm rubber and you're glue" strategy.

Some would argue that had we not spent the trillions of dollars we have spent on these three wars, things would be worse. This is an assumption, not an argument. While it is possible the assumption is correct, it should not be presumed so. Our government has never tried anything else in its approach to these three wars. Indeed our money has not gone to fix any causes of these three issues, but rather it has been used to assist those suffering from the symptoms of these three issues. That assistance is what costs so much money.

Our war on poverty is more of an effort to help the poor, not to get rid of poverty. Our war on drugs is more an effort to help lower crime rates, or help drug addicts caused by the drug trade, not to get rid of drug use. Our war on terrorism is more an effort to help find and catch terrorists before they commit their act, not to get rid of the cause of terrorism. It should be obvious to all of us, our current efforts fall short of solving anything. We're just trying to mitigate the damage. Mitigating the damage, or helping those affected by these three issues is important. However, our government's approach to problem solving never goes beyond that step.

We're not attempting to prevent the existence of poverty, drugs and terrorism. We need to refer back to that quote from Einstein about doing the same thing over and over again and expecting different results. It seems to me these three wars are repeatedly using the same single approach and expecting different results. Shouldn't "common sense" dictate that if the trillions of dollars we have spent over the past fifty years to solve these problems hasn't worked, maybe we should consider other approaches, or at least a different way of spending the money. Shouldn't we at least talk about it?

I am sure there are folks all around the country with good ideas who could think of more effective ways of spending all that money. But our government is so big that trying to navigate through the system takes a lifetime, or a politician. And sometimes even they can't help. Big government has resulted in a bureaucracy that is huge and daunting. Most of us regular people don't have the patience, the time, or the ability to get through the red tape. Bureaucracy means huge office buildings, thousands of employees, procedures, counter-procedures, processes, forms, supplies, transportation needs, staff development, and the list goes on and on.

All of this results in pay grades and levels of employees that seem to be endless. This leads to the lack of accountability in big government. Big government is the birthplace of, "That's not my job." It is full of duplicate, triplicate and googlicate oversight. I read a recent article that speaks to this very thing. Here's a quote from that article:

> *"The FDA oversees a cheese pizza and its ingredients, but if there is a meat topping the USDA becomes involved."* (USA TODAY, *"Obama proposes a single agency to oversee U.S. food safety"* by Christopher Doering; 02 Feb, 2015).

The article also explains that there could be up to a dozen agencies involved within the USDA and FDA. Imagine you had a complaint about finding a hunk of meat in your cheese pizza and wanted to go the government. It is laughable. This is just one example of what could be thousands, of how our government lacks efficiency. Is the size of government causing inefficiency, or is inefficiency causing the growth? I don't know, but shouldn't we be finding out and getting answers. Shouldn't our government want to resolve these things?

Imagine the following scenario: Currently a woman named Debbie, living in Phoenix, AZ pays taxes to the federal government to help people in need throughout the country. While some of that money will help a person named Mike, living in Jacksonville, Florida, certainly, some of that money might be used to help a person living across the street from Debbie. Conversely, some of Mike's neighbor's taxes could be helping Mike. Essentially we are paying someone in DC to give our money to our neighbors. The system seems very inefficient.

The more you think about it, it becomes almost criminal. The money the government takes from Debbie will first be used to build a new office building, fill it with furniture, buy supplies to put in and on the furniture, hire some people to sit in that furniture, create and buy forms for those people to pass to each other, hire supervisors to watch the people sitting in that furniture passing those forms to each other and then, finally, give some of the left-over money to help Debbie's neighbor. If you want to talk "common sense" what about just allowing Debbie to give money to her neighbor rather than spending millions of dollars to take Debbie's money with only a fraction of it getting to her neighbor? At the very least, that qualifies as inefficient and ineffective.

Big government and politicians would have us believe they are protecting us from big business. There are those in big government who claim we are all slaves of big business and that big business is making profits off us. Big government's solution: Take more money from us to fund efforts to prevent big business from making profits off us. Huh? What is that about? They want to protect us from being gouged by big business by gouging us first. Then corporations spend more, then the government spends more…over and over…more and more… If Mr. Spock came back in time and discovered this he would forever stop claiming he is half human. The absurdity of it all would overwhelm him.

Our government is stuck in a time loop much like the Enterprise in "Cause and Effect" (*Star Trek: TNG;* S5, E18), in which the same action results in the destruction of the Enterprise over and over again. We are seemingly destined to make the same mistake ending in failure over and over again. Regardless of the political party, our government always grows. The two major political parties only differ on how to spend the money, not whether to spend the money. As a result, candidates are more loyal to their political party than The People. Without breaking free of this time loop, fifty years from now our government will have spent hundreds of trillions of dollars, maybe even a quadrillion dollars on these "wars" and we will still have poverty, drug problems, terrorism, and who knows what else. All the while, the average Jane, or Joe, like me, will have less choice and fewer options. In short, we will be less free.

Government is important for any society. However, a free society is not defined by a government that can function only by taking more from The People. It is not defined by a government that is run by party bureaucrats rather than regular citizens. A government run by two children throwing temper tantrums does not define a free society. We The People are at the mercy of a government full of bureaucrats who are not accountable to anyone. While the *Star Trek* universe offers little insight into the day-to-day function of government, it offers many examples of people being free to make their own choices.

Giving individuals the power to make decisions and removing all outside influence and interference from those decisions is a step our counterparts in the *Star Trek* universe took. It may not be the *only* way to get to a future as portrayed in *Star Trek,* but if we want to take control of our future, it begins by taking control of our present. We simply need to decide who should have control, big government or the individual? In the *Star Trek* universe, the individual has that control.

The illusion of a "free market" and a "free society" is a great accomplishment on the part of marketing and advertising folks, whether for the private sector or the government. They have built these two illusions and hundreds of millions of Americans believe them. That fact alone is depressing, but what is worse is that there is a third illusion hidden within the first two: The illusion that big business and big government are some how different. The reality is they are the same. They work together. Big business buys political support. Big government gets…you guessed it, financial support. Large companies influence legislation and, in some cases, even get government subsidies. Politicians get money for campaigns and votes. And the marketing makes it happen.

An example of this is our Supplemental Nutrition Assistance Program. Commonly known as food stamps. I don't think anyone would deny food stamps help people. Certainly some conservatives would argue too much is being wasted, or some folks are gaming the system, or that some folks don't actually need the assistance. However, even the staunchest conservative would concede there are at least a couple hundred people, maybe more, in our country who need the help and for whom it actually is the difference between eating and going hungry. For the sake of argument let's say there are 1,000 people that actually need the help (I personally believe the number is much higher, but I want the conservatives to finish the book).

Currently big business, as it relates to the food industry puts sugar into most of our foods. I won't go into the complete list here (look it up online, it's amazing), but some examples: Canned soup, crackers, canned meats, mustard, salt, hamburger buns…the list includes many things not traditionally linked with sugar. Nutritionists will tell you it is not good for you and contributes to the obesity problem in America. Of course our Department of Health agrees. However, our government subsidizes the sugar industry. It even artificially controls the high price of sugar and this can influence the cost of groceries. Food stamps are used to purchase these items full of sugar, along with the items we know are bad for us… junk food, ice cream, etc. Our FDA has approved the sugar content in all these items, in spite of its bad effects on our bodies that the Department of Health warns us about. Then the USDA—knowingly—gives people money to buy this food that is bad for them.

It is all marketed as a program to provide nutritional support for those in need, when in reality it is being used to buy some foods that have nothing to do with nutrition. The government looks good because it is "helping" the poor. The companies that produce and sell these items effectively receive government money, through food stamps, as well as private money from the non-food stamp recipient which all goes to their bottom line.

It is a win-win for big business and big government, and lose-lose situation for the taxpayer and the person receiving the food stamps. Profits go up and the shareholders make money. Politicians get re-elected as "compassionate" folks and the status quo is maintained. Meanwhile, taxes go up and the obesity rates among the poor grow, as do diagnosed cases of diabetes. And, again, it's all marketed as a good program. That's the power of marketing.

There had to be some discussion between government and business that went something like this:

Gvt: You guys are making some pretty terrible food.

Bsn: Yeah, but it's cheap so we make a lot of money.

Gvt: Do you now? We could use some of that money. Hmmm…I'll tell you what, you make the stuff and we'll give it to the poor people. We'll make the workers pay for it. But, we want something in return.

Bsn: We're listening.

Gvt: We like being in charge of things and we're going to

need money to keep us in office. How about you guys helping with that.

Bsn: What if someone finds out?

Gvt: Are you kidding? That'll never happen. We own things around here. We'll make sure anyone who looks into it will get lost in a maze of paper work they need to file. We'll also make several agencies responsible so no one will know what the hell is going on.

Bsn: That sounds great. It's a deal.

Gvt: Good. Nice doing business with you.

Bsn: Same here. I think this is the beginning of a great friendship.

Food stamps are only one example of big business and big government working together to get what they want at our expense. There are special interest groups, political groups and activists groups that will almost always take one side of the equation and cite it as the "demon." "Watch out for big business." or "Watch out for big government." These groups of sane, rational citizens have come to hate each other over the illusion that big government and big business are different. The reality is, there is no real difference. Big business and big government in many cases are partners.

They sit back and laugh as we point fingers at each other while they collect more profits and get re-elected. It's easy for them because our education system is a failure in terms of developing self-actualized adults. We are trained early to do as we are told. And we do. None of us are left alone to make our own decisions, when that is exactly what we should be striving for to reach that Star Trekian future. Big business and big government need us to be dependent. They thrive on our dependence. If we were truly free to make our own choices, they would not exist as they do today.

In "The Ensigns of Command" (*Star Trek: TNG*; S3, E2) an

earth colony needs to be relocated or it will be destroyed by the Sheliac. When Data informs the leader, the leader insists he will not go. Data's response: "That is your decision." Data works hard to change the leader's mind and, in the end he succeeds. But the decision was always the leader's not Star Fleet's. Moreover, in a discussion about where the colony would like to be relocated, the leader of the colony tells Data they like being independent. Data responds, "The Federation will offer as little or as much help as you desire." COME ON! That would never happen with our big government or big business. The government bureaucracy would eat the colony up and spit them out into some forced housing project. Or some corporate developers would be constantly beaming company representatives to the leader telling him why their community is "perfect for them" and offering cash incentives.

What we know as a free market and free society is an illusion. Like the Enterprise crew described at the beginning of this chapter we are seeing exactly what someone wants us to see, and the people that have created the illusion will not simply remove it... they make a lot of money with it. Until we empower individuals to make their own choices and remove outside influences we will not really have a free market or a free society. I believe it is something our government and society need to rethink. It is something The People should demand.

Chapter 4

News for Sale

A young Captain Harriman of the U.S.S. Enterprise (NCC 1701-B) introduces his visitors to the press by telling them it is not often that he gets to introduce living legends. Immediately the press surround Kirk, Scotty and Chekov. The questions fly to Captain Kirk: "It's been thirty years since a ship named the Enterprise did not have you as captain. How do you feel about that?" "What have you been doing since you retired?" As the reporters circle around Captain Kirk, his friends help get him away from the crowd and the focus goes back to Captain Harriman.

The newly christened ship is about to leave space dock for the first time. Captain Harriman shares with the crowd how he used to read all about Captain Kirk's adventures when he was in grade school. Harriman then invites Kirk to give the command. At first, Kirk refuses, but the young captain insists and all the cameras and recorders point to Kirk in anticipation. After a brief silence Kirk stands and says, "Take us out." There is applause and the press records the historical event twenty times over.

That is the only actual footage of the press in the future. At first glance it would appear to be similar to our press today. Cameras rolling, tricorder-like devices are pointed at Kirk and the press asks questions that are very similar to those we would hear from our reporters today. Obviously the press does exist in the future, and one can assume it is free.

It may be difficult to make the connection of how having a free press might assist in the goal of building a society of self-actualized citizens who have gotten rid of poverty, hunger and war. The answer is simple: Information is important, and the ability to manipulate and control what information is dispensed is very powerful. Whether you are trying to learn a musical instrument, or the meaning of life, your pursuit demands that you have access to all relevant information. In terms of our society of the future, the focus would be on improvement in all aspects. The only way to move society forward is to understand what is happening around you, evaluate what is working and what is not working, and make the appropriate adjustments. Getting unfettered and complete access to that information is very important.

In today's America there is a free press. That is, reporters, photographers and journalists who qualify are given special rights and privileges to allow them access to public events, historical moments, and even actual combat. What they have observed can then be reported to the general public so that we can stay informed and aware of important events. In America today, however, although the reporter/journalist is free to observe and ask questions, it is the editors and owners of the media who decide what events will be aired and how they are framed. They also decide which specific questions and answers among those a journalist may have asked will be shared with the public. In this context our free press turns into a power machine. Those in charge seem to consider only two options: print what sells, or print what they want to sell. In both cases, for the most part, objectivity in the press takes a second seat to dollars and agendas.

I no longer read newspapers or watch television broadcast news. I live in China and get all my news from the Internet. I do watch clips that purportedly are clips from broadcast TV, and although I have no reason to doubt it, I have never verified that. All of the means by which we get our news—broadcast TV, cable TV, print, periodical, radio, cyber, or whatever else exists—are part of the media. As I understand it, the basic structure of the commercial media is designed around building markets in order to entice advertisers to pay the media outlets for advertising space or time, thus supporting the particular media outlet. In short, it is necessary for commercial media outlets to develop and build a constituency that provides advertisers with a good market to which their product can be sold.

In this regard the media is like any large corporation. Like the advertisers that use their services, the media has a product for sale: the news. Selling this product can earn quite a profit. This is not the way the founders intended. The notion of free press as it is mentioned in our Constitution is that politicians in particular are to be held under a microscope of scrutiny. The press was designed to be The People's "spear" if you will, to guarantee the government would not screw them, that politicians would not screw them, that laws were being followed, and that everyone was playing by the rules. Even in a government "of The People" there was fear that greed and corruption would seep in. Our founders wanted a champion for The People. So the free press was one of the five freedoms specified in the First Amendment of the Constitution.

One could make a reasonable argument that constitutionally speaking, the free press is what we might refer to as investigative journalists today. These people spend their lives seeking the truth and telling the world about it—at least in theory. But this effort can cost a lot of money. So, early on newspapers (and later electronic media) expanded to build markets big enough to draw advertisers. Depending upon the medium, you can now get soft news, entertainment, sports, weather, people's opinions, cartoons, community information and a whole slew of other stuff from your newspaper or "media outlet." The reason for this is to build their market of readers/viewers/listeners. They can then sell advertising and use the money to pay for investigative journalism…the search for the truth. Not the facts, but the truth.

I need to digress for a moment with a personal story that

might help make the distinction between facts and truth. I had a discussion with a friend online about this issue. This friend works for a newspaper, and he mentioned that as a journalist his job was to present facts not to interpret them. That sounds reasonable, doesn't it? However, I pointed out that presenting facts is different from the truth, unless all facts are presented, in context and with equal weight.

I was a victim of this when I was a school principal. A local paper printed an article stating that I, by name, refused to help a parent who came to school to discuss an issue concerning his child being bullied. In the article it mentioned that not only did I refuse to talk to the parent, I also kicked him off campus. Those are facts, I did refuse to talk to him and I did kick him off campus. However one little fact was not printed. The parent was armed with a side arm. (In fact, the police were called and he was arrested. Another fact that wasn't printed.) The paper printed facts, but not all the facts. So when a journalist says all they do is present facts, then the question should be, "Who decides what facts will be included, and how each fact will be weighted in regard to the overall story?" When I think of truth, I think of it in the sense of, "the whole truth and nothing but the truth." That is what good investigative journalists will do. They will follow a lead wherever it goes, present the all facts, and only the facts in the total context of the story, and readers will draw their own conclusions. In a best case scenario, the hard news sections are beholding to no one and nothing. These hard news sections are as relentless in their investigations as they are in their objective presentations.

There might be a couple of drunks sitting outside of a Circle-K somewhere in America who believe that, but aside from them, all of us know that is no longer the case. Media outlets have discovered that, in addition to selling space to their advertisers, if they tailor their news to accommodate their audience they can make even more money. This is especially true regarding political news. In today's America you have but to mention a specific network, journal, or newspaper and the informed reader or viewer already knows what kind of slant he will get.

In the *Star Trek* scene mentioned above, the young Captain Harriman asks the legend Kirk three times to give the order. The exchange was:

> Captain Harriman: "Captain Kirk. I'd be honored if you'd give the order to get under way."
>
> Captain Kirk: "Thank you very much. I...I..." (As he said this, he shook his head no.)
>
> Captain Harriman: "Please, Sir."
>
> Captain Kirk: "No, no, no..."
>
> Captain Harriman: "Please, I insist."
>
> Captain Kirk: "Take us out."

It is a simple exchange. If you watch the scene there are some gestures by Captain Kirk, shaking his head no, kind of dismissing the second request by a wave of his hand, and after the third request he looks briefly at Chekov and Scotty before rising and giving the "Take us out" command. All very friendly and very common. Simple scene. Right? However, the current state of our press, under the direction of management, would attempt to shape or slant this exchange, to create a narrative they can sell. Liberal management would shape the exchange to fit its narrative. Conversely, conservative management would do the same. If Captain Kirk were a known conservative and Captain Harriman a popular progressive, we would hear two very different accounts of this exchange depending upon the outlet.

On FOX we would hear about a young, incompetent captain who couldn't even take the new Enterprise out of space dock. We would hear how, the venerable and well-decorated Captain Kirk, after trying to encourage the disrespectful Harriman to do the simple task himself, was badgered repeatedly by the young upstart, probably in hopes that Kirk would embarrass himself. We would have some Special Reports questioning whether Star Fleet is promoting people into important positions before they are ready to take charge. There would be accusations of government corruption and waste within Star Fleet. They would air a special on Captain Kirk and all the wonderful things he has done in his career, only to be insulted and publicly harassed by this Harriman jerk.

The outrage would spill into sympathetic media, and radio talk shows would invite friends of that punk Harriman on their show to find out if he has always been incompetent. They would want to explore how he became so indignant. Focus groups would be assembled to get feedback on how the rest of the country felt about this young upstart insulting such a great Star Fleet officer. Polls would be taken on whether or not Harriman should be fired, or at least demoted. Petitions demanding a public apology would be circulated. FOX would stay with the story until they "got to the bottom of it."

On the other hand, MSNBC would openly question Kirk's motives for being so obstinate. Why reject a simple request from a young captain representing the future of Star Fleet? Why would he want to try to shame the new captain in front of his crew? Is Kirk self-obsessed, or is there something more to it? Maybe Kirk was deliberately trying to stall the departure of the Enterprise. Maybe the short, fifteen-minute ride to Pluto would reveal a problem with the ship that Kirk did not want exposed. Maybe, Kirk, the thirty-year puppet of Star Fleet, knew there were design flaws in the ship, the result of short cuts taken to save a few bucks at the expense of the crew, just another example of corporate greed.

Experts would be brought in to display ship design and how one short cut could cost lives. Contractors would be interviewed to find out if they knew, or ever worked with, Captain Kirk. There would be charges of collusion and deal-making…the kind that puts everyone at risk. All of Kirk's past missions would be called into question. After all, if he was willing to risk lives just to pocket a few extra bucks at the christening of Enterprise B, perhaps his real missions were also all a lie. Perhaps HE is a lie. Special Reports would identify all the people Kirk associated with in the different shipyards throughout the world. Who was making the most money off of Kirk's greed? MSNBC would air rallies around the country of outraged citizens who could have died because of his greed. Signs held by protesters with verbiage like, "Kirk the Jerk" or "Boldly going to the bank" and "Beam this up….asshole" would be displayed across America. Poor working people would yet again be victims of the powerful and wealthy.

That is the state our free press today. Politics is big money and the media is a big money machine. Each invented story brings in huge amounts of cash. The media love both sides of politics. Liberals and conservatives are either targets or benefactors, depending upon the media outlet. The more they marginalize their targets, the more support (money) they get from their benefactor. That's good business for them, but bad luck for Americans. As a result, media outlets attract a kind of captive audience who watches what they like because they like what they hear. This works well if you're talking about a sit-com. I really enjoyed "Happy Days," but never was a big fan of "Laverne and Shirley." I watched what I liked and tuned out the shows I didn't like. In any discussion I had with friends it usually ended after one or two sentences and someone saying, "Oh, okay. Whatever. Let's go for a beer."

Manipulation of viewer or reader response may be harmless when it involves entertainment, but the same approach is used with serious news. Programs begin to target their viewers (for ratings and money). The full context (the truth) of any news item becomes secondary to the need to satisfy their audience. (This may be the cynic in me, but when it comes to making money, in a sense business has adopted a notion that doctors practice: Do no harm! Unfortunately, CEO's generally apply this to the bottom line, not

the viewer.) As a result, programs that are purportedly presenting you with facts frequently lie, distort, omit or otherwise shape
what the viewer hears and sees. This process has been refined after
years of practice and getting feedback from focus groups. The media know much more about stage presence, demographics, buying patterns, viewing patterns, sound bites and catch phrases than
they do about presenting the truth.

The damage this causes becomes evident if you talk to regular
viewers of these kinds of broadcasts. If you want to see how damaging this is, simply put a regular viewer of Rachel Maddow in
the same room with a regular viewer of Sean Hannity. Ask them
to have a discussion about which of those two people is correct in
the way they present the news. Give them thirty minutes, then let
them leave. See if they go out for a beer together. It's more likely
they will have hurled names at each other and leave the experience
even more convinced about the stupidity of the other side. This
process of catering to the viewer is creating two opposing camps
of Americans who find less and less in common.

In "Let that be your last Battlefield," (*Star Trek*; S3, E15), the
last two members of a race from the planet Cheron want to kill
each other because they look different, and for 50,000 years they
have believed that difference defined who they were. They are completely entrenched in their ideology. When they return to Cheron,
it is only to discover that their entire species is dead from this
conflict. Rather than try to find peace, they escape the Enterprise
and continue their quest to kill each other on the planet below.

Uhura comments that it doesn't make any sense. Spock responds, "To expect sense from two mentalities of such extreme
viewpoints, is not logical." These two people, Lokai and Bele, had
been taught to hate each other until it consumed their reason and,
in the end, presumably their lives. One can only imagine how the
press on Cheron reinforced the hate over the centuries.

Manipulating the news can create divisions in our society that
can result in extremism. The media have learned how to take news

and shape public opinion. Rather than a viewer just observing the event, whether it's a debate, committee hearing, or speech, and then drawing her own conclusions, the media will immediately have color commentary and analysts telling us what people meant. Because the viewers are being specifically targeted for their ideologies, the programs reinforce how they think and further separate those who agree with their position from those who disagree. This division has gotten quite extreme in America today. In no small part, this is due to the bias in the media.

In the simple scene of Captain Kirk and Captain Harriman described above, the viewers, readers, and listeners of current media outlets would eagerly tune in to their source of news and, for possibly weeks, be fed what to think and even what to do about it. Like a drug addict and his dealer, in our current world there is a kind of co-dependency relationship between viewers and the media, both viewers and media feeding and supporting their ideologies which breed distrust and even hate among Americans. This chasm can be exploited by people in positions of power. A politician can use it to solidify a voting block. A corporation, or special interest group can use it to influence legislation by creating PAC's (Political Action Committees). As a result people with opposing views on any issue are driven further and further apart.

We are no longer presented with the truth. We are given facts that have been handpicked to advance the narrative of the highest bidder. If MSNBC was purchased by the Koch Brothers, programming would change. If FOX was purchased by George Soros, the programming would change. The same holds true for CNN, ABC, CBS, NBC. Whether it's TV, the Internet, print, or radio, it would take no more than one hour of watching, reading or listening to tell me to which party the owners belonged. (I want to reiterate I am talking about political news, or any news that can be used to advance a political ideology.)

The source of the money that funds the media outlet decides what the "news" is and how it will be presented to us. As I mentioned in the previous chapter, big business and big government work together to create false realities. In turn, they control the media to sell and maintain these illusions for direct profit, or indirect profit through political gain.

As a result, the news is not only misleading, it becomes so wrapped up in ideology that it can be very confusing to the reader/listener. Because of this bias, real issues are ignored in an effort to effect a person's political leanings. During the writing of this chapter, there were a couple of events in the news that demonstrate this point. At a Hillary Clinton speaking event, a frustrated attendee who was laid off at HP expressed his natural frustration about it by saying he would just like to strangle Carly Fiorina (A Republican primary candidate). Hillary's response was to laugh and say that she wouldn't stop him. At about the same time there were students at Mizzou (University of Missouri at Colombia) protesting suspected racism, and one of the student leaders said that "safe spaces" were needed. She went on to say she was tired of hearing about Free Speech.

In this timeframe, I heard conservatives and progressives argue with themselves at different times. They also agreed with each other at different times. In the first example, conservatives were arguing how Clinton's response was not appropriate. Anyone who suggests strangling someone should be called out. When Clinton did not do this, conservatives argued, the message is that threats are okay. However, conservatives took issue with the demand for "safe spaces" on campus, and said people have the right to free speech. Progressives argued the right of free speech in the case of Hillary Clinton and insisted the reference to strangling wasn't meant literally; the person was just joking. In the Mizzou case, in one video I watched on FOX (online), the progressive on the show defended the notion of "safe spaces" and the student's concerns by saying, "words hurt." She went on to say that trying to insure that everyone feels safe is important and should not be discounted. In one case, it's just a joke, in the other, "words hurt."

The issue was and is free speech. However, because media outlets are directed to advance ideologies rather than talk about issues, conservatives and progressives argued in favor of, and against, free speech on two separate news items. The principle of free speech was meaningless. Who was saying what was important. That is how "news" is brought to us. It is biased and it is whored out by the corporate pimp with the most money. You would think that the notion of free speech would be almost sacred among members of the press, but that is not true. Ideology is sacred. Free speech? That's just used when it supports the ideology.

At one of the colleges (dormitories) at Yale, prior to Halloween, a student group sent out a notice asking students to be sensitive to other cultures when deciding on the costumes they would wear. A teacher there sent out an email suggesting that trying to limit how others want to express themselves may not be in the best interest of a society that is supposedly based on free speech (and free expression). Some students got very angry about this and called it racism. (That's a whole other issue we'll talk about later). The husband of the teacher, also a professor, was explaining to a group of students in the quad area that what his wife was suggesting was not racism, but just an acknowledgement that trying to control how others express themselves is contrary to free expression and free speech.

One student in particular became very angry and indignant, vehemently yelling at the guy for not supporting the need for a "safe space." She also took a step toward him and let her backpack slide off her back to the ground. I mention this because when I was a school principal there were two sure signs of a fight: "Stepping up" to someone and dropping your backpack. If this had happened on my campus, I would have intervened. She was that upset. In her mind, he was placing students in danger because he supported the idea of free expression even though he knew that maybe, possibly, someone might, could be, offended or feel uncomfortable by another student's costume. How dare he make the campus unsafe!

Among journalists the right of free speech should be held equally high with the right of a free press. To me, any suggestion for controlling either should be considered a step toward totalitarianism or even fascism in the minds of journalists. That is not the case. Very little was said about this incident.

At a different university, for a different reason, the same argument for "safe spaces" was again made by students. The university was Mizzou (The University of Missouri at Columbia). The event was a protest against the school administration for allegedly moving too slowly on some issues of racial slurs. The students held a protest and a student reporter who was trying to cover the event was blocked and refused access to the area the protesters were occupying. At one point a teacher was trying to prevent the student reporter from accessing that area. When she told him he had no right, he responded by saying he did, in fact, have the right as a member of the student press, and that it was specifically guaranteed in the Constitution. The teacher's response was to ask protesters to help her. She said she needed "some muscle" to help her prevent the reporter free access to reporting the event.

If we had a free press in its true sense, I would think reporters would have descended on that campus. They would have held this teacher up as the poster child of censorship and fascism. Investigative journalists would find out exactly what classes she taught and would interview as many people as possible to determine how much influence she might have had on the students. Investigative journalists might even have checked into other campuses to see how widespread the issue was. That did not happen. However, she did apologize and a few days later resigned.

If we had a free press, one would think the outrage and danger of a teacher at a university with an excellent journalism program telling students that a free press doesn't have rights, coupled with the incident at Yale in which the support of free expression was interpreted as racism, would have gone "viral" as they say. That a teacher called for "muscle" to help her! You would think journalists would not ignore that. That a young college student lost her temper with a teacher who was supporting free speech—again, where are the journalists? Many would think free speech is a pretty big thing in the U.S., but the press didn't seem to be much interested. It was like a small burp at a frat house in an evening of beer chugging.

The day after the event at Mizzou on November 10, 2015, I went online and took screen-shots of several news outlets. The screen shots were of what I could best describe as the electronic front page of the media outlet. (Although the front page of a website can hold quite a bit more than a traditional newspaper.) This is by no means meant to be a definitive study, it is just an observation. As such, you may draw whatever conclusions you wish. Because there were a variety of articles concerning Mizzou, I included the title of the article.

MEDIA OUTLET	TOTAL NUMBER OF ARTICLES	MIZZOU RELATED ARTICLES	ARTICLES
ABC	20	0	
CBS	22	2	"University of Missouri no stranger to racial tension"
			"Threats prompt increased security at University of Missouri"
CNN	21	1	"Threats prompt increased security at University of Missouri"
FOX	22	4	"PRESS FREEDOM ISSUE Mizzou prof resigns after clash with student reporter"

MEDIA OUTLET	TOTAL NUMBER OF ARTICLES	MIZZOU RELATED ARTICLES	ARTICLES
FOX			"VIDEO: Media under siege on Mizzou campus"
			DISCIPLINARY ACTION: Students at University of Missouri asked to report 'hateful,' hurtful' speech"
			OPINION: University of Missouri, Yale, and a cultural revolution"
LA Times	15	2	"Threats on social media rattle University of Missouri campus"
			"Would University of Missouri students have needed to go to such Extremes if they were Jewish?"
NBC	25	1	"Mizzou teacher who tried to boot journalist apologizes"
NY Post	32	2	"University of Missouri has the world's worst journalism professor"
			Real Missouri 'Concerned Student 1950' speaks, at age 89
Wash. Post	19	3	"Missouri football shows how sports affect social change"
			"Can colleges protect free speech while curbing voices of hate?"
			"Missouri professor apologizes for confronting student journalist"

Summary: The day after an event in which a professor at a journalism school asked for "muscle" to prevent a student reporter from covering a school protest, here is how the media outlets above reported the incident. For that day, the eight outlets above displayed a total of 176 articles on the 'front page' of their websites. Of that total, 15 articles reported on Mizzou (about 8.5%). Of those 15 articles, 8 articles had to do with free speech; Roughly 53% of the relevant articles, or 4.5% of the total number of articles presented that day. However, you can see FOX presented 4 articles on the issue of free speech. If FOX is removed from the mix, of the154 remaining articles, 4 refer to the incident, or about 2.5% of the articles covered the event. On the other hand, articles concerning the allegations of racism at Mizzou received twice as much coverage, about 5% (again without FOX).

Assuming that decisions needed to be made concerning what the front page would display, one would think concerns about free speech might take precedence over articles like the following (these all appeared on outlets listed above that had no story about the Mizzou incident): "Secret Service arrest man for firing a sling shot at the White House." "Apple iPad pro: What you need to know." "Cheerleader gives football coach dad the game of his life." "Photographer startled by Milky Way encounter." "NFLer accused of taunting a police dog." In terms of news, shouldn't a story about a journalism teacher at a journalism college asking for muscle to prevent a reporter from reporting the news make the cut, compared to articles such as those just cited? Viewers and readers of these outlets only received what the owners wanted.

So, from the start, we know the truth is biased. But that is only the first punch. Our "free" press has a combination-punch routine to keep the truth at bay. The second punch: We have to hear from "experts" about what it all means and what to think about it. We have to listen to testimonials from people who are supposed to help personalize the event, or the people around the event. We need to listen to activist groups and what they think. And all of this is done in ways to make it appealing; funny personalities, warm personalities, probing personalities, engaging personalities…people that we have been trained to "trust" tell us what it all means and what we should think about it. This is all very deliberate and very important to keeping an audience, or maintaining a bottom line. The truth is lost to the dollar and honest debate succumbs to pandering.

This tactic is not only more successful when the population is not self-actualized, I would argue it can only occur with a population that has been educated to do what they are told. Numbing the mind in school is the first step to keeping it numb for a lifetime. The media simply continue the process each day they present news.

As I mentioned previously, big business and big government work together. They use the free press to help numb all of us and condition us not to expect the truth. Whether it's the food we eat, the programs we watch, or the news itself, the free press is used to sell the agendas of big business and big government, no longer protecting The People. The press, driven by agendas that have nothing to do with protecting us, present us with information that is slanted in such a way as to define how we should live and what we should believe.

Without any real examples of this in the future, it is hard to say how those in the 24th century would have responded. There are, however, many examples in the *Star Trek* universe of how important the truth is, as well as how pervasive the notion of transparency is.

In *Enterprise*, Captain Archer uncovers a secret listening post hidden by the Vulcans near the Temple, P'Jem, that was being used to spy on the Andorians ("The Andorian Incident," S1, E7). Rather than placate the Vulcans, their only real ally as they begin star travel, they insist the post be revealed and dismantled. In *StarTrek: TNG*, "The Hunted" (S3, E11), the Enterprise was asked by the Prime Minister of Angosia III to catch an escaped convict. When they caught him and heard about possible wrong doing, they investigated and discovered the truth. They did not just simply return the prisoner. Also in "The Wounded" (*Star Trek: TNG*; S4, E12), Captain Maxwell was trying to expose a possible Cardasian plot and violated the treaty. Captain Picard was placed in the position of catching Maxwell. The Cardasians were highly suspicious of any Star Fleet effort to catch one of their own. To ensure transparency, Captain Picard invited the Cardasian captain on board the Enterprise to observe Picard's efforts to find and detain Captain Maxwell. Worf objected for security reasons, but Picard insisted.

It appears in the 24th century transparency is commonplace. When Kirk appears at a Star Fleet disciplinary hearing after saving the world from some alien probe that was evaporating the oceans, he and his bridge crew stand before the panel with hundreds of onlookers. (I presume they were representatives from the many planets that make up Star Fleet.) A younger Captain Kirk also finds himself in front of a disciplinary board in *Star Trek* (2009) with what appears to be hundreds of cadets from the academy. In both cases there are no lawyers. It is not an unreasonable assumption that the hearings are recorded, or logged and available for general review. Certainly within Star Fleet, logs are kept. Perhaps this complete willingness to air laundry from the beginning helps prevent laundry from getting too dirty.

Neither one of these scenes gave a hint of reporters, press hounds, public outcries or any of the publicity vehicles that we typically see today. Without the press being used by big business and big government to advance their agendas, perhaps events occur and are simply interpreted by the citizen...a citizen who is self-actualized and who strives to improve herself. Rather than the event being reported in sound bites and catch phrases, perhaps camera feeds, accessible to anyone who wishes to view, present events live, in their entirety and viewers think whatever they choose to think.

I believe it was in the 1970's when there was an experiment

with broadcasting NFL games in their entirety without anyone "calling the game." No John Maddens, no Howard Cosells, no Chris Collingsworths…just the game. It didn't go very well as I remember and henceforth broadcasters were forever joined with NFL broadcasts. I am sure there were many focus groups and other efforts by the networks to help them determine the success of this experiment. I can tell you that I didn't miss the jabber. If memory serves, my friends and I just flipped on the stereo and created our own commentary.

We were well versed in football. We knew the teams, we knew the players, we knew the importance of each game and how it would affect the fourteen game season. (That was the old season.) We understood what was happening on the sidelines and we understood basic defenses and offenses as well as the strength of each team.

In a way, regarding football, we were self-actualized. We could provide a context for the games. Maybe the "news" should be just that: information that is new. The next day it is replaced by more "news," rather than rehashed and reshaped to advance ideology. Perhaps in a world of self-actualized, free-thinking individuals there is no longer a need to hear talking heads tell us what and how to think. Perhaps news is presented in full without commentary, only to viewers who seek it. News only becomes as big as the viewers choose it to be, not the media outlets.

The closest to this in the political news arena is C-SPAN's House, Senate and Hearing cameras. The viewer can watch whatever portion of a floor vote, debate, or committee hearing they wish. There are no commercials, no talking heads, just the government working (or perhaps not working) live for the world to see. Maybe that is what the free press looks like in the 24th century. Perhaps when the citizenry are self-actualized and we no longer have to worry about poverty, hunger, money and war, when the only want that needs to be satisfied is self-improvement, all the biased information we are being fed today will not exist. Maybe our counterparts in the future have a free press that simply presents what is happening and each citizen simply chooses what to make of it.

Part II

Chapter 5

Here Today, Gone Tomorrow

T he USS Enterprise makes its first contact with the Children of Tama. The main view screen comes on and Captain Dathon, of the Tamarian ship opens the discussion.

Captain Dathon: "Rye and Jarin at Luca. Rye of Luwani. Luwani under two moons. Jiri of Umbaya. Umbaya of crossroads at Lunga. Lunga at sky grey."

Captain Picard: "Captain would you be prepared to consider the creation of a mutual non-aggression pact between our two peoples? Possibly leading to a trade agreement and cultural exchange. Does this sound like a reasonable course of action to you?"

Another bridge officer from the Tamarian ship starts to laugh and says, "Good day at Tamic."

He is interrupted by Captain Dathon who says, "In winter." The officer immediately stops laughing.

Captain Dathon continues, "Shaka when the walls fell. Darmok at Tanagra."

The other officer starts to say something and is cut off by the captain. "Darmok and Jilad at *Tanagra*."

Suddenly Captain Dathon and Picard are beamed off their respective bridges down to the planet they are orbiting.

This is the opening scene from "Darmok" (*Star Trek: TNG*; S5, E2). In this episode we learn that the Tamarians communicate by referencing important events of their history. Although English is being spoken, the Enterprise crew are baffled because they can't understand the context in which it is used. At a briefing prior to meeting the Tamarian ship, Picard learned that Star Fleet had already had seven encounters with the Tamarians, all apparently as confusing as this one. As a result one Star Fleet officer insisted that the Tamarian language was incomprehensible. Picard commented, "In my experience communication requires patience and imagination."

This is what is required for this chapter. I am going to discuss issues that we experience today, but I will be looking at them through the lens of the future. As such, when you first read this section, you will understand the words, but you may have a difficult time accepting the ideas. We have all been taught what to believe and what is "normal" in terms of our society and our culture. As we look at these issues through the lens of the future we may discover a different norm. The notions of how our future counterparts would view these issues might appear to be as meaningless and disjointed as the initial conversation between Picard and Dathon. However, if you are patient and are willing to use your imagination, in time it might start to make sense.

Before I begin, some caveats:

1. I am not an "ist"… economist, sociologist, psychologist, theologist, constitutionalist, or whatever. I will be discussing current issues using conjecture and observation. No empirical evidence has been collected. However, the assumptions I make are consistent with what we know of *Star Trek*. I want to reiterate that our future is a future in which everyone has shared values. Moreover, institutions encourage those values. Those values include individual responsibility, a desire to improve one's self, self-respect, and pride in one's ability to achieve.

2. Going through this process will once again step on ideological toes. Whether you are a *Star Trek* fan or not, try to

remove your personal, political and social biases as you read this. Step out of this reality and try to look at this as if you were observing it, not judging it, kind of like Jordy and Ro in "The Next Phase" (*Star Trek: TNG*; S5, E24), where they are out of phase with everyone else and are looking in on events. Remember I will present issues from a world that is disconnected from what we know now, one that has left behind many of the problems we have today. The purpose of this chapter is to provide the landscape of the future. In later chapters I will attempt to provide details as to how it all might work.

3. The issues below are in no special order and are not intended to address all the challenges we face today. However, they do address issues that have been in the news for the past several years, (many of them for decades).

- Jobs/Economy
- Taxes
- Race relations
- Gender inequality
- Abortion
- Immigration
- Drugs
- Religion
- The 2nd Amendment
- Gay Marriage
- Global Warming

Jobs/Economy

In the future there is no minimum wage, there is no job lock, there is no income-inequality, there is no unemployment, there are no unions, there is no one percent, there is no big business and there is no big government. Why? There is no money. Without money fueling capitalism everything has changed. Well, not everything. Individuals still own property and still provide goods and services. In *Star Trek* (2009) we can see many people working at the shipyard in Iowa as Kirk leaves to join Star Fleet. In that same movie we see people working in a bar. Someone, or some business, built the motorcycle that Kirk gave away to one of those shipyard workers. So, jobs do exist, but the job "market" is clearly different.

In chapter two I talked about how the public school system today is designed to produce worker bees: get a good education and get a good job. In the future, without money, education transforms from a system of indoctrination and training, to exploration and discovery. Children in the future are learning how to learn and how to achieve. They are learning skills, not content areas. In a sense, no one ever finishes school. They complete a phase of their learning process and move into another. From elementary, middle, and high school, they go to trade schools, colleges, universities or less formal settings. From there they go into apprenticeships, internships and partnerships. They begin collaborating with others, sharing what they have learned, and challenge themselves to go further. They seek others' perspectives and input. They live their lives gathering information, observing, and pushing themselves to experience growth and gain expertise.

All of this is done without earning one penny. The obvious question is, how? I will offer an idea about that in the next chapter. For now we will simply look at how jobs are affected in an economy without money. Big business and industry needs trained employees. Without money, big business is gone, but businesses still exist. Moreover, schools are no longer training large work forces. So how are jobs created and filled? We know in the *Star Trek* universe, individuals are empowered and make many, if not most, of the decisions that affect their lives. That leads me to assume that whatever the economy of the future is, it is not controlled by a large bureaucracy empowered to make decisions for members of society, a common characteristic of a communist or socialist government. We also know that capitalism as we know it is gone.

However, of those three possibilities, capitalism, or some form of it, would offer the best fit. Webster defines "capitalism" as "a way of organizing an economy so that the things that are used to make and transport products (such as land, oil, factories, ships, etc.) are owned by individual people and companies rather than by the government." We know that in the future, individuals own property. I cited several examples of that in chapter one. Autonomy is respected, individuality is respected, and choice is important. The system that governs our future has to be one that honors individual choice and ownership. Perhaps there is some hybrid form of capitalism in the future.

In the future our schools teach us to be individual learners and to achieve on our own. The government of the future reinforces this practice by empowering us to make our own choices for our lives. Without big government and big business defining our society, we would be left to define it for ourselves. One possibility might be that business is local. So Kirk's motorcycle, or the bar where Uhura is introduced, could be the result of one local economy among many. There might be thousands of small fabricating shops throughout the country; national chains and franchises may not exist. (I am going to use conjecture just to give you an idea of how it might work.)

Kirk could have bought his bike from a dealership located twelve miles from his house. However, it isn't just a dealership. They actually make the bike, or most of it. Kirk's bike has a unique kind of suspension. It's innovative. The designers of the suspension system went to school with some kids who had new ideas for how to build a lightweight frame for motorcycles that offered more efficiency as well as safer design qualities. These people got together and started talking about collaborating and building their own bike. They approached their educational facilitator and got some names of people who were working on a new polymer tire that provided safer travel.

These kids, working together, formed a partnership. They shared a common passion and started building bikes. Since money is not a factor, they were not worried about bottom lines. There was no need to build a large factory, find investors, no bank loans, and no market-share discussions. They simply focused on building their idea of a great bike. They only made seven or eight a year, but with each one completed they improved the process.

One of them knows this kind of wild guy named Jim who likes to ride bikes. He calls him up and tells him about what they are doing. Jim comes by and likes what he sees. Jim has been credited for work he has done in school as well as his community. He uses those credits and drives off with a bike.

It's a similar story for the bartenders. They are not working for a franchise. It's not a TGIF. They are owners of their own establishment. This story is repeated hundreds of thousands of times across the country. With big business and big government out of the way and an economy not dependent on money, individuals share passions and develop them into enterprises that can build local communities.

Jobs are replaced by personal interests. Rather than earning money, people earn credits for how they live and what they do. These credits can then be used for goods and services. As I explained in chapter three, people don't want as much as we do today. Marketing and advertising are gone. Creating a need where none previously existed is gone. Wealth is not defined by what you have, but rather by what you do. We are no longer living to consume. There is no need for jobs as we know them today. People learn skills in school, they learn how to achieve, how to work with others, and they apply that knowledge to their lives…forever. People don't need thirty pairs of shoes, three flat screen TV's or four cars. Like Arlo Guthrie's line in one of his songs, "Some of them just want to ride a motor............cycle."

There are jobs that fill needs for all members of the community: education, health care, emergency services to name the most obvious. Certainly there are people for whom these types of jobs are perfect. However, it would be a stroke of luck if individual passions of the people within a given community matched up exactly with all the needs of the community. In the three examples above, it's easy to imagine filling teaching roles, or nursing roles and even policing roles. But what about all the support services: cleaning, maintenance, record keeping, etc.?

The community would complete these tasks in a kind of community service program. Individuals would be credited for the time they participate in their community. As a result the job market would be much more fluid than it is today. Rather than one janitor working forty hours a week, perhaps one week there are four people who fill that role for ten hours each and they are credited for their time. For the next week there might be ten people who are credited for four hours each.

The job market and workforce is ever changing. Time is the currency and people are credited for the time they commit to sustain the community, regardless of the particular task. As a result, one person may perform many different tasks over a year, or may focus on a single task. The decision would be determined by the individual and her community's needs. The economy is not driven by government or business, but by communities and needs. Self-actualized individuals would seek out opportunities to participate in the community and fill the needs of that community.

Because material wealth is not the goal, however, the time they commit to the community is determined by the need to complete the task, not the need to make more Tomoney. They are then credited for their contributions to the community and earn time to pursue personal endeavors. Unlike people of today who seek to earn money so they can buy more stuff, our future counterparts contribute to the community to earn credits that give them time to work on personal growth and personal interests. In a sense, the ability to sate our own personal curiosity is the goal. Time is what we most value and giving away large chunks of it every week for money would be seen as wasteful.

Taxes

Taxes obviously are strongly connected to the economy. Without money, taxes no longer exist. The role of government is as limited as possible and filled much like the community jobs cited above. One example would be public transportation. We no longer pay taxes to hire people to manage a department responsible for building roads and vehicles, or hire drivers and maintenance crews. We no longer have to worry about the bureaucracy that grows from the need to provide employees with regular raises, benefits, hiring policies or firing polices. Moreover, we no longer have to deal with the politics of it all. Where the roads will go? Who will benefit from a new highway? These are the kinds of questions that often lead to the infamous deal-making practices of current politicians.

All of this evolves away to a much simpler process in which people earn credits. Their jobs are also very flexible, and the workforce very fluid. The people with a natural proclivity or personal interest that overlaps with community needs might become the supervisors of a project, or a particular aspect of the project. These people are spending their time doing exactly what they want, not because it's their job. They don't get up and think, "Oh, no. It's only Tuesday. Four more days to go." They do it because they love it and they want to become better at it. Their job satisfaction is high.

The other workers also benefit. There may not be many people who love digging ditches, but there may be many more who would be willing to commit a couple of hours a week just to earn some credit for participating. A large project may have thousands of different people committing various amounts of time. They are no longer angry about having to work four months to pay off their inevitable taxes. They work to get credits enough to give them the time they need, and they are gone.

This whole issue of taxes has become moot in the future.

Race Relations

In the future, race is not defined by color. It is defined by species. There is only one race: human. The NAACP has either closed its doors and boarded up the windows, or they have changed their organization to the NAAP (National Association for the Advancement of People). Their focus is the impact of humans on our planet and they are actively involved in the preservation of our environment.

There is not one episode in the entire *Star Trek* franchise in which a character refers to another by the color of his or her skin or heritage. When Ro first joins the crew of the Enterprise and goes into Ten-Forward for the first time, she does not ask Riker, "Who's the black lady behind the bar?" Captain Jainway doesn't introduce her 1st officer by saying, "This is my 1st Officer, Jakota. He is a Native American. No one comments on Keiko's pretty yellow skin. No one refers to Q as a powerful white guy. References to skin color just don't exist.

Race is also not identified by heritage. Jainway never says how happy she is that her communications officer, Mr. Kim, is Asian. Nor does she refer to her chief of security, Tuvok, as an African-Vulcan. Worf does not introduce his parents to Captain Picard as his Russian parents. No one asks chief engineer, B'Ellana Torres about her Hispanic father. Race is just not an issue in the future. Prejudice is considered primitive. In "Let That Be Your Last Battlefield" (*Star Trek: TNG*; S3, E15) Chekov and Sulu have a brief discussion that reveals this fact. They are having a discussion about the hate Lokai and Bele had for each other simply because of their skin difference. In a final bridge scene Chekov says, "There was persecution on earth once. I remember reading about it in my history class." Sulu responds, "Yes, but it happened way back in the 20th century. There's no such primitive thinking today." In the *Star Trek* universe, Martin Luther King, Jr's dream has been achieved.

Of course there are two events that have occurred in the *Star Trek* universe—a nuclear war and alien contact—that have made it obvious that skin color means nothing. Our future counterparts understand that color does not designate a new race, but rather demonstrates the breadth of a single race. Without having lived through these events, it might be more difficult to see this truth. But it's not impossible. Many people living today would like to stop using color as a reference to others. Perhaps they can help the rest of us see this simple truth without having to annihilate each other or wait for alien contact.

In any event, this issue has become moot in the future.

Gender Inequality

I believe the biggest sub-issue of the greater issue of gender inequality is the pay gap between women and men. In the future, without money, the pay gap is obviously no longer an issue. The broader issue of women not being permitted to participate, and not being accepted in roles that are seen as exclusively male, is evolving away as we speak. In the *Star Trek* universe, gender roles have been completely erased. Women are everywhere! Pilots, engineers, doctors, officers, cooks, bartenders, security chiefs...you name it, you can see it. There are too many examples to cite them all. Any fan will tell you that in *Star Trek*, possession of a vagina does not preclude a person from doing whatever she wishes.

This issue has become moot in the future.

Abortion

Abortion is an individual choice. I am sure it is legal in the future. However, I am equally sure it is a rare practice...perhaps even very rare. One evolutionary step humans have taken in the world of *Star Trek* is to respect life. Not some life, not life that is convenient for us, or even understood by us, but all life. In "Home Soil" (*Star Trek: TNG;* S1, E17), an inorganic life form is discovered. Dr. Crusher tells Picard that two measurements used to determine organic life forms are reproduction and growth. She is convinced that this new life form, completely inorganic, has both, and as such it should be considered life. This awareness results in Picard bringing an abrupt end to an important scientific project with broad implications for humans. But reverence for life dictates that such ethical steps must be taken. This kind of respect for all life would surely transfer to humans, making the willful destruction of human life a very rare act.

We have eliminated war and murder in the future. In the episode, "Justice" (*Star Trek: TNG;* S1, E8), we learn that we have eliminated capital punishment as well. Wesley Crusher violated a law on Rubicun III and the penalty was death. Picard intervened and sought mercy, explaining that earth no longer practiced capital punishment.

In terms of abortion, there are two telling examples of unwanted pregnancies in *Star Trek:* "The Child" (*Star* Trek: *TNG;* S2, E1) and "Unexpected" (*Enterprise;* S1, E4). Deanna Troi, Ship's Counselor in "The Next Generation" and Commander Tucker, Chief Engineer in *Enterprise* (a male) were impregnated by aliens. In both cases abortion was not sought. (Although Worf did suggest it as an option, it was only because the alien fetus could possibly pose a threat to the ship. As Chief of Security, Worf was simply doing his job.) In regards to Trip's pregnancy (Commander Tucker), abortion was never discussed. The discussion was how to remove the fetus safely. In a future that respects life and has gotten rid of other forms of the willful destruction of human life, it would be absurd to believe we would continue to regularly practice abortion.

It is important to note that in both cases the choice belonged to the individuals involved: Troi and Trip. It was respect for life that drove each individual's choice. Much like with many behaviors that we seem to practice regularly today—public displays of outrage, crime, drug use, alcoholism, etc.—human behavior has evolved in our future. While choice does exist, the well balanced, educated, self-actualized, life-long learning species we have become has not only conquered war, hunger, poverty and want, it has helped us conquer one of the most insidious behaviors that humans suffer from today: Men have learned not to think with their penises!

All of the behaviors that lead to abortion today—poor planning, men thinking with their penises, passion, immaturity, men thinking with their penises, alcohol, defective contraception devices, men thinking with their penises, peer pressure, acts of violence, and men thinking with their penises—are not exhibited, or rarely exhibited in the future. With self-actualization, responsibility, self-respect, education and strong support from families and communities these behaviors fall by the wayside as a step in a natural process. This results in eliminating the need for abortion.

This issue becomes moot in the future.

Immigration

One hundred percent of Americans support immigration. We all understand that as a nation we are the "mutt" of the world. Indeed, we celebrate that fact. The real issue is about those who come to our country illegally, or stay in our country illegally. That is to say they violate the law. Sometimes, however, these laws are violated by people who need to escape serious circumstances and may even be fleeing for their lives. In the world of *Star Trek*, humans are described as Tarens as we are from the planet earth. We are one people who live in various parts of the planet. There are borders and there are countries, but nationalism and territoriality to the point of conflict seem to have disappeared. All people from all countries live in a world without war, hunger, poverty and want…and no need for money. If you take away the circumstances from which people want to escape, in most cases they will stay with their families and live a happy life right in their own community.

I am sure the process of migrating from one country to another is much simpler and much less significant in the future. If the goal of our future counterparts is to improve their lives or their communities, they are not going to be fighting over resources or territory or religion. They are going to be focusing on helping each other.

In the example I used to describe how Kirk's motorcycle might have been built, maybe the classmates who got together are from several different countries. Their "class" could have been a digital classroom. Their class project could have been an international collaboration of five or six students working on this new suspension system. Upon completing the class, one of the group members may have brought up the idea of getting together, and just by coincidence Iowa was chosen as the meeting place. (The group could just as easily have begun their work in Koh Samui, Thailand.) Next thing you know, Kirk has a bike!

The issue of immigration has become moot in the future.

Drugs

As Lieutenant Yar explained in, "Symbiosis" (*Star Trek: TNG*; S1, E22) when she was talking to Wesley Crusher about her home planet, "When there is so much poverty and violence, some see drugs as the only escape." Get rid of poverty and violence, like we do in the future, and the need for drugs as an escape evolves away! Add to that a self-actualized citizenry that strives to improve themselves and drugs actually become an impediment.

In the future, drugs no longer play a part, and the issue has become moot.

Religion

Religion may still exist in the *Star Trek* universe. The references are conflicting. However, if it does, its role is much less significant and much less visible than it is in today's world. In *Star Trek: The Wrath of Khan"* (1982), Dr. McCoy becomes angry when he hears about the Genesis device and says, "According to myth, the earth was created in six days. Now, watch out! Here comes Genesis! We'll do it for you in six minutes!" This suggests, for McCoy at least, religion is a myth. Yet in "The Man Trap" (*Star Trek;* S1, E2), Dr. McCoy is forced to shoot an alien life form that is sucking all the salt out of Kirk. Before doing so he says, "Lord forgive me."

In, "Who Mourns for Adonis," (*Star Trek;* S2, E2), Kirk meets a being on Pollux IV who says he is the god Apollo. Later, in a discussion Kirk says, "Mankind has no need for gods. We find the One quite adequate."

In "Who Watches the Watchers" (*Star Trek: TNG*; S3, E4), the Enterprise is tasked with resupplying a Federation outpost observing the Mintakan people on Mintaka III. Due to an accident, members of the crew are forced to reveal the Federation's technology. Picard becomes worried that the exposure has "set back" the Mintakan people to an age of religious belief. However, in *Generations* (1994), Picard gets trapped in the Nexus and finds himself in a fantasy of having a family and celebrating Christmas. In, "Far Beyond the Stars" (*Deep Space 9*; S6, E13) Commander Sisko's father, Joseph, quotes from the bible.

With the conflicting referencing of religion in several of the franchises, it becomes apparent that religion exists on some level for some, but it plays a much smaller role in the future. It is safe to say, however, that to whatever extent religion exists in the future, it is respected. Spirituality is respected in the future. Whether it is Klingon, Vulcan, or even our Native American, there are many examples of the various crews supporting the traditions and spirituality of Worf, Spock, Jakote and others.

Indeed, the support becomes participation. In "The Cloud" (*Voyager*, S1, E25), Jakote helps Jainway find an animal guide. This respect for spirituality is very strong. In "Emanations" (*Voyager*, S1, E8), the crew discovers alien corpses inside of an asteroid. Before scanning them, Jakote suggests they be left in peace. Mr Kim says the scientific knowledge they could gain might be invaluable. Janeway decides not to move, scan, or otherwise disrupt the bodies. Their respect for culture won out over the pursuit of scientific knowledge. This is a testament to the importance our future counterparts place on individual choice.

In the future, religion may evolve away. Certainly the influence religion has on our daily lives today does evolve away. Churches no longer have collection plates. They no longer have the ability to sell God to everyone. Much like with the corporate world in which large corporate restaurants are replaced by "mom and pop" joints that survive on word-of-mouth advertising, we no longer have the corporate church. There are no more national chains of religions that open a new restaurant (church) on every corner. We no longer have globally organized religions telling us how to live. Local communities may have groups of individuals who get together and share, but that would be the extent of it. More likely, religion would kind of be similar to sex in that we would keep it behind closed doors. Individuals would no more carry a Bible, Koran or Torah around in public than they would flash their genitalia in public. In any event, whatever people believe or don't believe is respected. Persecution and condemnation are gone.

In the future, religion as an issue has become moot.

Guns

The real issue in America today in terms of the right to bear arms, is the number of deaths caused by guns—sometimes falsely referred to as "gun violence." (Guns are not violent, guns are not peaceful, guns are not happy, depressed or schizophrenic. They are just inanimate objects.) If there were no victims from gunshots, it would probably not be much of an issue today. That is why it is not an issue in our future.

Gun ownership in the future is legal and practiced. In "Broken Bow" (*Enterprise*; S1, E1), a Klingon crash lands on a farmer's field in Oklahoma. The Klingon is being chased by two Suliban. The Klingon manages to kill the Suliban, but the farmer comes out with a plasma rifle and shoots the Klingon.

However, in the future I believe there are few people who actually buy guns. In order to understand this, it may help to look at what motivates humans in the 21st century to buy guns. The four primary legal reasons people buy guns are: Personal protection, collecting, hunting, and to prevent a tyrannical government takeover.

In the future as depicted in *Star Trek*, the need for personal protection has greatly decreased. Crime is virtually non-existent. (Stun phasers would be available for those few who feel the need for protection.)

While there might still be collectors, collections would be more similar to historical collections. Arms and munitions manufactures would have been winnowed down to a very few (similar to saddle making companies today), and probably would have been replaced by local gun makers.

While hunting might exist, this too could be on a much smaller scale. We know meat is still consumed. In "Lonely Among Us" (*Star Trek: TNG*; S1, E7), the Enterprise is taking two alien delegations to peace talks. In a conversation with one of them, Commander Riker says, "We no longer enslave animals for food purposes." He goes on to explain that what looks like meat is, "as fresh and tasty as meat, but inorganically materialized, out of patterns used by our transporters." This would suggest that meat is still eaten. However, in the event we actually develop food replicators, the only people who would still hunt for meat would be those who choose a lifestyle that embraces nature rather than technology.

Even if food replicators are not available, the general diet would be healthier and probably include less meat. Moreover, the future economy would not support large corporate ranches, farms, and stockyards. They would be more local, and this approach would also have an impact on the meat we eat, possibly further reducing the number of hunters needed, and some of those hunters would likely be bow hunters.

In terms of those people who believe they need guns to prevent the government from taking over, there would be many fewer of them since government no longer takes from the people. It serves the people and is much smaller.

The one exception to these four groups is police officers. However, as any *Star Trek* fan will tell you, for Star Fleet at least, phasers are usually defaulted to stun. It would be logical to assume for our police force the same would be true. Much like other rights we have today—the right to yell in people's faces, the right to drink alcohol, the right to watch TV, the right to buy things we don't need, the right to live beyond our means and so on—the right to own a gun would be of little interest to most of our future counterparts.

Given this reality, this issue has become moot in the future.

Gay Marriage

In the latest presentation of *Star Trek*, "Star Trek Beyond" (2016), we see our first example of a gay couple, presumably married, when Sulu meets his husband and daughter at the Yorktown space station. It would appear gay marriage is legal, accepted and practiced...and no one really cares. Individual choice is respected. No one in the future cares who you marry, whose hand you hold, and with whom you smile when you see a cute little puppy dog in the window. In the great scheme of things it makes no difference.

This issue has become moot.

Global Warming

Our future is not concerned with global warming. Our future counterparts have survived our current practices, which are now damaging our planet. They have learned the importance of living in harmony with the earth. They live a life that promotes health: individual, family, community and planetary. Today's global warming issue can be closely linked with human consumption. In the future our need to consume is balanced with our understanding that respecting all life means respecting the eco-system as well. Our economy is no longer driven by profit, but rather by improving the human condition.

By getting rid of want we develop a lifestyle that helps us focus on what we are doing, not what we have. This mindset would apply to how we live our lives in the home as well. Smaller homes and fewer wants result in less energy use. Moreover, technology advancements make us independent of fossil fuels. I can't tell you exactly how personal transportation is fueled. When you watch either *Star Trek* (2009), or *Star Trek; Into the Darkness* (2013), you can see individual cars, motorcycles, busses, a trolley, and air-barges. Certainly the future has flying vehicles and hovercrafts…even a "hover gurney" in one scene from *Star Trek: Into the Darkness*. Some appear to be powered by some magnetic, or perhaps anti-gravitational, field.

Kirk's bike gives off a hum of some sort. Perhaps it is magnetic; it certainly isn't gasoline powered. While electric vehicles might be a bridge to energy in the future, they also have a negative impact on the planet. Hence, it is more likely that solar, wind, current, electro-magnetic, and natural geo-thermal energy sources, are more commonplace. In the world of *Star Trek*, photons are generated by colliding matter and anti-matter and then converted to electrical power. There is also the real possibility of fusion. Suffice it to say, fossil fuels will, at the very least, be greatly reduced if not completely eliminated as sources of energy. Regardless of what the energy source is, it is important to remember that the demand for energy consumption will also be greatly reduced.

Because we no longer have a drive to own things, and because everything we own demands energy to be produced and transported, the fewer items we own, the lower the demand for energy. Today, the transportation industry has the largest impact on our environment in terms of carbon emissions. This includes the obvious: human travel. However, when we think of transporting goods that we are taught to want, I am sure that alone adds up to millions and millions of gallons of fuel per year to ship billions of items around the world. Remove the need to buy unnecessary things and we no longer need to transport so much. That alone would have a large impact on our environment.

Lastly, the individual consumer is focused on improving himself and his community. The practice of burning energy almost 24/7 by watching TV, playing video games, computer games, tablet games, phone games, watch games—and the soon-to-be-invented electronic game embedded on the inside cover of books—has been replaced by actually living life. In the future we use *human* energy to get us through the day.

This issue has become moot.

Much like the seeming disjointed conversation we heard from the Children of Tama, all of these issues seen through the eyes of our future counterparts would not make sense. They would just not exist. Although it might be difficult to take in, the future doesn't have to be three hundred more years of doing the same thing. If we can change who we are and become that self-actualized society, then what we see as issues today could all but disappear. In the coming chapters we will take a more detailed look at what a self-actualized America might look like.

Chapter 6

A Credit for Your Thoughts

The crew of the Enterprise watch in wonder as large-scale magnetic field changes in the Sun at the center of the De-Los system produce gigantic, violent flares. Captain Picard puts the ship on Yellow Alert as a precaution. Commander Riker comments, "The violence of these eruptions is awesome." Suddenly, there is a distress call from a damaged freighter, the Sanction, orbiting the planet, Brekka (the fourth planet in the system). Communications are garbled as a result of the solar eruptions, but the ship's orbit is decaying and the ship is falling into the atmosphere, burning up.

The solar activity prevents the Enterprise from locking on and limits the transporter. As the Sanction begins to enter Brekka's atmosphere Lt. Yar tries to save the six passengers. When she engages the transporter only cargo containers from the ship materialize on the transporter pads. Picard cannot believe it! The ship begins to disintegrate in the atmosphere and Picard tells Lt Yar to lock onto any life forms on the ship. She locks onto all six passengers, but only four materialize on board the Enterprise. Two were lost because of the interference from the solar activity. Riker apologizes to the four as he explains that the other two are gone. He said, "If you had come instead of the cargo, you could have all made it."

One of the passengers, Romas, in a panic, asks, "You did save it, didn't you?"…referring to the cargo. We learn that the cargo is a medicine called Felicium and is very important. Two of the passengers, Romas and T'Jon, are from the planet Ornara. They are bringing the medicine to their planet. The entire population of Ornara is infected with a plague that has lasted for two centuries. The Felicium mitigates the symptoms of the plague, and the Ornarans need the medicine regularly to keep them alive.

As the story develops, however, we learn it is all a lie. Felicium is actually a narcotic and the Brekkans, aware that the plague is no longer a threat, have built their entire economy around processing it. (A key ingredient can only be grown on Brekka.) Ornarans, thinking they are suffering from a plague, and need regular injections, have committed their world's economy to producing goods to trade to Brekka for the drug. For two hundred years the Ornarans have been hooked on Felicium.

While the Ornarans are the only race in their planetary system to have developed space travel, their addiction to Felicium has caused them to be lax in the maintenance of their ships. Now, after the destruction of the Sanction, their fleet is down to one ship back at their home planet, Ornara. But the ship is in bad shape. Some parts need to be replaced, and the Ornarans can no longer repair it. Picard says he will help. During the trip from Brekka to Ornara, Dr. Crusher uncovers the truth about Felicium and the Brekkans. She and Picard confront Sobi and Langor, the two Brekkan passengers.

Picard tries to convince Langor to tell Romas and T'Jon the truth, but Langor refuses. Brekka's whole economy would change and Langor is not prepared for that. Picard cannot tell the Ornarans because the Prime Directive mandates non-interference with local trade. Picard is forced to go along with the lie. As they approach Ornara, the four passengers are with Dr. Crusher and Picard. Langor graciously announces that he will give this shipment of Felicium to the Ornarans for free. Langor also thanks Picard for providing parts and helping to repair the Ornaran's last ship.

Picard then surprises all four of them when he tells them he will not help them repair their ship. The Ornarans, T'Jon and Romas are stunned. If they cannot repair their ship, they will be unable to get their "medicine" in the future. As they are ready to be transported down to Ornara, T'Jon says, "Captain, I hope you realize what you've done to us." Picard responds, "Of that you can be sure." The four are beamed down. Picard knows that when the Felicium runs out, the Ornarans will go through withdrawal, but they will survive and learn they no longer need the drug. Dr. Crusher tells Picard she could have made it easier for them. Picard responds, "Painful as it will be, the people of Ornara—and the people of Brekka—must shape their own destinies." ("Symbiosis," *Star Trek: TNG*; S1, E22).

When I first watched this episode I remember thinking what it would have been like on Ornara when they first learned that they no longer had the plague. They had lived with that lie for two centuries. What would it have been like to learn they are free from a life of fear, a life deprived of choice, a life controlled by others. I can't help believing it would have been an exhilarating and liberating feeling. Like a great weight being lifted.

We are also living a life based on a lie. Unfortunately, this is a lie of our own choosing. And just as on Ornara, some have learned to use the lie to their own advantage. So much so that we have all come not only to accept it, but like the Ornarans, we have become hooked. Like any addict, we will do whatever is necessary to get our fix. In fact, chasing after our fix has become a central pillar in almost every culture. The chase? Jobs!

Of the approximate 3,000,000 species of life on this planet, there is only one species that values, brags about, complains about, and otherwise makes a big to-do about working for other people for the majority of their life…and that species is thought to be intelligent. The world doesn't need jobs, the life cycle doesn't require jobs, the eco-system wouldn't break down if there were no jobs. Indeed, I could make a great argument for how our planet would be better off without this need to work to make others rich.

We are conditioned from an early age to become good workers. Some of us would brag about our father's jobs when we were kids. In school the all-too-common question, "Why do we have to study this?" usually got a response similar to "Because I said so." However, if we pushed the issue, teachers and parents would explain to us that doing well in school would help us to get a "good job." And that's what we all wanted, right? A good job with a good salary would get us a good life, and we were all taught that a good life was defined by how much stuff we owned and how much money we had. We see the good life on TV, in movies, and in print. We are barraged daily by TV, movies, and print to remind us what the "good life" is.

And for this we require money. It is this addiction to money that has made it easy for some to promulgate the idea that jobs represent the best way for us to work together, that somehow it is necessary to sell ourselves to the highest bidder. In reality that is all nonsense.

That is not to say we don't need to work together and complete tasks to support our communities. Working together as a community is important. But, the need for jobs is a fiction created by industry. Workers are a commodity. WE are a commodity. Just like a rancher might raise his cattle on special grains so he can become more profitable, WE are raised in an education system to make us more profitable to corporations. As mentioned earlier, Barbara Business and Gary Government have worked to develop a system that produces worker bees: Us. We provide labor for business and generate tax revenue for government. As a result, Barbara Business becomes wealthy, Gary Government becomes wealthy and we?…we become slaves and do as we are told. Like the Ornarans who believed they needed Felicium, we believe we need money…and to get it, we need jobs. The notion of money and currency was invented as a convenience. Early human communities simply swapped goods and services to help each other. For instance, a farmer would grow more than he needed for his family and trade the rest. This worked well in small villages. The wheat farmer and his neighbors could simply remember transactions and when crops were harvested each farmer, using their crop as currency, would settle their accounts.

As villages grew, the number of traders increased and more goods became available. People would exchange a variety of goods throughout the year. It not only became difficult keeping records, it was very inconvenient. One person might pay in barley and another would pay in chickens, yet another would pay in fish. To make it easier, these communities established objects—shells, animal teeth, or whatever—that were given a common value and made it easy for everyone to keep track of all the exchanges. These objects could then be exchanged later. They were used as currency. They had no intrinsic value, they were more a means to keep track of all the transactions. However, these objects only worked within a particular community. Trading outside the community was difficult.

As villages grew into cities, and kingdoms developed, it was necessary to create something that had intrinsic value and could be used beyond local communities. Kings and other leaders decided on using precious metals like gold and silver as currency. They were portable, durable, and easily divisible. Only the wealthy and powerful could actually mint them, making it very difficult to counterfeit. Money made it easy to keep track of transactions as well as provide a common value, which opened more markets. Fast forward to today. Although currency no longer has intrinsic value, it is still used. This means of trade for goods and services has become embedded.

Currency and money is part of almost all human cultures on our planet. Barbara and Gary have learned how to get a lot of it. There are those who would argue this is the fundamental flaw in capitalism. Some want to destroy capitalism because they believe we would be better off without it. But they miss the point. Getting rid of capitalism and replacing it with socialism, communism, Buddhism or marijuana-ism does not get rid of money. It may change how it is gotten or who gets it, but the chase would continue and the need for worker bees would still exist. The masses would always be at the disposition of the wealthy. Capitalism simply puts the power of the economy in the hands of the people. Thus anyone can create a product, provide a service, or own land and become part of the economy. This breeds innovation and creativity. It inspires dreams. In a society full of self-actualized citizens striving to improve life, capitalism seems to be a natural fit. The challenge is that our current economy is based on dollars.

The currency of today's capitalism is money. As a result, a lot of money has been made. As I mentioned in an earlier chapter, companies have learned how to create false needs in order to generate more money. In that sense, capitalism is very successful. Unfortunately, with money as the currency, the natural behavior to support it is consumerism. However, if innovation, creativity and dreams are focused on earning dollars, then new thoughts, ideas and products are only developed if they are marketable. Which means they need to be consumable and/or profitable.

By definition good ideas that are not seen as profitable get ignored regardless of their value to others. For example there are certain readily available and cheap medicines that Big Pharma "ignores" because they aren't profitable. Hence little research is done and doctors won't prescribe these medicines because of the lack of research. This emphasis on profit has caused great harm to humanity and to our planet. Moreover, it has created a huge gap between those who are good at either making or selling marketable goods and services and those who are not.

As an example, an author can make good money writing books. But the publishing house that is good at marketing and selling the book makes a lot more money. The same thing applies to any industry. That is what Wall Street is all about: Selling financial products to the masses. Sometimes the consumer makes money, sometimes he looses. But a good seller, or broker, always does well. They can sell short and make money when others lose money.

This difference will always generate an income gap, and the gap will always grow. It is generational. Babies born into wealthy families will have better access and more opportunities than babies born into families with little money. Anyone who tells you the system is rigged is correct. But, if they suggest they know how to make the system fair, they are wrong. There will always be a disparity of wealth. The only real solution is to fundamentally change the system. We must end the chase for money.

We have been enslaved by this system, and like the Ornarans with Felicium we have learned to accept it. Many of us live a life based on the pursuit of money because our culture not only encourages it, we glorify it. We imagine money will allow us to buy all the things we need and our problems will be solved. Money will make us more important and it will make us feel more valuable, even smarter. Hence, people with a lot of money become our idols. We live vicariously through them, and often this reaches the level of absurdity.

Take a pop singer, let's call him Dave. Dave has a good voice, maybe a great voice. That's it, that's the only difference between Dave and the next guy. However, a savvy agent (driven by money) and a good record label (driven by money) can build an empire around Dave. Dave makes millions. He buys a house with 250,000 square feet, thirty-two cars (one with a swimming pool in the trunk), owns a private jet and travels to his island home in the Caribbean on the weekends. He drinks caviar shakes and uses toothpaste with ground-up diamonds. All because he can sing. Now that he has money, we love him. We follow him. We listen to him and we try to copy him.

In fact we will pay him more money just to let him show and tell us how rich he is. Magazines will pay him money to take pictures of all the cool stuff he has in his house. And we will buy those magazines. TV shows will pay Dave to brag about his house and wonderful trips and we love watching. At a concert Dave might wear a pair of purple pajamas that have green stripes made with llama hair and open holes in the top so his nipples are exposed. The next day, we buy a pair because we love Dave. He is rich. He must have insight that the rest of us lack. The record company owns dozens of radio stations, so we can hear Dave sing to us anywhere, anytime.

TV talk shows pay Dave to come on and tell us how wonderful his life is. Dave jokes about the time he spent $1,000 giving his dog a hair cut only to discover it was his neighbor's dog. What! How silly is that! So he had to pay *another* $1,000 to get his actual dog's hair cut, and you can bet this time he had his maid make sure it was the right dog. "Ha, ha, ha, ha, ha!" goes the audience. Everybody laughs because Dave is funny. He must be, he has so much money!

Dave is such a good singer he wins awards. Awards from who? Glad you asked. Awards from his record labels, awards from other pop singers, and awards from us because we love him so much. Before Dave became a pop singer, he worked in a warehouse. His friend, Mike was going to college. Mike's major was political science, but Dave didn't care for it. He said he always had a tough time with science and didn't like having to dissect a frog in high school. But now he is rich so when Dave tells us what's wrong with our country, we listen and nod our heads like a bunch of bobble-head dolls in the back of a 1965 Ford Galaxy. His money has made him intelligent and insightful and a group of us are pushing to have him run for political office.

The system is now rigged for Dave. When Dave puts his money in a bank, he will get high interest-rate returns. Dave has lawyers to help him pay fewer taxes. Dave gets free clothes, free shoes, and free cars, just to show them to us. Dave doesn't have to wait in line for anything anymore. He gets great seats at concerts. He gets free food in restaurants and free drinks in bars, just for showing up. Dave's kids will go to any university they want. Their teeth will be straight and they will never be ashamed of their clothes. As a favor, they'll get cast in TV shows or movies, they'll travel and see the world, they'll never wish for a heater in their home. Their children's children will have even more opportunity.

For the rest of us it is different. The only time we get high interest rates is when we borrow money. The interest on our deposits, compounded every one hundred years, will come to about twenty-seven cents a year. We worry about doing our taxes correctly because we fear the IRS. We buy our clothes from discount stores or second-hand shops. We consider ourselves lucky if we can afford to go to one concert a year. We use coupons to eat at fast-food places and drink wine from a box. We hope our car doesn't break down. When we get older we continue to live pay check to pay check. Dave and his family get richer generation after generation, and we get poorer.

Certainly people can work hard and move up the system, or catch a lucky break. However, with a public school system designed to build worker bees, with fractured families, with Barbara Business doing her best to sell us what we don't need and Gary Government taking as much as he can from us, with TV and video games, drugs, alcohol and all the other distractions, picking oneself up by the boot straps is much more difficult than it should be. Innovation is hard to come by after a fourteen-hour workday is capped off with a microwave fish dinner. So we collapse in a chair, flip on the tube and scan the channels. Fortunately for us there is a special program and Dave is singing. We relax and nod off, only to face the same routine tomorrow.

Spending generates debt and debt generates more dollars. That is why banks, corporations and governments work together to develop a culture of consumerism. Anything is sold for any reason. Make-up companies selling make-up that makes you look like you're not wearing make-up…what the heck is that! Perfectly good blue jeans are deliberately ripped creating many holes and then the price goes up!

Then there is the insidious side. Think about products like, *I can't Believe it's not Butter.* So, butter is either bad or too expensive.

Rather than just stop using it, companies get approval from the government to make some synthetic, additive and preservative-filled grease for us to eat. Those that can't afford natural, get chemical. Health issues for the poor increase and that widens the gap between the haves and the have-nots.

With dollars as the fuel, there will always be some people with more and some people with less. That is the "playing field" that we always hear needs to be leveled. Issues like minimum wage, income inequality, free college, tax reform, less business regulation and even job lock are cited as needing to be addressed to level that field. All of these ideas would actually do very little in the end. Either prices or taxes would go up, or both.

Most importantly these efforts maintain the status quo of promoting consumerism to generate dollars, which simply creates the same problems down the road because consumption would not stop. Twenty-five years from now there will be calls for a thirty dollar-an-hour minimum wage, free life insurance, free dental insurance and there will still be protests of income inequality. Twenty-five years after that, let's go to a sixty-dollar minimum wage—and on and on and on. Of course a hamburger will cost twenty bucks. And we will buy it! The cycle will never stop.

Even non-economists like myself understand that with money as currency, the only target is the bottom line. Increase costs in anything and prices will go up. I'll use the French fry-o-meter to explain. When I started working at McDonald's I earned minimum wage: $1.30 per hour. At that time an order of French fries cost 20 cents. That means I could buy 6.5 orders of fries for one hour of labor. Fast forward to today. The minimum wage is $7.25. The cost of a regular order of fries is $1.00. Today I can buy 7.25 orders of French fries for one hour of work. Minimum wage has increased by a factor of 5.5. The cost of French fries has increased by a factor of 5. That's a pretty close relationship.

If we increase minimum wage by a factor of two what do you think will happen to the cost of fries? Everyone will make more money, but they will need to because prices will increase. The only thing that is a constant is the bottom line. PROFIT! Using dollars as currency will always develop behaviors that support consuming. Regardless of cost, government and business will find ways for us to consume until we consume our planet to one giant dirt ball. At that point someone will probably find a way to market dirt!

But, what if something else could be used as currency for capitalism. What if a capitalist system was as successful with this other currency as it has been with money? What if the behavior that earned this new currency actually supported our families, our communities, and our environment? And what if this new currency provided equality for all with no gap? Everyone would have the same amount of currency and the same ability to practice the supporting behavior. Remember that beginning sequence in *Star Trek* where it talks about going someplace that no one has been before? Well, strap yourselves in and, like Captain Picard at his first meeting with Captain Dathon, open your mind as far as it will go…Engage.

Time.

What if time was the currency for capitalism? Regardless of how many dollars you have, you only get twenty-four hours a day, one hundred sixty-eight hours a week. That goes for everybody. And, what if the behavior that was needed to support this new currency—time —supported your family, your community and the environment and all of it was your choice?

In short, what if how we lived our lives added value to the time we have and that time could be used as currency? What if, based on our choices throughout our lives, we were credited for our time and that credit could be exchanged for goods and services? This system would apply to individuals, businesses and government. The more often any individual or business practiced these behaviors the more credits they would receive. I'm talking about behaviors that have been defined by society as necessary for improvement, individually and collectively, a pre-established set of behaviors that anyone can develop and practice to gain expertise.

Don't put the book down yet. Take a breath and remember, it's a whole new world in the future. All citizens have had equal access to education. (Chapter Two). Our society has recognized that doing what is best for the future, requires that we focus on what is best for the children. Caring, cooperation and compassion for each other and all life is not taught in classrooms, but demonstrated daily by our actions throughout our communities. Our purpose is developing each child to his or her full potential so that as children become adults, communities become stronger. All of our behaviors and choices are driven by our desire to nurture our next generation so the human race can continue to grow.

Drugs, alcohol, TV, advertising, marketing…all are gone. Investment has transitioned from investing dollars to investing time. Likewise, return on investment is not measured in profit, but in growth. People respect each other and themselves. Pride in what we own has been replaced by pride in what we do. As a society we have learned that competition is more meaningful when we compete with ourselves. This promotes personal growth, and that is the goal. We have recognized as a species that at some point in the future this planet and our solar system will die, but there is no longer any need for us to hurry that process along.

Given what society could become as portrayed in the *Star Trek* universe, moving an economy away from money and consumption to a collective effort of peaceful coexistence with all life, is an evolution that should not be laughed off. I make no claims that what I am about to present is the way to get there, but it is a possible way that is achievable. More importantly, it raises questions we should be addressing.

The path we are on now produces a certain kind of future. Change the path, and we change the future. Take a look at a street scene from *Blade Runner* and compare it to a street scene from *Star Trek* (2009). That is what I see as the difference. I believe the path we are on now will lead us close to a *Blade Runner* future. We can change that path. The future portrayed by *Star*

Trek is possible. We just need to think differently.

The question becomes where to begin. Perhaps we can begin by asking, what does it mean to be human? In a future without advertising and marketing, without TV, newspapers, magazines and radio constantly telling us what we need, we have re-discovered that our real material needs are simple: food, clothing and shelter, the same things we have needed forever. These needs require energy to produce. Obviously, energy will be an important component of this discussion. We also have needs that are not material. We have left the nomadic wandering behind, we are a communal species, so there is a need to belong to a group, a community. We know humans are curious. There is a need to sate our curiosity without sacrificing our other needs. So food, clothing, shelter, energy, community and discovery are important for us.

As self-proclaimed god of the world, I have decided the six areas that we will shape our behaviors around are as follows:

- Carbon footprint
  - Energy
  - Food
  - Clothing
  - Shelter
- Community
- Curiosity

In our new system, success at these behaviors will earn you the thing you most want: time. In addition to these behaviors, as god, I will assign a rubric that will quantify each individual's success at practicing these behaviors. As a point of reference, in today's world consumerism is the behavior. If you have a good job and practice consuming well, your bank loans are at lower rates, you're qualified for more credit on your card, you can buy nice homes, provide a better education for your children and you will get what you most want: money. In short, practice the right behaviors and you will be rewarded.

Our future counterparts recognize the importance of our environment and the need for us to be caretakers, not takers. This point is made clear in *Star Trek IV: The Voyage Home* (1986), where we caused the extinction of the humpback whales in the 21st century, which would have led to the destruction of our planet in the 23rd century had captain Kirk and his crew not gone back in time to save the whales.

It would be reasonable to assume that having a small carbon footprint would be valuable. The human needs for food, clothing and shelter would be a measure of how Earth friendly your behaviors are. Moreover, the type of energy you use, as well as the quantity would be important. The goal for each citizen would be to have a black belt in their carbon footprint. Below is a possible rubric:

CARBON FOOTPRINT

RATING	WHITE BELT	ORANGE BELT	GREEN BELT	BROWN BELT	BLACK BELT
POINTS	<12	13-18	19-24	25-29	30

Here is how points are earned.

BEHAVIOR RUBRIC

POINT VALUE	1	2	3	4	5
SHELTER (square feet)	>2,001	1,501-2,000	1,001-1,500	501-1,000	<501
TRANSPORTATION	>60%	50-59%	40-49%	30-39%	<30%
HOME ITEMS	<60%	60-69%	70-79%	80-89%	>90%
HOME ENERGY	>4:1	3:1-4:1	2:1-3:1	1:1-2:1	<1:1
FOOD	<60%	60-69%	70-79%	80-90%	>90%
CLOTHING	<60%	60-69%	70-79%	80-90%	>90%

DESCRIPTORS

Shelter:

This number represents the number of square feet per permanent resident in the home.

Transportation:

This number represents the percentage of time you use fossil fuels when you leave home. This does not include using mass-transit.

Home items:

This number represents the percentage of items in your home that were produced or manufactured within a fifty-mile radius of your home.

Home energy:

This number represents the ratio of electrical items per permanent resident in the home. This number does not include items for basic meal preparation (refrigerator and stove/oven) since a home with one person would need the same appliances as a home with six people. This would place homes with a small number of residents at a disadvantage.

Food:

This number represents the percentage of food eaten by permanent residents of the home, purchased from the community food exchange.

Clothing:

This number represents the percentage of clothing that is completely natural. This includes fabric, coloring and any design. This is measured for each permanent resident of the home.

Let us consider two homes, both of which have two adults and two children.

Home A: This home is 1,800 square feet. The residents own a car but it is only used about 5% of the time they leave their house. The two children walk or bike where they need to go. The father is a teacher and uses the bus to get to and from work. The mother walks to work. Everything in their house, except two computers and one phone has been produced or manufactured within a 50-mile radius. Outside of the kitchen there are only three electrical appliances: two computers and one phone. The mother is a horticulturist and works in the community food exchange (See appendix A) where they get about 95% of their food. All of their clothing is made of natural fibers, usually cotton or wool or a mix. They are all natural colors and are very plain. When we apply their life-style to the behavior rubric, it looks like this:

DESCRIPTION	VALUE FROM BEHAVIOR RUBRIC	POINTS EARNED
SHELTER: This home has 1800 square feet. Divide this by the number of people in the home (1800/4= 450).	<501	5
TRANSPORTATION: They only use their car for special occasions. This accounts for about 5% of the time.	<30%	5

DESCRIPTION	VALUE FROM BEHAVIOR RUBRIC	POINTS EARNED
HOME ITEMS: Only 3 items in the entire house were produced more that fifty miles away from their home.	>90%	5
HOME ENERGY: Four people live in the house, only 3 electrical items.	<1:1	5
FOOD: More than 95% of what they eat comes from the food exchange.	>90%	5
CLOTHING: All of their clothing is made from natural fibers with no artificial coloring or print.	>90%	5

As a result of their life-style the family in this home have earned 30 points and have a "black belt" for their carbon footprint.

Home B: This home is 2,000 square feet. They use their car for local errands and drive about 50% of the time when they leave their house. Many of the items they buy are produced over-seas. (It is important to note that buying something over-seas hurts your score because the transportation of those goods damages the environment. This is not a matter of patriotism.) They own a total of twelve monitors, computers and phones. They like to eat out, but they also get about 70% of their food from the food exchange. Like the family in house 'A,' all of their clothing is either cotton or wool or a mix and are all natural colors and are very plain. This is what it looks like using the behavior rubric:

DESCRIPTION	VALUE FROM BEHAVIOR RUBRIC	POINTS EARNED
SHELTER: This home has 2000 square feet. Divide this by the number of people in the home (2000/4= 500).	<501	5
TRANSPORTATION: They use their car about half of the time they leave the house.	40-50%	3
HOME ITEMS: Only about 15% of the items in their home have been produced less than fifty miles away from home.	<60%	1
HOME ENERGY: Four people live in the house, each of them own their own phone and their own computer. They also have 4 monitors in the house, for a total of 12 items.	3:1 – 4:1	2
FOOD: About 70% of what they eat comes from the food exchange.	70-79%	3
CLOTHING: All of their clothing is made from natural fibers with no artificial coloring or print.	>90%	5

As a result of their life-style the family in this home has earned 19 points and have a 'green belt' for their carbon footprint.

COMMUNITY EXCHANGE

Work in the community exchange is where your time is credited. The credits you earn depend on the amount of time you work. The ratio of credits earned vs. hours worked increases the more hours worked.

COMMUNITY EXCHANGE CREDIT TABLE

Hours worked per week	<15	15-19	20-24	25-29	>30
Ratio (hours to credits)	1:1	1:1.5	1:2	1:2.5	1:3

The community exchange is made up of industries that are defined and divided by purpose. They are industries that support both local and national concerns (in the *Star Trek* universe, global). Working in these industries is where individuals earn credit. The community exchange includes the following departments:

Cultural Department:

This includes the arts. However, only the producers of art. Advertising and marketing is not an art. Artists, musicians, playwrights, etc. can exhibit their art at local community centers and have them streamed to national audiences. All products: movies, books, displays, etc. are free. However, artists can earn credit as they develop their skills.

Community Department:

This includes the education, health, housing and clothing industries. It is also includes all of the support industries. For instance, time spent building a school is credited. Time spent growing cotton is credited. Time spent cleaning a classroom is credited. Time spent working in a nursing home is credited. All of the time needed to provide the services above is credited.

Infrastructure Department:

This includes the transportation and communication industries. As with the welfare department, time spent in all support industries is credited. For instance, the transportation industry would include everything from building a car to building and maintaining a road.

City Services Department:

This includes police and fire departments, waste disposal, and utilities. Time spent in any and all of these endeavors is credited.

Science Department:

This includes research and development for all other departments. Some examples would include a molecular biologist developing a new treatment for a disease, a psychologist developing new protocols for treating psychosis, a chemical engineer developing a new type of road surface that is impervious to weather, or an engineer designing a new type of conductor for high-volume data transfer.

Logistics Department:

This includes the organization and administration necessary to coordinate the raw materials needed for all the departments above.

The time committed helping in any of the industries mentioned above is credited. However, the rating one earns for their carbon footprint can impact the credits earned:

- White, Orange and Green belt: No impact

- Brown belt: Total credits earned increase by a factor of 2.0

- Black belt: Total credits earned increase by a factor of 4.0

Using this formula we can go back the example of the two households above. House 'A' is rated as a black belt. In house A the mother is a horticulturist and the father is a teacher. Both adults in house 'A' work fifteen hours a week. The ratio of credit earnings is 1:1. Together they are credited for thirty hours a week (2 x 15 = 30). However, house 'A' is a black belt. This means the time they are credited is increased by a factor of four (30 x 4 = 120).

House 'B' is rated as a green belt. In house 'B' the mother is a carpenter and the father is an engineer. Both adults work 25 hours a week. The ratio of credit earnings for house 'B' is 1:2.5. Together they are credited for one-hundred and twenty five hours a week (2 x 25 = 50; 50 x 2.5 = 125).

As we can see, house 'A' is rated a black belt. Their credited time of 30 hours is increased by a factor of four, which comes to a total of one hundred and twenty credits. House 'B' is rated a green belt. They receive no increase in the number of credits they earn. In this example it is easy to see the importance of earning a higher rating in your carbon footprint: The smaller the carbon footprint the better.

Children can also earn time credits. These credits do not impact the calculation for the adults. Let's assume in house 'A' the children are aged nine and fifteen. All schools have a peer-tutoring program. A student's performance must reach mastery level in order to qualify as a tutor. The nine-year-old girl has mastered her speaking and writing skills. She is a student tutor and works with students needing help in those areas. She tutors for about three hours a week, and she earns three credits. The fifteen-year-old is working on a school project with students from around the world. The project is an effort to increase the efficiency of collecting biogas from compost heaps and converting those gases into energy to supply homes. He spends two hours a day working on his project...he earns ten credits a week. The credits the boy and girl earn are calculated using the carbon footprint rating of the household. The thirteen credits are increased by a factor of four for a total of fifty-two credits. This is the basic structure of the economy. Time has replaced money and is used as currency. Time spent helping in the community exchange is credited, or earns credits. Contributing to the community, like the boy and the girl in the example, also earns credits.

However, even in this system there could still be people who see earning credits as a competition and latch onto that. Instead of living life chasing the dollar, they chase credits. In that regard the future could present the same issues we see today with a little twist. We might have a credit-gap rather than an income-gap. For example, above if the adults in house 'A' worked thirty hours each for a total of sixty, the initial calculation of the community exchange table would increase their credits earned by a factor of three. The sixty credits earned would become one hundred and eighty. With their carbon footprint rating of "black belt," the one hundred and eighty credits would be increased by a factor of four. This would amount to seven hundred and twenty credits a week, significantly more than the one hundred and twenty credits in the example. Black-belt earners might get caught up in working as much as they could to earn more credits. To address this problem, the system would need something to govern this behavior.

Once more: Time.

Remember the goal of our future counterparts is to improve themselves, and in order to improve anything, time is necessary. As a piano player I understand that the more time I commit to practicing and playing the piano, the better I will become. To encourage this, the system has one final rubric that quantifies and rates the time people use for self-improvement. The fewer hours one goes to work the more hours one can devote to self-improvement.

Currently an average workweek for a full-time employee is about forty hours. In the future that would be way too much time to give to someone else. That is not to say no one commits that much time to his profession. Being a captain of a starship, for example, is a 24/7 job. However, if that is one's passion…well, you know what they say. If you love what you're doing, you never really work a day in your life. Looking at all of the opportunity available in the community exchange, many people would spend long hours with their passion and, while it might look like work, it would all be voluntary.

Our future counterparts have developed a system in which work is not a job. It is not something they have to do to earn money. For them, work provides opportunities for growth as well as a place to develop skills. However, their time working is balanced with time they use to further develop skills on their own. The balancing of these two kinds of time, the community exchange and personal time, is purely up to the individual.

Captain Picard (I am sure this applies to all Star Ship captains) commits all his time to his ship and his service. That is how he enjoys life. He doesn't punch a clock, he doesn't worry about salary or why a different Star Ship captain takes so much time off. He is living life on his own terms and, for the most part, doing exactly what he wants. There are a few times throughout his career when he seems to question this, but he always comes to the realization that his work is what he wants…his work is his life. That is his choice.

Even with a system that allows individuals to choose how they balance their time, there is the possibility of "credit junkies" trying to earn as many credits as they can. Here is where the final rubric comes in. The system encourages personal time by establishing a rating for the amount of personal time each person earns. For this example I will use the same rating system that was used for the carbon footprint. The more personal time you have, the higher your rating.

COMMUNITY EXCHANGE WORK TABLE

RATING	WHITE BELT	ORANGE BELT	GREEN BELT	BROWN BELT	BLACK BELT
Community exchange hours worked per week	>30	26-29	21-25	16-20	<16

At first glance this table seems to be in conflict with the Community Exchange Credit table above. In that table the longer you work the more credits you earn. But, the goal isn't to earn credits, the goal is to contribute to your community and still have time to improve your life and the community. To the extent possible the goal is to give each person individual choice as to what they do with their time. In this system you are rewarded for living a lifestyle that is more harmonious with our planet. You are encouraged to work in industries that advance that effort and you are also encouraged to use time for your own growth, to balance the two.

Even in this system there is still a market: A credit market—remember credits represent time and time is the currency. People have to worry about having enough credits to use for medical care, or a new car or trip to a neighboring solar system to visit friends. And, as with any market, there is a corresponding black market. People could still get stuck in this system. Moreover, credits can only be used for goods and services provided in the community exchange. If you want to collect cars, clocks, art, guns, coins, or anything else, credits will not necessarily help you. (I want to clarify something. When credits are used…they are gone. They are not traded, or spent. They do not go to someone else. Unlike a dollar that can be used over and over again, once your credit has been applied for a good or service, it evaporates.)

There is one final component of this system that addresses these two issues. It gives individuals peace of mind. They would no longer have to worry about having enough credits to use for something they need or to receive an important service. They could also use credits outside of the community exchange.

Any citizen who earns a black belt for their carbon footprint AND a black belt in the Community Exchange Work Table has a few pretty cool things happen. First, their credits can now be used for anything outside of the exchange. Secondly, the hours they commit to the community exchange are now matched, hour for hour, for *all* goods and services provided in the Community exchange. It is a bit confusing with the Community Exchange Work Table. The short version would be there are formal hours and voluntary hours.

The formal hours are hours a person "works" on a specific project, a collaboration with others with a specific goal. These hours are used to rate the individual and to earn a particular belt. The voluntary hours are accrued by the individual by helping in any field or industry in the community exchange and have no impact on the Community Exchange Work Table (I will provide a concrete example shortly).

Credits outside of the community exchange would have a value that is set by a market…perhaps another planet uses klochlespiels as currency. They would work with the Federation to establish an exchange rate with Federation credits. Maybe one credit = Four Klochlespiels. Whatever the exchange rate would be, Double Black Belts could participate to the extent they continue to earn their credits.

The voluntary hours accrued by an individual would have real value inside the community exchange. Every hour they volunteer provides them with one hour of time from the exchange. I will use the example of house 'A' from above to demonstrate how this would work. Remember in that house the mother is a horticulturist and the father is a teacher. They both work less than fifteen hours a week for their black belt rating in the community exchange. Their lifestyle earned them the other black belt for their carbon footprint. (It is important to note that these black belts are not permanent. One can easily lose either rating depending upon his or her behavior.)

The mother's formal hours include her work on a project to restore part of a rain forest that was devastated by a disease. The father's formal hours include his work as a high school project coordinator for seniors working on developing a new organic polymer used in tires to provide better traction and longer wear.

When both parents finish their work week of less than fifteen hours, the mother volunteers time working on a project to develop medicinal plants that can be grown in some of the harsh environments that exist in several planets in the galaxy. The father volunteers time at a university teaching linguistics and studying how two particular species from different solar systems have an almost identical phonetic base, yet completely different meanings. They both volunteer their time working on projects near and dear to them that provide them satisfaction and growth in their fields. The hours worked in these endeavors accrue.

For the sake of argument let's say they both volunteer about thirty hours a week, sixty hours a week total. Let's say they volunteer for about forty weeks a year for a total of twenty-four hundred hours. Since this family has earned a double black-belt rating, these hours can then be used for goods and services provided in the community exchange. Whether they need an operation, a new vehicle, or new clothes. Their credited hours can be used for those goods and services. Moreover, the credits they earn "working" (the initial one hundred and twenty credits) can now be used outside of the community exchange. Lastly, as double black-belt earners, they are eligible for awards and honors as well as special postings when they distinguish themselves in their fields. This includes getting published, being invited to make speeches, and participating in special projects throughout the industry. Only double black-belt recipients can run for political office.

Double black-belts are the "stars" of the future. To put it in present day terms, the only people eligible for Academy, Emmy, Golden Globe, or any awards would be double black-belt earners. Heisman trophy winners, music awards and any awards that we have today would only be awarded to double black-belt earners. The whole concept of celebrity would be predicated on being a double black-belt earner. In terms of today's world only double black-belt earners would fill the pages of People Magazine, Vogue, Playboy, Newsweek, Time, etc. These people would be the only people we see on TV talk shows, news interviews and all other forms of broadcast mediums.

Money and possessions would not factor into celebrity. Life style and contribution to the community would be the new "rich and famous." Our social heroes would all be double black-belt earners. The only universities eligible for accreditation would be those whose entire staffs: teachers, professors, administrators, janitors, cooks, everyone, were double black belt earners. The same would be true for all secondary education entities. The only private business endeavors eligible for incorporation would be those entities whose entire staffs consist of double black-belt earners.

The foundation of our society would be built upon double black-belt earners. Since everyone would have equal access to education and have twenty-four hours in a day, everyone would be capable of becoming a double black-belt earner. All would be challenged to contribute to the community and improve themselves.

The pop singer, Dave, described above, would have to be a double black-belt earner to be recorded. All the employees of the record label and the agency his agent belongs to would have to be double black-belt earners. The same would apply to any radio station or TV program that played his music or talked to him. Dave would receive no money for any of his songs, singing or celebrity. Rather than talking about his big house, car collection, private jet and the funny story of spending $1,000 to groom the wrong dog, Dave would be telling us how he found ways to improve his life style, to reduce his carbon footprint even more. Or he would be talking about his music.

All the other stuff we see and hear with celebrities would not exist. Red Carpet walkers wouldn't be celebrated for wearing $50,000 dresses, or $1,000,000 jewelry collections around their necks, or the $250,000 car they drove up in. All the stuff that means nothing to humanity would no longer be celebrated. As double black-belt earners, they would wear clothing made of natural materials, they would not own jewelry, certainly no make-up, and they would probably arrive in some form of mass transit, or possibly a solar-powered bike.

Socialism, communism or our current system of capitalism all require using Earth's resources to generate more wealth. Moreover, all of these systems create disparity. This disparity will inevitably end up in discussions about how to redistribute the wealth, or to whom the wealth belongs. Within the system I described above, the need to use Earth's resources to generate wealth would disappear. Rather than talking about redistributing wealth, this system would completely redefine how wealth is expressed. Within this system everyone would have equal access to that wealth.

I would like to provide you with a case study of our future. Meet the Yang's. Wade and Mary Yang are married. They have two children, Jose and Hiroko. Mary's father, Isaac also lives with them. Wade is forty-four years old and is a teacher. His specialty is linguistics. He also loves to play the piano. Mary is forty-nine years old. She is a horticulturalist. She works closely with medicinal plants. Her older sister died from an infection that was detected too late. As a result, Mary has a personal interest in using plants to aid the body in providing an early defense system against infectious diseases. Mary also likes to write short stories. Jose is the oldest child. He is fifteen years old and attends high school. He likes science very much and also likes to run and he likes to draw, especially comics. Hiroko is nine years old. She is in elementary school. She loves taking pictures. She spends a lot of time taking pictures of trees. She also likes music and plays the guitar. Mary's father, Isaac, is seventy-four years old. He is retired. He is confined to a wheel chair as a result of an injury years ago. He used to work in construction. He likes the fresh air and gets outside as often as he can.

They live in an ergonomic home made of recycled cargo containers. The home has 1200 square feet. This does not include an outdoor living space that is multi-purposed throughout the year. Their neighborhood is made up of many similar homes all nestled against a large stretch of hills. The school that Mr. Yang works at is about three miles from the house. It is the same school that Jose and Hiroko attend. The three of them ride an electric cart, much like a golf cart to school in the morning.

Mary works at the community garden and rides an electric scooter to work. The cart, the scooter, and Isaac's wheel chair are charged each night in charging pods powered by solar panels. The community is provided energy by vertical-axis wind turbines positioned at the top of the hills surrounding their homes. The VAWT's provide enough energy for lighting the home in the evening as well as running the pump for their well from which they get their water.

Like all homes in the community, the Yang's house has a terminal that allows for optional use of the local power grid. However, their use of the power grid is very small, about 50 kWh per month. (That's about 1/20th of what a home in America uses today.) They own a small refrigerator, a washing machine, a range, and two computers, which are connected to the grid. (They share the washing machine with three of their neighbors.) The heating and cooling of the house is achieved through a variety of energy-efficient technologies: Strategic venting, insulated materials, positioning the house to optimize the use of each season's natural climate, shade and sun directors for the outdoor living space, portable walls and even wearing more clothes in the home during cooler months. (These are technologies that are available today. Who knows what new technologies will have been developed in the future.)

They shop for food almost daily. They don't buy frozen foods. All of their food comes from the food exchange. (This portrayal does not account for the use of replicators. If they exist two hundred years from now, the food exchange would be much different. However, I am working on the assumption they do not exist.) The food exchange is not limited to produce. It also includes a large preserve in which animals can be hunted and used for food. There are no meat sections in super markets. Those who want to consume meat are required to hunt and butcher their own meat. Their meals are simple and are prepared at home. Fast-food restaurants do not exist, and the Yang family rarely eats in restaurants in the community.

Local carpenters made all of the furniture in the house. In fact all of their home items except the computers were manufactured locally. There are several small manufacturing plants that make appliances, fixtures, furniture, ceramics, glass and other needs located close by to the community. The plants are run on an as-needed basis and might be closed for several months of the year. The entire Yang family wears clothes made of only natural fibers and materials that are grown and processed locally. As a result, the Yang's have earned a black belt in their carbon footprint.

Having small manufacturing, processing and food producing businesses located locally has resulted in a community manufacturing and production plan (CMP plan) that insures needs are met. This requires consumers to plan their needs, making impulse buying a thing of the past. Families project their household needs and work as a community to develop a CMP plan throughout the year. Scheduled bazaars for clothes or household items are held through out the year. Families are more self-sufficient in terms of maintenance and repair, and do-it-yourself projects are also taught throughout the year.

The consumers of goods set the market and the producers of goods only respond to the market's needs. They are not chasing profit, they are chasing time to improve themselves. These small companies keep very small inventories. There is no advertising and marketing push. While it is recognized that consumption is necessary, it is done with awareness and caution. The community understands the serious impact consumption can have on the environment.

Mr. Yang works at his son's high school. That is his formal job, and the hours he spends there are used to calculate his rating in the Exchange Credit Table above. He goes in every morning for a couple of hours. His role is project facilitator. He facilitates the collaboration between students and outside experts and reviews project progress with students. Some weeks he may go to school seven days, other weeks maybe just a couple of days. The project determines his schedule, but he never works more than fifteen hours a week. Salary, wages and benefits no longer exist. It is not a consideration for any company, business, school....or employee.

With the emphasis on self-improvement, a much more fluid work force is created. The nine-to-five model is gone. Forty-hour workweeks are gone. Jobs as we know them are gone. A single job of today may be handled by six, seven, or more people in the future. Jose's school where his dad works may have several hundred teachers, maybe thousands that work there, all of them working less than fifteen hours a week. Some of the teachers may work only five or six hours at Jose's school and another five or six hours might be spent working at another school, or perhaps as a police officer, or perhaps as a construction worker.

Each citizen will choose how he or she contributes to the community. As long as their formal jobs accrue no more than fifteen hours in a week and citizens are part of the community exchange, they can do whatever they wish. Working less than fifteen formal hours keeps their community exchange status as "black-belt." This is the key factor to insuring peace of mind for each citizen. Once their formal commitment is met, each citizen can focus more on specific interests in their personal growth.

Mrs. Yang spends three afternoons a week working at the food exchange. She works in the orchards inspecting trees, insuring they and their fruit are healthy. She works four or five hours a day, but never more than fifteen hours a week. She chose this work because she enjoys the outdoors. There are hundreds of people, who help out in the food exchange. Each of them has chosen specific roles for their own reasons.

Hiroko and Jose work hard at school. Jose's school project is developing a technology that captures and stores biogas from compost heaps. This stored energy is converted for household use. If his project is successful, households around the world can be more self-sustaining without adding to their carbon footprints. Hiroko is nine years old. She has demonstrated mastery-level skills in speaking and writing. As a result she is a peer tutor at school. She helps other students practice and improve these skills.

Jose's project, like all school projects has real-world applications. All time spent on project work is calculated into the Exchange Credit Table above. Hiroko's peer tutoring time is also eligible. These hours do not impact their parent's formal hours. That is to say, both parents' formal work hours remain at less than fifteen. As a family, the Yang's have a status of double black belt.

When Wade finishes his formal assignment at the high school, he takes the public shuttle up to the university. He spends several hours a day working on a project in which he has personal interest. He and his team are trying to analyze and determine how two geographically separate cultures developed a similar phonetic pattern in their respective languages. Mr. Yang was formally trained in linguistics. He has been fascinated with this phenomenon for years and finds himself spending many hours a week on this project. Sometimes he misses the shuttle back to his children's school, which forces Jose to drive the cart home. Wade then takes the last public shuttle that gets him close to home and walks the rest of the way.

When Mary Yang finishes her formal assignment at the food exchange she takes the shuttle to the community's science facilities. As a horticulturalist with a specialty in medicinal plants, she spends her time working to develop an organic compound that will assist the human immune system in the early detection of invasive bacteria. Her research is advancing medical knowledge in the area of natural medicine. Her sister's death is the motivation, but as her project advances, medical care improves without the need for chemical processes that are more damaging to the body or the environment, which helps everyone in the community. Mary's father, Isaac, is retired. He spends his afternoons at a local community center. He helps with community event scheduling. He doesn't have to, but he likes the challenge. As a self-actualized citizen, nothing is more enticing than a good challenge.

When all is said and done, the Yangs spend more than sixty hours a week, above and beyond their formal assignments. Additionally, the children and grandfather are credited for about thirty hours a week. As double black-belt earners these hours are banked each week. The Yang's like to travel and they usually take about twelve weeks every year to do so. As a result, the Yang family accrues about 3,600 hours (or credits) a year in the Community exchange. As double black-belt earners, all the credits they receive from their formal assignments can be used outside of the exchange.

The 3,600 credits they receive can be used within the Community exchange at a one-to-one ratio. The credit value of goods would be determined by the time it takes to produce the product. For example, it might take a local plant thirty hours to produce a washer, or eighty hours to produce a car. The Yangs can use thirty of their credited hours to get a new washer when the time comes. The credit value of services would include both the time it takes to produce the goods needed for the service as well as the time it takes to perform the service. For instance, a surgical procedure at a hospital would include the time it took to produce the surgical instruments, the hospital space, the support equipment and other goods needed to perform the surgery. Additionally, the time of the doctors and nurses would be included.

For things like hospital space and instruments, there would be rated value. Obviously, the time it takes to build the entire hospital would not be used, but rather a percentage of the time that represented the operating room, recovery room, the production of a surgical bed, etc. It might look like the following:

Surgical Instruments	40 hours
Hospital Space	
Operating Room	20 hours
Recovery Room	20 hours
Drugs	10 hours
Time in Operating Room	7 hours
Time in recovery	96 hours
Doctor	21 hours
Nurse	131 hours
Out-Patient Care	100 hours
Sub Total	**445 hours**
Less Exchange Hours	140 hours
Net Total	**305 hours**

For a seven-hour surgery, obviously a major surgery, the Yangs would use 305 credits. The net total reflects the hours of formal work required to provide the surgery. The line item of "Exchange hours" represents the time that others volunteered. Maybe one doctor was not formally working. Perhaps a couple of nurses registered their formal hours as custodians at a local business and volunteered time as nurses for their own personal interests. Volunteer time is not calculated into the total. With the Yangs averaging 3,600 credits a year it is easy to see that after only a couple of years and from then forward, health care would not be an issue for them. Because this model encourages citizens to spend personal time advancing their knowledge in their areas of interest, their bank of accrued credited time continually grows.

If you think of it in terms of today's citizens, we work very hard, and some of us have two or three jobs. When we get home we are tired and usually will relax in front of the TV. According to Neilson, on average Americans watch twenty-eight hours of TV each week. In the future, we formally work less than fifteen hours a week, and that might be at two or three different places. Our TV watching hours are replaced with time spent advancing our knowledge in our specific areas of interest. When we come home we are not burned out from the day. Couch potato time turns into fun time. We can explore our hobbies and other interests. For the Yangs this means getting creative.

Most evenings Mr. Yang arrives home with his two children. His wife, Mary is already home. Mary and her father are preparing dinner. Wade joins them and they share their day as they finish preparations. Jose goes to the garden and checks on the compost heap and the device he is working on in school designed to collect and store the biogas. Hiroko helps getting the table ready for dinner. After dinner Wade spends time at his piano working on some songs he is writing. There is an upcoming music event at the local community center and he will perform.

Mrs. Yang sits outside and puts some finishing touches on a story she is writing. She is a member of the creative writing club in her community and will share her story for open discussion next month. Jose finishes some work on his project in the back and then joins a few friends to do a sunset run. Hiroko is in the outside living space with her mother. She is reviewing pictures she recently took while on a field trip with her class. She will submit them to be displayed at an upcoming photo night at the local community center.

Art is not commercialized. Those who produce it, simply share it. In a society without money, intellectual property rights do not have a dollar value, they are provided simply as recognition. Making sure the artist is properly recognized is important. However, making money from what the artist produces is no longer practiced. As a result, artists, musicians, painters, writers, poets, et al openly share what they produce at free community events. There is no one flooding the market with a particular song, no one telling us how good it is, no one focusing on the performer and telling us where he lives, what he does, what he wears. Dave, the pop singer does not exist. People who like listening to him will listen to him. Period.

Without commercial radio and TV, music and film productions are simply made available (via streaming) to the public. Some people will watch, some will not…they may, or may not recommend it to their friends. Artists, like all citizens, will work in the exchange. Those who work less than fifteen hours earn a black belt. If they have a black belt for their carbon footprint, then the hours they spend producing a song, video, or movie accrue just like those for any other citizen. The time spent on projects is important, but the final product has no commercial value. The popularity of a project may validate an artist, but it will not make him rich and famous. Any associations or organizations that would like to formally acknowledge any artist, can only do so if the artist has earned a double black belt.

With the chase for dollars eliminated, art is for art's sake. Money is no longer the great equalizer or oppressor. Everyone has twenty-four hours a day from which to choose how to invest his or her time. The "field" no longer needs to be leveled. Without the incessant barrage of advertising and without marketing companies trying to create false needs to generate sales, consumerism in all industries is gone. With this distraction removed, the Yang's have no need or desire to "keep up with the Joneses." Without credit cards and the false need to borrow money, people are much more independent. When unexpected needs arise, the family looks to itself first, and then to neighbors to help out.

Communities share resources and ideas. Drugs, alcohol and other chemical agents are not used. Crime is not an issue in the community. The community becomes more like an extended family. All the members of the community share common values that support self-actualization: initiative, responsibility, accountability, industry, pride and integrity. As a result, issues of concern are not defined by the color of skin, age, or whether you have a vagina or a penis. Stereotypes have disappeared. There are just people doing their part in the community.

Corporate churches are also extinct. With no one telling the members who to hate, or who to kill, who to judge or how to love, individuals privately choose their own way to honor their spirituality. With each citizen recognizing how important individual choice is, the desire to meddle in others' choices has been removed. We have learned that spirituality is a personal journey not a public quest that needs to be championed or denounced. Public policies are guided by the need to have a healthy planet, a healthy community and healthy lives. Our collective mind-set is focused on future innovations and solutions, not the assignment of blame and self-recusals of participation. Empowering each individual has freed us from commercial, material, physical and spiritual competition.

The Yangs live in a world that presumes logic and efficiency. Function over form. That is not to say that style and individual expression are not present. However, these are accomplished without risking the environment, and are driven by internal desires, not external pressures. With a society of independent thinkers and independent doers, the government does not collect money from Mr. Yang only to give it to his neighbor. Communities help themselves. The "disadvantaged" don't exist. Citizens simply take advantage of opportunities as they see fit. People help each other because they see a need, not because they see a reward.

What I have just described is not utopia. It is humanity. Or what it would be if we didn't make things hard on ourselves. I remember when I was young someone told me that it takes more muscles to frown than to smile. So why isn't everyone walking around smiling? It's easier. We don't smile because we learn not to.

We are reminded daily of things we don't have or can't do. We face a daily drudgery of working for someone else so we can get some "American Dream" as it has been defined by others and forced upon us. From birth we are taught to accept our current system. Just like the Ornarans believed they needed Felicium, we believe we need money, and jobs are the best way to get it. Big government and big business have worked together for years to develop a school system designed to create us—work drones.

Their efforts have been very successful. The evidence is in the belief that a system such as the one described above could never happen. In reality, however, the system above is much easier to accomplish than our current system. Our current system is the result of a concerted and relentless effort to control our thoughts, behaviors and our perceptions all for the sake of money. Trillions of dollars have been spent to do this. We are so accepting now that we will do the insane because we are told to. Conversely, we will refuse to accept possibilities that are readily available and, I would argue, more aligned with our natural development.

The whole notion of consumption is rational to us because we have been taught to accept it as rational. Implicit in that teaching is that non-conformity is radical. Tell your friends you don't want to participate in giving gifts—birthdays, holidays, whatever—and see what happens. YOU are the one with a problem. You're a Grinch, you're selfish, stingy, conceited…you are something that is not desirable.

The "utopia" I described above is simply us living as humans without the conditioning. Without the man-made invention of money, we could very easily have evolved into a society much like the one I described. Humans are a communal species. Humans are intelligent. Humans are curious. Humans are innovative. The society described above is built on those concepts.

All that prevents us from moving toward a different future is our mind-set. Life is not supposed to be so hard. We are the only species on the planet that chooses to make life so difficult. Money is a vehicle for many to pervert the human existence on our planet. And while it may be challenging at first to change our mind-set and transition to a society without money, it would not be difficult to live in such a society. Indeed, it would be a much more relaxed life-style. If you want an idea of how it might feel, just relax your face and let the natural smile emerge.

Chapter 7

Enough With the Donkeys and Elephants

As Captain Picard concludes discussions with the Prime Minister of Angosia III, the Prime Minister tells him that the development of the mind and the cultivation of intellect is an important part of their society. Picard returns to his ship with Riker and comments, "I think they'll make a fine addition to the Federation."

The Prime Minister then contacts them asking for help. Danar, an "extremely violent" prisoner has escaped the prison colony on Luna 5 and Picard is asked to help find and return him. Picard agrees and, after some clever attempts to avoid capture, the prisoner is finally apprehended by the Enterprise. Danar, a former soldier, intrigues Counselor Troi, who begins to uncover his background. We learn that he was one of many citizens who underwent a government program to build a "perfect soldier" during their past war.

When the war was over, the soldiers had trouble re-integrating into society. The Prime Minister tells Picard they were "resettled on Luna 5 for their own protection." He adds that they were given a "fine quality of life." Picard responds that even the most comfortable prison is still a prison. The Prime Minister adds that agitators like Danar forced them to add guards to the colony as a matter of internal security.

Meanwhile, Danar escapes the Enterprise, liberates other soldiers from Luna 5, steals a ship and is on his way to Angosia III. The Prime Minister becomes very concerned and again asks for Picard's help, telling him that "We aren't equipped to handle things like this. That is why we created *them*." Picard and his team beam down to the planet and meet the Prime Minister in his council room.

Although the Prime Minister considers the escaped soldiers dangerous, Picard insists they are victims. The Prime Minister reiterates that it was the will of the people to resettle them. Other members of the council reinforce that, telling Picard there was a referendum and the people chose resettlement. However, when Picard asks if there was any effort to reverse the effects of the conditioning, he's told that studies were done, but never tried. One council member adds, "Besides we may need to use them again someday."

At this point, Danar and other soldiers storm the council room and surround everyone. They are armed. Picard does not challenge them. The Prime Minister turns to Picard for help, but Picard has his landing party beamed back to the ship. Once back, Picard comments that if the Angosians can successfully negotiate with the "terrorists" in the next few minutes they will demonstrate substantial growth as a people and he will recommend their membership in the Federation.

This episode of *Star Trek: The Next Generation* ("The Hunted," S3, E11), reveals that even thoughtful and intellectual societies can be persuaded to believe something that isn't true. When this happens, an entire society may use rationalization to support behaviors they would otherwise find reprehensible. The Angosians did studies and held referendums to imprison their own people. There are no details as to how the referendums were conducted, but it is safe to assume they were sold as being fair, with everyone believing that they were making a moral choice. They rationalized that it was for the safety of the very people they imprisoned. In

American political terms, the Angosians did some "spinning" of the truth to help convince the people to make the choice they did.

Spinning the truth is the ability to frame information to support a particular agenda. This can be done by omitting some facts, presenting some facts out of context, emphasizing certain facts over others, distorting facts, and of course, just lying. In American politics spinning the truth is commonplace. We even have "spin-doctors." These are people who are especially adept at not telling the truth. (This is in the context of the truth, the whole truth and nothing but the truth.) Facts, statistics and direct quotes are the perfect ammunition for good spin doctors to reshape the truth and advance agendas. Indeed, We The People pay the salaries of spin doctors. Elected officials use our money to hire spin-doctors to lie to us.

Skillful politicians, with the assistance of these spin-doctors, can create false narratives, which can then be used to persuade us to vote in a particular way. Much like the Angosian people—who I am sure truly believed what they were doing was in the best interest of the very people they imprisoned—we use our vote, based on these false narratives, to advance particular agendas. In America today, both major political parties, Democrats and Republicans, compete for their version of the truth, creating their own narratives to persuade voters.

In general terms I believe that competition is a good thing, but only if it is open to everyone. In a political system in which there are only two major political parties the competition is effectively limited to two points of view. This gives the false impression that there are only two sides to any problem, or only two solutions to any problem. This competition between Democrats and Republicans for "the truth" has evolved into a very dangerous situation. Both parties have convinced Americans, falsely, that only two solutions for problems exist.

As things stand now, without the support of either party, winning elections is nearly impossible. Whether it's for a state office, Congress, or for the White House itself. Therefore, candidates must join a party and gain acceptance there first. With only two parties competing, and both of them wanting to distinguish themselves from each other, it is only natural that their differences have grown wider over the years. As each party seeks to claim the truth, they must inherently also claim that the other party is wrong. Moreover, as we see in American politics today, not only is the other party's platform wrong, the individual members of the other party are wrong. In fact, they are probably lying. Indeed, each member of the other party is probably a liar, not to be trusted, perhaps even un-American.

As this process continues, the natural evolution of a two-party system is for each party to blame the other for the problems. Issues would solve themselves if the other party would just dissolve or acquiesce. Each election cycle demonstrates a stronger push by both parties to alienate the other. Party platforms move further away from each other, as do the politicians themselves. Personal attacks replace honest disagreements, and rather than defending policy choices, politicians end up defending their behavior. It has become personal! When a politician states a policy he supports, he is branded a socialist, a racist, a xenophobe, a religious fundamentalist, etc. There is no honest discussion about the policy. Just name calling. All of this is done in an effort to win elections.

To the extent that each party is successful in marginalizing members of the other party, more power is gained through more congressional seats or more White House wins during elections. That becomes the goal: gaining party power and winning elections. Politicians no longer work to solve problems for their constituents; they simply work to gain party power. With only two parties, politicians have a simple choice. Once they are in a party, they can either try to advance their career by trashing the other party, or lose their own party support and melt into political history.

Ideas are replaced by ideology and ideology gains importance. What one does once she is in congress or the White House is not as important as what she purports to believe in. Unfortunately for America, this process has two devastating results: extremism thrives and compromise withers.

In an effort to further distinguish themselves from the other side, politicians move further from the center. In a system where ideology trumps ideas, individuals push further away to demonstrate their allegiance to the ideology. As a political party, each party must accept these steps further and further away from the center for they dare not impede the advancement of the ideology. As servants of ideology, politicians can ill-afford to be seen as unwilling to go along with the party line as it moves further away from the center.

This results in what I call the "shattered windows" approach to politics. This is the notion that each party must continue to accept all extremists in order to justify accepting any extremist. Shatter all previous boundaries! Regardless of how few people might be affected, a new extreme grows the party and validates previous less-extreme viewpoints. Both of these outcomes are welcomed. Sometimes new extremists become their own voting block and gain power quickly within the party with which they identify.

Events also influence this process of special interest groups as well as pushing the envelope in terms of extremism. In the 1960's America experienced the Civil Rights movement and the Vietnam War. These events greatly influenced this process of the development of special interest groups. White hate groups like the KKK started killing and bombing. In response, new hate groups like the Black Panthers were born. Non-violent special interest groups, such as feminism and gay rights were also born. Emotions were high and most groups were aggressive in pushing their beliefs. In the mid to late 1960's partnerships brought anti-capitalist groups and anti-war groups together to form very extreme groups. The Weather Underground are an example of this. Like the KKK, they used bombings to make their points. These kinds of extreme groups infiltrated both political parties and helped accelerate the move away from the center.

With each step further away from the center, compromise becomes less likely. Ideology becomes a measure of allegiance. Working with someone on the "other side" becomes suspect and is often seen as weakness or betrayal, even leading to damage to a politician's career. It is framed in one of those hard-to-get-out-of corners: "If we're right and they are wrong how could you possibly want to agree with them on anything?" Rigidity replaces flexibility. When you apply this rigidity to trying to govern a nation, it becomes dangerous.

When only two parties control the entire country and their choices become mandates for the nation, we are all at risk. Honest differences are replaced by a kind of political fundamentalism. American freedom as we know it is in danger. As this process further separates the two parties, Americans not bound by ideology become the victims. Since the two parties are the only way to win an election most Americans find themselves having to choose the lesser of two evils.

With each election cycle, Americans are given more extreme choices to make. Anyone considering not voting for a Democrat or Republican might be open to criticism by his ideologically driven friends. On a personal note I have voted for a Democrat or Republican only twice —1976 and 2008. When I choose not to vote for either major party's candidate and I share that information with ideologically driven friends, I am often told that I am "wasting my vote." Those same friends sometimes try to convince me to vote for their party's candidate using the logic that it will prevent the other party's candidate from winning. And we don't want that! When you think of how dangerous that is, it can be scary. Where once conservative and liberal ideals were both valid and helpful to our country, we are now at a place where we must choose one over the other. Moreover, we are thought of as being wasteful for voting our beliefs. That is the danger of the two-party system.

To demonstrate how absurd this is I will use an issue that is near-and-dear to me: personal health and fitness. I am forever battling my weight. Some years are good, some years…not so good. Over the past 20 years in particular, while I have learned a lot about general fitness and weight loss, I haven't always taken advantage of that knowledge. Anyone who has ever dealt with this issue and has done just a small amount of research has learned a very basic truth: Fitness requires attention to both diet and exercise. In the same way, both conservative and liberal ideas need to be a part of the political discussion. Ignore either one of them and the health of the nation is jeopardized.

If our current two-party system was applied to the fitness industry, there would be only two types of fitness trainers, and we would be forced to choose one. Let's pretend the conservatives adopted the ideology that diet was the only path for fitness, and liberals adopted the ideology that exercise was the only path for fitness. Where would that leave Americans who want to get into shape?

Conservatives would introduce bills in congress targeting diet. They would tell us what foods to eat and how often and in what quantities…so far not too bad. However, as this would be their ideology, they would condemn liberals who spoke of the importance of exercise. They would stop any liberal effort in Congress to pass any laws relating to exercise, because for conservatives exercise is not just wasteful, but an impedance to becoming fit. Conversely, liberals would only put forward legislation that supported exercise, and would frame efforts to improve diet as being harmful.

Conservatives would support public efforts to limit the construction of fitness centers that included exercise equipment. Radical conservatives might even bomb gyms. And, while most conservatives would condemn the bombing, they would understand the motivation. They would seek to attack liberals who "threatened" our well being by their radical ideas of exercising and working out. They would find out-of-shape people who exercised three or four times in any given year (which would obviously have little effect on body weight) and try to paint them as representative of the failed practice of exercising.

On the other hand, liberals would push for expansion of gyms and the training equipment industries. They would spend—I'm sorry "invest"—tax dollars on start-up ventures that had new ideas for designing or producing weights and/or equipment. They would raise the corporate taxes on the food industry. They would levy more taxes on food items, and use the revenue to provide an entitlement program to help the poor exercise their "Right to Exercise." And the followers would chant, ERTE! ERTE!

Protestors would line up in front of supermarkets with signs that read, "F#!#*k Food" or, "Eat This" with a swastika below it. They would compare restaurateurs with Nazis. Traffic would be stopped and police cars trashed because of the oppression protesters felt from the Food Nazis. Some liberals would condemn the behavior, but nonetheless champion the message. Hollywood actors would join the fight. They would use the kind of logic that only Hollywood has and argue that cavemen also ate, and haven't we evolved since then?

Both sides would not only debate each other with their misplaced logic, they would condemn each other personally for their betrayal to American ideals! They would stop listening. They would resist change. They would spend their time in caucuses of people who shared their perspective. This would strengthen their resolve and embolden them to move even further away from compromise. This process is supported in behavioral psychology by the attribution theory. I am over-simplifying here, but this theory suggests that beliefs influence behavior, which in turn strengthens our beliefs, and so on.

In this scenario, as the government became more divided and their legislative zeal grew, the only beneficiaries would be the companies involved on either side. A conglomerate that owned exercise equipment manufacturing companies as well as food producing companies would love it. Profits would soar. Other companies would position themselves to do the same. Cash from these companies would pay for politicians' campaigns. To the extent campaigns were successful, policies and new laws would be bought and paid for. Each election cycle would bring more radical ideas from which companies could profit. These corporations would buy media outlets to help fuel the fire and increase profits. They would sit back and laugh as Americans verbally assaulted each other…every assault would be another dollar.

As a result, rather than having a government that is effective in supporting the efforts of Americans to stay fit by addressing both diet and exercise, we would have elected officials who are not only distrustful of each other, but potentially dangerous to the average citizen. Rather than helping John Q Public, our government would be aiding Wall Street and large corporations.

I admit I was having some fun with the exercise vs. diet debate, but the end result of divisiveness and distrust is exactly what is happening in our partisan approach to government. Liberals and conservatives have become so entrenched in ideology that they no longer have genuine interest in solving problems, just advancing their ideology. Advancing the ideology gets them re-elected.

That has become the political reality in America under a two-party system. Both parties spend all their efforts in gaining political power. According to the Federal Election Commission, an estimated $7 billion dollars was spent on campaigns during the 2012 election cycle. Through September 2016 the FEC reports the amount spent for that election cycle was 7.2 billion dollars. Their final report has not yet been published, but surely it will be a higher amount. Billions of dollars spent by two political parties to condemn each other, to spin the truth in their favor and convince Americans to vote for them, or at least vote against the "other side."

Where once we had the Republicans wanting to champion America by stoking the push for industry to grow the economy, and the Democrats wanting to champion America by stoking the push to insure no one was left behind (much like the offensive and defensive squad of a football team: sharing a common goal, but playing a different role), both parties are now fighting each other.

They are unwilling or unable to recognize the common goals we have as a nation.

Both parties have been spinning the truth for so long that they have not only fully accepted the spin, the spin is all they see. For the convenience of building voting blocks, whole groups of people have been distilled into single personalities. Conservatives and liberals have essentially created an amalgamation for each group. These representative people are all they see. Nothing else exists. They live in a binary world of their own creation in which national issues are defined by these amalgamations. Whether it's the economy, immigration, abortion, or whatever, Republicans and Democrats only see two people, created by their own spin, regardless of how absurd. Here are a couple of examples of this:

Illegal Immigrant

For the conservative, meet Carlos. He is an illegal immigrant. He is a member of La eMe (the Mexican Mafia). He regularly crosses the border to bring drugs into our country. He is very violent and has no problem murdering for hire, or as a means to "send messages." He disdains American values and is here simply to support his gang. He has no job of course, and he is usually stoned. He lives a life of crime. For recreation on the weekends, he usually goes to the park and rapes a couple of women (probably young coeds) and beats two or three innocent children.

His day job is to break into apartments and steal from hard-working Americans. In the evening he steals social security numbers and gives them to coyotes. Honest, hard-working American lives are regularly destroyed by identity theft. Moreover, he will use a stolen identity to vote, and always votes for a Democrat. If he is caught, he is released immediately because he lives in a sanctuary city. As a result he is never held accountable for his actions. He also sticks his tongue out at the American Flag every chance he gets.

For the Liberal, meet Magdalena. She is an illegal immigrant from the poverty stricken country of El Pooro! She was sitting in her home with her nine children when a death squad broke into her hovel and began shooting her children. She escaped out the doggy door of her hovel with three of her children and made it to America. She managed to find work. She works six jobs, all of which have rich white bastards exploiting her. She gets up at 2:00AM to start her first job and doesn't get home until 1:00AM the next morning. For all her hard work, she earns twenty-seven cents a day. She uses this money to support her family. They live in an old refrigerator box in a ditch by the road. All three girls are exploited by rich white bastards and earn an additional nine cents a day for twenty hours of work. Amazingly, the mother reports her income and pays more than $100,000 a year in taxes. She loves America and her dream is to have the Stars and Stripes tattooed on her forehead…and her daughters' foreheads!

Abortion

For the conservative viewpoint, meet Bambi. She wants an abortion. She likes to whore around and is way too busy to be bothered with a child. She understands that contraception costs money, but she can get free abortions. She is taking advantage of a special at the demon-possessed Planned Parenthood Center. Currently she can get $2.00 for every fetus, so she is going for a record four abortions in as many months. She will use the eight dollars to buy some supplies to make protest signs that read, "My body is a temple! Government keep your hands off!"

For the liberal position, meet little Carrie Ann. She wants an abortion. She is a nine year-old girl who was raped by her older brother. Her father is an abusive alcoholic who works at a bank, and her mother is a society bitch, too busy to take care of her own child. Both parents have taught her that God's will must be obeyed. This means she will be killed if she gets pregnant before marriage (But that is only if her parents find out.) On top of that she has a horrible disease: Bellyitis Circumfrencia. If her belly grows as a result of pregnancy she will die a horrible death. The only way to save her life is to get an abortion!

StockBroker

For the conservative ideology, meet Ken. He is a stockbroker. He works twelve to fourteen hours a day helping middle class clients invest what little money they have to build a nest egg so they can send their children to college in the future. The money invested by average American citizens is used for companies to expand and grow jobs so that more Americans can join the middle class. These new jobs also help take hard-working poor people off the streets and give them dignity as human beings. With this new income the working class (that just went to the middle class, that is on its way to well-to-do class) buys more goods and services and the economy grows even more. As companies increase profits, the Boards of Directors take handfuls of cash and throw them out of the top floor of their building. This is so the money will trickle down to the people on the street. Things would be even better if the damn government would stop trying to regulate these "builders of a nation."

For the Liberal position, meet Dick. He is a stockbroker. He spends $200 for a pair of socks. As he goes to work, he steals money from the blind homeless guy on the street looking for help with his next meal. He yells, "Sucker" as he walks away. He spends most of his day learning how to side step regulations in order to increase his cut of the pie. The rest of his workday is spent with his colleagues designing Ponzi schemes and collecting lists of suckers from whom he can con money. He likes to go to the mall with his friends and laugh at all the suckers who actually have to shop there. The only poor neighborhood he has ever been in is the one he just bought with some investors with the goal of turning it into a parking lot. When asked about what will happen to the poor people living there, he smiles and says, "Hey, there will be some covered parking sections. Don't know if they'll be able to afford the hourly rate, though. Heh, heh, heh."

Okay, these examples are exaggerated, but the point is liberals and conservatives have been spinning the truth so long they now live in world in which caricatures created by their own spin, no matter how ridiculous, are more real to them than people. Regardless of the issue, conservatives and liberals already have preconceived positions from which they will not move, from which they cannot move. The two-party system has aided in the creation of a rigid power structure. One that must be obeyed if a politician wants to get elected. Any politician who attempts to walk away from these rigid and preconceived positions risks being abandoned by his or her own party. As a result, young politicians who show promise in the party are quick to champion the party's ideology. If there are several young ambitious politicians, then there is a competition that pushes the particular issue further from the center. After all, they don't want to appear similar to the other party. They need to show distinction. To the extent that young politicians are successful at advancing a particular issue, the party adopts the issue and moves their ideology even further from the center.

Politicians have learned that the party apparatus is made up of constituent groups (voting blocks) that represent varying degrees of sway within the party. Politicians try to gain the support of these groups by becoming champions of their causes. They learn quickly how to change the "truth" of any issue and present it as a kind of sacred mission within the party. They spin the issue until it "sells" by gaining traction. Gaining the endorsement of these groups improves chances for election, or re-election. To this end, politicians will use spin, not only to better frame their position, but also to try to damage their opponent's position.

This can be a difficult task because most issues are not simple to define or to solve. However, both political parties have spent decades distilling difficult issues into only two solutions. This makes spinning much easier for them. They have used fear and greed to garner support from many Americans. These "political zombies" have voted the party line and will continue to vote the party line…forever. You may know some of them. I do. I have no idea who will run for president in 2028, but I know some people (providing they're still alive), who will vote for the Republican candidate, and I know some people who will vote for the Democratic candidate. I know how they will vote twelve years from now. That should scare everyone.

Both political parties also know. They have their armies of zombies who do as they are told. All that the Democrats and Republicans have to do is continue to use fear and greed to keep their zombies in line. To do this they simply need to continue to spin the truth.

The power brokers from both parties understood a long time ago the best way to do this is by controlling information. One obvious way is to buy the press. Newspapers, TV networks and other news outlets have been purchased by the rich and powerful as a means to help their particular party spin the truth. There are five corporations—Viacom, AOL/Time Warner, Disney, News Corp and Clear Channel—that own almost all of the radio, news, print, music, movie, cable, entertainment and production industries in America.

The CEO's of these five corporations align themselves with political leaders and as part of the ruling elite, decide what truth we see and hear and how often we see and hear it. As both political parties continue this struggle for power, the political zombies from both sides become more blinded to the truth. They live on the spin. This is great for the political parties, but not so good for America.

Part of the process of spinning the truth is to create distractions. This includes attacking people personally, which has become the norm for American politics today. Issues have taken a back seat to attacks on character. In today's America the effect of the two party system is tragic. It has resulted in both parties supporting the candidate with the best chance to win, not the candidate with the best qualifications. This includes not only minor political positions, but even the position of the president of the United States.

We live in a supposedly advanced free nation and are a species that is supposedly intelligent, yet our two-party system has driven us to argue that people should not vote based on principle and what they believe in. We should vote on the lesser of two evils… two evils, I might add, that have become worse and worse with each new election. Two hundred and fifty million American voters are being told to vote for the least bad person because that is our only choice! About half of that number have stopped voting altogether, leaving the other half to make decisions for our country. Within that half, the political zombies do as they are told regardless of how absurd. Many of them will vote their party rather than make their own choice. Indeed, the committed zombies actually believe it is their own choice.

As mentioned many times in this book, the future as represented by all the *Star Trek* franchises is one in which individual liberty and rights are paramount. Citizens are self-actualized, responsible free thinkers. Problems are solved by the use of logic, planning, and cooperation. I think it is a safe assumption to say that spinning is not a common practice in the future, as it does nothing to solve problems, and it would be ineffective with a self-actualized citizenry. Without the motive of profit, I have no doubt that it has evolved out of our politics in the future.

Our future counterparts have learned that different approaches to a problem don't require conflict, but rather cooperation. ALL input and ideas should be considered and discussed as part of the process of solving any given problem. Solutions that worked would be chosen over solutions that didn't. In the future, attention would be focused only on results and progress, not ideology. The gridlock we are forced to live with today would be seen as primitive and counterproductive.

On Angosia III when the Prime Minister and the Council were forced to look at their decision of "resettling" their soldiers, what the viewer didn't see is the council members pointing fingers at each other and trying to escape responsibility for bad decisions. The members calmly accepted their circumstances as a single group of responsible leaders, and as an optimist I believe they worked out their differences with the soldiers and worked to reintegrate them into their society, their families and their homes. That same optimism leads me to believe we can evolve out of a political system in which two parties spend billions of dollars to gain power, spin the truth to suit their own agenda, and divide our people rather than serve their nation.

Chapter 8

United We Stand, Divided...

The USS Enterprise arrives at Klavdia III to pick up a young person who is destined to be the leader of Daled IV. Daled IV has been locked in a civil war for decades. This new young leader has been trained and is charged with finding an end to the violence. Her parents were on opposing sides of the conflict and it is believed she is the only one who can bring peace. In a conversation on the bridge, Picard tries to discover how the conflict started, but there is no direct information. When Data is asked to speculate, he says that they had "developed disparate cultures which is the cause of most wars" ("The Dauphin," *Star Trek*: TNG; S2, E10).

Even in the future, war exists on some planets. However, on earth we have ended war in the future. With little direct evidence that can be seen, it is difficult to try to identify exactly how this was achieved, but Data's answer suggests that disparate cultures are probably not an issue for the earth of the future. The United States is a good country to use for this discussion because we are made up of cultures from around the world and we are not a one-world society yet. Economic disparity notwithstanding, to the extent that the primary culture is able to integrate the various other cultures, common goals are easier to identify and work toward.

Diversity is a strength. It broadens perspective, offers new ideas and enriches a culture. I have traveled to, and lived in, several countries and I am the better for it. However, diversity can become a political tool. It can be used to slow or even prevent cultural assimilation. In our current political reality of polarization, it becomes even easier to use diversity as a means to divide our common culture.

As I demonstrated in the last chapter, our two-party system has learned to spin a reality that is designed to gain power, not serve; to place blame, not solve problems; to use fear, not knowledge; to control information, not enlighten. All for greed! In short, in the quest for more money and more power (or both) our two-party system has divided our politicians and those "political zombies" from either party to a point that our government no longer functions correctly. Gridlock is commonplace. Finding solutions is rare. Differences are highlighted in any national discussion.

Unfortunately, this practice of division has become a huge industry in itself, and its power is not lost on some Americans. Pushing emotional buttons can be very profitable. Using fear as a weapon and "spinning" as a strategy, there is money to be made. The division that is so obvious in our government is like a cancer growing in our society. Special interest groups have learned how to use this weapon and strategy to advance their "cause" (code for "making profit"). Learning from our politicians, some Americans actually use polarization as a strategy. Their goal is to divide, to marginalize, to demonize. (Politicians refer to this as "playing to the base.") In the real world, this encourages further division.

Special interest groups have much smaller bases and can afford to be more radical in both their rhetoric and their actions. In a nation of so many different cultures this strategy of polarization is being used by both politicians and special interest groups not only to impede assimilation, but to create more division. On one side, radicals will argue that failure to assimilate—sounds like the Borg doesn't it?—is a danger to the country. On the other side, the argument is that those supporting assimilation are de facto attempting to strip individuals of their unique cultures.

Using the polarization strategy to raise money, fund campaigns, and gain power, both sides have no room to move in terms of compromise. Seeing both sides of this issue and being reasonable is seen as caving in, and is not an option for these groups. As a result, any politician who has pitched his or her tent in "Camp Ideology" has only one response to those who disagree: "Kill them, before they reproduce and multiply!" That might be a bit harsh, but the result is the same: Dissenters are the enemy and are to be fought and conquered on any political battlefield in which they present themselves. Discussion stops, and gridlock begins, for any politician dare not endanger her/his re-election bid. "Long Live The Party" is code for "To hell with the nation."

As a result of this constant warring between conservatives and progressives, little is done to bring us together as a nation. Usually, the only time that happens is when we have suffered a great tragedy. But only if the cause of the tragedy doesn't invade "Camp Ideology." Natural disasters tend to bring Americans together, and 9/11 brought Americans together. However, some tragedies, like Sandy Hook, invade "Camp Ideology," and as quickly as Americans start to come together, our politicians and special interest groups work feverishly to pull us apart again. As they say: When it comes to political gain, no tragedy goes unnoticed. I might add that recently even natural disasters are being used to push political agendas. On his website, "Bloomberg View," then New York City's Mayor Michael Bloomberg, used Hurricane Sandy as a platform. He suggested that the hurricane might have been caused as a result of global warming and that it "should compel all elected leaders to take immediate action."

With each passing year the process of polarization leaves fewer and fewer clues to what America represents. Indeed, if you ask one hundred people that question today you will probably get one hundred different answers. As I said, diversity is a good thing in the context of people sharing a common goal, whether it is a nation, a company, or a football team. Having diverse ideas, perspectives and input increases the chances for success. However, when there is no longer a shared goal, diversity can become an impediment. If disparate cultures can be a reason for war, as Data suggests, what effect would splitting a culture apart have on the society? Perhaps it could be as devastating as war…perhaps civil war.

Some important components of culture include language, beliefs and traditions. Beliefs can be both spiritual and social. For instance, a shared value system, or a shared work ethic is important for a cohesive culture. It is very easy to see these components at work on board the USS Enterprise. While we may speculate that some specific differences (like uniforms) may differ from earth culture at large, it is a safe assumption that the cultural values and beliefs of the Enterprise crew members from earth are shared by citizens back on earth.

There are some basic commonalities among our future counterparts that bear notice. All Star Fleet characters in all the *Star Trek* franchises respect individual liberty, including individual thought. Respect for life is very important in the future. Families and education are important. Working together to solve problems is common practice. That effort begins with good communication, which makes language very important. Finally, duty is important. In the context of the civilian culture, duty would translate as work ethic.

When a culture shares common values, it becomes a stronger culture. Generally speaking, with shared values and traditions comes shared respect, shared understanding, and more likely than not shared goals or vision. To the extent values and traditions are not shared, a culture becomes weaker and its very survival may be threatened. National efforts to resist common values or to champion the differences within any culture can accelerate the process of division of that culture. Thus making it weaker.

An example is the issue of women's rights, which began to take center stage in the 1960's and 1970's. Much like what we did when the Civil Rights Movement achieved school integration, adults looked for solutions that helped adults. Getting women in the workplace at all levels—entry to management—was important. This was like exploding dynamite at the very foundation of pre-existing women's roles. (You know, keeping women in the kitchen "barefoot and pregnant.")

Over a decade or so the movement succeeded somewhat. Women were out of kitchens and baking was left to pre-packaged, microwave delights. The act of making babies, however was still commonplace. In fact, the increased availability of "the pill," along with the free sex movement, quickly accelerated…well… sex. Pregnancies among single women increased. Those women who got pregnant and did not want the fetus, suddenly had the legal option of abortion (January 22, 1973: Roe v. Wade). Those who wanted to keep the baby saw daycare centers growing across the country. Additionally, as the stigma of divorce faded, we have had steady growth in single-parent homes, from 8.2% in 1960 to 31.3% in 2014, according to the U.S. Census Bureau.

Women were on their way. However, like our efforts at desegregation, some one was left behind to deal with the fall-out: children. Again. In a just cause for females in our country, children became the unintended victims. Here is a full-disclosure digression. I am basing this notion of children being "victims" on the research—ALL research—that addresses raising children. (I talked about this in more detail in Chapter 2 when I discussed education.) Volumes of research support the notion that stable homes which include two loving and caring parents are better for children than homes that include one loving and caring parent (Brown, 2004; Carlson & Corcoran, 2001; McLanahan & Sandefur, 1994).

As the number of children being raised in single-parent homes increased, the percent of children raised in a home in which both parents were married dropped from 85% to 68%. Let me whisper this to you, I am not suggesting anything negative about women, regardless of their status. However I believe the research is important. If you look at research, it is better for the child—the child, not the adult—when he or she is raised in a stable household with two loving, caring parents.

Given what we know about the importance of a two-parent home, is there some other way women could have achieved "liberation" without children becoming the unintended victims? What if the movement was not framed as "Helping women break their chains," but rather, "How can the chains be broken without harming children?"

Perhaps rather than adding a new stigma to the term, "housewife," we should have really pushed for growing "house husbands." That term did begin as a result of the movement, but only in small circles of forward-thinking folks. What if politicians hadn't fenced themselves in at "Camp Ideology"? What if actual policies had been developed to nurture and embed house husbands into our culture?

What if companies had been given government incentives to develop and implement programs aimed specifically at training wives to share their husbands' jobs? A "couples job" approach. What if opportunities for women to enter the workforce didn't simultaneously build a negative connotation around the word and around the role of "housewife"?

The sexual revolution of the 1970's coincided with the increased enrollment of women at universities as job barriers came down. What if social efforts emphasized earning degrees and de-emphasized sex…or at least stressed the need for safe sex and not getting pregnant until young people were absolutely sure of their futures and their partners? (That too, came too little, too late.) Indeed, the exact opposite was true. Getting married suddenly became old-fashioned. Those that chose that path risked being called "square."

When children are involved maybe adults need to move cautiously. Perhaps at the time, the only way to "liberate" women was the way it was done. Maybe we can modify the movement now. As we have seen, our future counterparts recognize the importance of life and, in terms of humans, the importance of family and education. Our future counterparts would not support cultural change that risked damaging children's prospects for the future.

During the period in which more and more children were raised by single parents, the incarceration rate in this country increased by almost a factor of seven according to the Department of US Corrections. While I don't want to oversimplify the issue and I am certainly not claiming causality, I don't think it is a coincidence that in the developed world, America has the highest rate of children being raised in single-parent homes, and the highest rate of incarceration. Moreover, both of those statistics grew in roughly the same time frame: 1960-2000.

Those who might see making this argument as an attack on women represent the result of the politics of polarization. There is no way what I just said can be seen as a simple thought or an idea. To the extent that you are part of the feminist movement, your first response may be to see this as an affront to women because this argument places you in conflict with your politics...politics that were first driven by special interest groups and later adopted and nurtured by our two-party system. Despite research, despite facts, this argument could be, and often is, dismissed as sexist and the people who suggest this argument are framed as having enlisted in "the war on women."

It is interesting to me how many people can see that damaging our earth is not good for the future. These people push for policies that may cause some humans discomfort, all in the name of protecting earth. Shouldn't we at least consider doing the same for our children? Are they not as important? Can't we see beyond our politics and realize that supporting policies that are harmful to children is not in our best interest as a species. If that means the adults suck-it-up, then so be it.

There can be no denying that the traditional family of the 1950's is much weaker than it was. (I want to emphasize that by "traditional family" I don't necessarily mean June and Ward

Cleaver. While most research reinforces the importance of married, biological parents raising their children together, ALL research suggests than having two loving, caring adults—any gender—who can provide a stable home environment is better for a child.) When it comes to parenting a child, two is better than one.

As a component of our culture, the weaker the family structure becomes, the weaker our culture becomes. In our current polarized political environment, an honest and open discussion begins to be framed as some kind of assault, or even a war! This attitude creates a problem that can never be solved. Either side sees the other as an enemy, and conceding anything is seen as a weakness. Winning the argument becomes more important than solving a problem. As special interest groups push further apart from the center, the likelihood of solving this issue fades even more. And worse, our society becomes weaker.

Another fundamental component of any culture is language. A shared language provides a common context for idea exchange. Nuances in a shared language give special meaning that can only be understood by those who share the cultural context of the language. Much like Captain Dathon from Tamaria (See Chapter 6). If you watch any episode of any *Star Trek* you will quickly notice one thing in terms of their language: They all speak the same English—what I call Star Trek Common English (STCE). What I mean by that is their syntax, their grammar, and even their enunciation is virtually identical. There are accents to be sure (more common in the original series than the later ones), but for the most part their spoken language is the same. There are two current politically driven efforts to insure that America does not use anything like the STCE. The first movement is framed under the notion of equality and centers around skin color. The second is framed under the notion of cultural respect and centers around immigrants.

When the Civil Rights Movement gained strength in the 50's and 60's, Reverend King spoke of a dream he had in which his children would not be judged by the color of their skin; that descendants of former slaves and slave-holders could sit down together "at the table of brotherhood"; that black boys and girls could hold hands with white boys and girls; that whites and blacks would enjoy the liberty, freedom and opportunity afforded all citizens of America. Others supported that dream. The notion that Americans of all colors were equal became a rallying cry for many across the country.

As the movement grew, desegregation was one of the efforts to bring the country together. (I spoke in more detail about this particular issue in Chapter 2.) Though the effort did put black and white children in the same classrooms, it did little more than that. It was cosmetic and staged to satisfy political interest. There was no real effort to systemically integrate education. The integration was on a policy level, not a cultural level. As a result, the underlying problem with the segregated and racist system that condemned blacks to what Reverend King referred to as the "lonely island of poverty," was never really addressed.

While both black and white students sat in the same classrooms, impoverished school districts that serviced an inordinate amount of black students were never really helped. Resources, materials and facilities remained limited at best. Teachers at these schools had less training and were paid much less. The "candy shell" looked nice, but the chocolate on the inside was still bitter. As time passed this policy level approach to integration grew, but culturally the opposite occurred. Racially identified subcultures grew. This left many blacks in classrooms with whites, but not integrating with any real meaning.

I can't explain in detail how the movement shifted, but it did. While structural integration of sports teams, clubs and other school organizations occurred, it was always at the policy level. After the meetings or games, black and white students tended to separate themselves in their more informal social groups. The language used by these groups when they were together reflected their colloquialisms as well as their spoken English used around their homes. Perhaps white groups stigmatized this difference in language commonly used by black students. A kind of "integrated" racism was begun that formed loosely around color.

Human beings all share a need to belong. As some blacks felt isolated from the white status quo, they found themselves virtually alone. (And these are young kids who can struggle even when everything is going fine.) Being isolated and targeted as "different" or even dumb was a huge weight to bear. Did you ever hear the comment that "kids can be mean"? Well, they can be. I am sure that back at home, black parents were beginning to feel the fallout from dealing with segregation at a policy level, not at a cultural level.

In response the movement added a component. In addition to gaining equality, new efforts were established that focused on trying to build pride among blacks and help these young kids with their self-esteem. Blacks certainly had nothing to be ashamed of, but remember, these were children. To be fair, there was plenty of white support in the political arena, but that didn't help a lot in the classroom. Political groups to support this new component grew. During this process of change, school achievement did not seem to mean as much. The new effort was more about helping the esteem of young black students isolated at schools. This effort influenced the black pride movement. Distinguishing blackness from whiteness became the focus. This furthered the notion of a "black" and "white" America.

Eventually black pride overshadowed a more straightforward effort for civil rights. As a result the Civil Rights Movement, which was an effort to place character over color was supplanted by reverting back to placing color first. As time went on, being proud of your color wasn't enough. Somehow being proud of being black (a good thing) morphed into an effort to deliberately avoid anything associated with being white. In an educational context, this included speaking English. In the 1980's there was a serious push to create a new language to be taught in schools: Ebonics. Concise, clear and persuasive arguments were made to allow blacks not to be held to the same standard as whites in a common English classroom. Some even insisted teaching common English was racist because white people spoke it first.

The effort continues today. I am not suggesting for a minute that Ebonics is wrong or improper. Many subcultures within America have unique dialects/slang. But offering this in place of holding all students to the same standard for learning common English in a classroom does not strengthen a culture. As you watch any *Star Trek* episode in which STCE is spoken, you can see the importance of this. Not speaking a common English serves to separate, not integrate. It insures that blacks and whites will never sit at the "table of brotherhood," that Reverend King spoke of, but rather have two separate tables. The absurdity is outrageous. You simply have to go to YouTube and type in "acting white" and click. There are many videos you can watch. The short version is this: Some blacks are accused of acting white when they strive to do well in school. This would include speaking a common English.

Rachel Geantel is an example of the kind of damage this approach causes. You may remember that name. She was a witness in the trial of George Zimmerman. Part of her testimony included reading a letter she had previously presented. (The video is on YouTube.) Rachel said she had a friend help write the letter so it would be easier to understand. And, as the letter is read you begin to wonder, if this is the good version, what was the bad one like? We also discover she cannot read cursive. In her spoken testimony we hear many grammatical mistakes. From my perspective as a white person who has accepted a common English (although I can speak some very unique versions around my friends) she was "different." She was a fellow American, a fellow citizen, but I had difficulty relating to her. This is not a good thing if you want a common culture.

A common written and spoken language is important from a cultural perspective. Whatever version we decide on should be taught to EVERYONE, and the same expectations should be applied to EVERYONE. Skin color should not determine how we communicate. From a logical perspective, what we currently teach in English Language courses might be a foundation. Then we can add to it in any manner we wish. However, once the curriculum is decided, ALL students should be required to demonstrate the same level of proficiency.

Upon achieving that level, people can choose how to communicate in their lives. Certainly we all have different social groups that may influence how we speak. I speak much differently when I am talking to a few of my friends about football than I did when I was a principal in my office talking to a parent about his child. That is choice, and that is fine. However, currently we are not giving whole groups of people the ability to choose. Hence we are leaving fewer doors open for them. It is absurd, and further divides us, to argue that it is their right to be held to a different standard because of their skin color. Some special interest groups are condemning future generations to this separation because of this misguided notion of equality.

Being in favor of a national language is considered by some to be xenophobic and racist. Depending on which special interest group you are listening to, anyone who supports a national language seeks to destroy the culture of others, resulting in trauma and humiliation. Those who favor a national language are portrayed as nationalists, or even fascist by some special interest groups. These groups seek to characterize a national language as being harmful to, and disrespectful of any citizen who does not currently speak English. There are some groups that suggest having a national language is oppressive.

As crazy as it sounds, that is the argument by those who are pushing their agenda further away from a common culture. However, in the future a common language is important. Either through Universal Translators, or communications officers like Hoshi Sato (*Star Trek: Enterprise*), or a crew that speaks STCE, effective communication is the only way any of our future counterparts on any version of the Enterprise solve problems. I will digress a bit and tell a personal story that may add a different take on this issue.

In 1990 I moved to Japan to live in a relatively small city called Numazu where I taught English at a private English school. Before I left the States I knew about six or seven Japanese words: Toyota, Honda, Yamaha, Suzuki, Kamikaze, Sansui…maybe that's it. Because Numazu was a small town, there were not a lot of foreigners. Most of the foreigners that were there, taught English. I worked at a private school close to the train station and I had never lived in a foreign country before. After just a few months I began to feel lonely. I had heard about a jazz bar very near my school and I decided to go.

The music was great, live jazz, and the beer was cold—I learned to love Kirin Lager! But, there was something else even nicer about the bar. I didn't know it at the time, but this bar was the foreigners' hangout of Numazu. It was full of English-speaking people from around the world: Australia, New Zealand, England, Canada and, of course, America. (By "full" I mean 12-14 people.) I could speak English at my normal speed and didn't have to wait for the listener to catch up. Conversely, I immediately understood what I was hearing. (In fact, this is when I learned that after losing the Revolutionary War, the Brits decided to change some English just to confuse the Colonies.)

It was great. I will not forget how much at home I felt the first night I went to the bar. It was the spring of 1990 and I could talk baseball, at a bar, drinking cold beer and listening to live jazz — just like home! JUST. LIKE. HOME! It hit me very quickly how strange it was that just outside the doors was this foreign country in which I felt isolated and a little lonely.

I don't remember exactly when, but at some point after my first visit to the bar I had this thought: Here I was living in a new country with a lot of new things to experience and my greatest experience to date was "being at home" in this bar. I resigned myself never to go again. (I did end up going back four or five times over the next five years.) I thought the best thing for me to do was to learn about Japan, and to do that I needed to learn the language. I tried on my own for about a year, practicing phrases and pronunciation. I decided I would memorize the phrases I needed to buy a train ticket to a nearby city and take the train alone…a little day trip.

After practicing in front of some Japanese nationals that worked at my school I decided I was ready to go for it. I went to the station window and confidently asked how much for the ticket to Mishima. I think I said it flawlessly. I was waiting to hear a cost, I had memorized the basic number system and was ready. The ticket agent spoke for only fifteen or twenty seconds, but I understood none of it. Try as I might, I couldn't figure out what all the extra words meant. I walked away and went to the ticket machine, got my ticket without speaking another word of Japanese. I had failed.

I realized that learning the language on my own, from "easy-to-learn" books was not enough. I decided to learn Japanese the way Japanese people learned: from the beginning. I enrolled in a Japanese Jouku school (cram school) in the evenings. My classmates were all between seven and nine years old. I learned how to write Japanese (Kanji, Hiragana and Katakana) from the 1st grade level up. All my classmates could not speak English, nor could my teacher. Two nights a week, on my days off, I was surrounded by Japanese…the language and the culture. I also hired a private teacher to help me grow my vocabulary.

After more than a year, I started to get it. I could read many signs in the streets and on the storefronts. I could ask directions and go shopping and actually ask questions rather than constantly point my fingers or mime what I wanted. Taking a train was nothing. I remember when I went to the train station to buy a ticket and asked about it, the ticket agent asked me if I wanted the green car or not. That could have been what I was asked more than a year earlier when I had gotten totally flustered. This time I told him "No," and added, "After all it is only two stops." He smiled.

By 1993 I was hanging out with Japanese friends and going

to places that they wanted to show me. Some of them, especially from school, could speak some English so the conversation usually flowed back and forth between both languages…and my vocabulary became more useful. In February of 1993 I decided to take a break and see parts of the world. My first stop was New Zealand. As I was taking the ferry from North Island to South Island, I noticed a Japanese girl sitting close to me. I had brought my Japanese grammar book and was looking through it. I decided to approach the girl and ask her a question I was struggling with.

Her name was Takako and we had a great conversation. I discovered she was visiting a friend on South Island. She told me about a concert at the end of March that she was going to. It was Paul McCartney. The concert was back in North Island, Aukland, to be precise. When she asked if I would still be in New Zealand, I told her yes. We decided to meet again the day before the concert, and we ended up going to the concert together. She could speak some English, but it was difficult, and she told me it was nice to find someone who could speak Japanese.

I got back to my school in December of 1993 and picked up where I left off. I had some great welcome-back parties from my friends. We caught up, I showed them my pictures, and life got back to normal. In 1994 one of my friends, Akemi, got married. She invited me to the wedding. I sat at a table with her friends. Most of them I didn't know, but that would change. It is customary at Japanese wedding receptions for friends of the bride and groom to stand up and say something about the couple, a toast.

I decided to say something. I went to the front of the reception room where the mic was and told everyone how Akemi and I met and how happy I was for her and her new husband. (All in Japanese of course.) I remember after my toast people from all around the room came to offer a drink. The common custom in Japan is to fill your friend's glass. My glass was full the whole night.

Later that year I was highlighted in a Yamaha piano school journal. I had been taking piano lessons and was asked to join a recital. I did so and, although very nervous, had a good time. My picture was taken and placed with a small story in a national magazine. It felt great. I left Japan in the spring of 1995. When I got back to America I was happy to reconnect with my family and friends. But, I also felt homesick. I stayed in communication with some friends for a period of time, but eventually lost touch with all but one: Akemi.

In 2015 my wife and I went to Japan to visit friends. I decided to look up Akemi. I wasn't sure her family was still running the same coffee shop in Susono. They were. When I entered, Akemi's mother recognized me immediately and welcomed me. She commented on my head being shaved. She told me Akemi was working in Mishima so I contacted her by phone and we made a date to meet the next day. Tears came to my eyes as I saw her come into the coffee shop. She smiled and teared up a little herself. We spent the afternoon catching up. I honestly felt like I was home.

I shared all this with you because I wanted to demonstrate that I am speaking from the heart when I say that learning a new language and immersing oneself in a new culture is not a loss, it is a gain. It is not traumatic, it is wonderful! By learning Japanese I am a better person. I had a more meaningful stay in Japan, made a life-long friend and experienced things I would never have experienced without learning the language. I like to think that perhaps I broadened the experiences of the people I met as well.

Yet, because special interest groups can profit and perhaps gain more political power, there are those who argue that having a national language is xenophobic, possibly even racist. I would offer this to those people: Allowing communities to exist without needing to learn English might be immediately accommodating to those community members, but it locks them out of a broader community, one full of new experiences, new thoughts and new friends.

In the name of protecting other cultures we are preventing our culture from growing. We are preventing the newest members of our nation from getting to know us on a personal level. We are not protecting their culture, we are building a wall between them and us. At the very time we should be welcoming them, we are abandoning them.

Our counterparts in the future are open to many cultures and experiences. As much as they respect individual cultures, they understand the importance of a common language. They speak the same common English. They do not see speaking a common language as a racist or xenophobic issue…that would be illogical. A culture in which a common language is not supported will splinter and eventually fracture. Context and meaning will be confused or even lost.

Those who see requiring a common language as a bad thing (and let me emphasize spoken, as well as written) are victims. They have been taught that learning a new language is an assault on theirs or someone else's culture. They are the political zombies who have been created in the process of the politics of polarization. As special interest groups gain power they will push further away from the center, which will only further fracture our society.

The last cultural component I will speak to is the notion of work ethic. In terms of American culture the notion of a good work ethic means that "you are in control." Your actions can create future opportunities or conversely result in mishaps. By taking responsibility for your actions you can plan your future. In short, apply yourself, work hard, and new opportunities will present themselves.

In the context of work, this means you can choose your career. Those of you who don't believe it is true have been duped into thinking you have no control, that great powers hover over you and oppress you and make your life miserable. Moreover, you have been convinced that only upon conquering your oppressor will your life be wonderful! Somehow, magically, the world will be a better place. So your efforts are spent on getting the "enemy."

In a free society, the world is, has always been, and will always be what you make of it. The operative word here is "YOU." The

American work ethic essentially supports this. No matter your lot in life you have control and can build a dream. Hard work, planning, commitment and perseverance will pay off. There is no oppressor, there is only your own decisions. In the context of our current society where money is important, this means working. As I mentioned in an earlier chapter, when money disappears the goal will change, but the ethic is essentially the same.

If you apply this ethic to work, you become upwardly mobile. Starting off in a minimum wage job, always on time, working hard, working well with others, having goals, committing yourself to them and not giving up will be rewarded with raises and promotions. Doing the same in school rewards you with grades. Doing well in both opens more doors for your future. I am not saying it will all be roses and fun; it can be tough, especially for those living in poverty, but it can be done. And America has demonstrated this generation after generation…until now.

For the first time in my life we are learning that the current generation will not be better off than the previous one. It has never before been that way for America. What has changed? I don't know the definitive answer to that question, but I believe it is wrapped up in the politics of polarization. With so many different special interests hiding behind "causes" we have managed to pick apart virtually every aspect of our past culture and use it as a means to further divide us. The political climate has led us to a place where we no longer look around us and see issues that need to be resolved, but rather people that are getting in the way. We have managed to throw the baby out with the bath water, and we're left standing outside in the cold.

We no longer see ourselves as being able to do anything on our own. With a fractured family structure, a failed education system and a government that never addresses problems, only symptoms, we have been enabled by the system to just give up. Somehow, in some way, we are victims. We use our jobs, our wallets, our skin color, our education, our nationality, our genitals or whatever as an excuse not to strive. We have been convinced the American Dream is out of our reach. So why try? Why plan?

Poverty is never pretty. However, it doesn't mean we must give up our work ethic. In 1960 the poverty rate was about 18%. It's about 15% today. While that is an improvement, it is no reason to break out the Romulan ale! Back then, the average savings was three times higher than today. Higher poverty, yet more savings. Why? The work ethic of our past was to take care of ourselves and plan for that rainy day. (I can't count the times I had to hear that stinking story about that stupid squirrel.) People lived without things that other people had. It might have caused some embarrassment, but we got over it. We all understood that it doesn't have to be like this for our kids. Just keep at it.

Now people can buy more stuff more quickly, but they have to deal with the fall-out: title loan companies ripping people off with outrageous interest rates; payday loan companies helping people cover the cost of an unexpected expense; the dreaded credit rating that tells us if we are human beings or pond scum. Many of us live a life that finds us worrying that one misstep might place us on the street. In the past, families were strong, people saved money, lived within their means, and did not live in the same kind of fear we live in today, at least not to this extent.

In the 1960's big business and big government grew out of adolescence. I think issues of race and poverty overlapped. In an honest effort to defeat institutionalized racism, government programs targeted those in poverty because so many more blacks had to deal with it. Rather than attacking the root cause in any meaningful way—lack of equal access to education—the programs simply offered money to help out. While the money helped those in need, it did nothing to prevent future generations from having the same need. Special interest groups organized around these government programs and maintained the false argument that it was only about race. As a result, people had a right to these programs and others that would grow from them. This was not charity, it was their right and those that did not support the government programs were racist. This impacted our work ethic negatively.

On the other hand, big business got together with banks and created the credit card. Now anyone could get a color TV or a new clothes dryer. Using the ad agencies to market this as helping everyone get the American Dream, credit cards helped all of us to learn how to live beyond our means. We could all keep up with the Joneses! Rather than saving for four months to buy something, we bought it today and used our card to "retro-save." Why save and plan when you can have it now? We were no longer working to save for that rainy day, we were working to pay off bills. Of course, the interest rates were making banks rich. This impacted our work ethic negatively.

As Americans got more comfortable getting money they didn't earn, or spending money they didn't have, the special interest groups and lobbyists made millions. Within the context of the politics of polarization, and while the rich got richer, our work ethic has been all but destroyed. Many of us no longer think we must earn a living. We believe we are owed a living. This kind of disparity within a culture is not healthy and only serves to further fracture our society.

If language, belief, and traditions are important for a culture to stay strong, we are becoming weaker with each new day. We have fractured our family structure and values, we have fractured our work ethic, and we don't have a common language. While I certainly don't blame the two-party system for everything, it was the two-party system that gave birth to the politics of polarization. Opportunists then moved in and nurtured this process. In the process of learning how powerful voting blocks can be, we have given up our individuality. We lapse into "group think" and have lost the notion of personal responsibility or accountability. With each new group, we move further away from the common ground that helps define us as a people.

Different groups of people struggled with the social upheaval of the 1960's. Struggling with change was a natural response, but certainly that struggle did not need to result in fracturing society overall. The cultural fracturing is the result of deliberately entangling issues of race and income with being "American." By obfuscating the truth and confusing citizens, special interest groups and lobbyists made money, and continue to make money at our expense. In the name of equality, we lower expectations in our schools. In the name of "rights" we do wrong by our children. Under the banner of "cultural diversity" we create cultural factions and pit them against each other. And, in the name of fairness we demand someone give us more.

The notion of being in control of your destiny is being replaced by consigning our choices to the decisions of others. Some may argue that this is a natural process for our culture to grow. I would not agree. These efforts to fracture our culture are deliberate attempts to push agendas for the sake of power or money, or both. Growth is a process that implies a natural evolution of getting stronger, becoming more cohesive, maturing and becoming more experienced. Unless you are talking about the growth of hate, there is nothing natural about what is happening.

Cultural diversity is a two-way street. In "A Matter of Honor" (*Star Trek: TNG*; S2, E8) we can see a little of the philosophy Star Fleet has incorporated into its procedures on this issue. Granted this is Star Fleet, not downtown Denver, but it does offer insight. This particular episode revolves around an officer exchange program. We can see the expectations of both the visitor and the host. On the one hand, Riker is assigned to a Klingon ship. In his preparation he learns to eat some of the delicious cuisine that Klingon Birds of Prey offer. On the other hand a young officer, Mendon (A Benzite) is assigned to the Enterprise.

In Riker's case he learns how his preparations weren't accurate when he discovered that eating "gagh" is better when it is alive. He learns this when he sits at a meal with Klingons, mixing with the new culture. A particular scene that places Riker at odds with his

Star Fleet oath involves Captain Kargan asking Riker where his loyalty lies. Riker responds, "I will obey your orders. I will serve this ship as First Officer. And in an attack against the Enterprise, I will die with this crew. But I will not break my oath of loyalty to Star fleet." His solution was to honor both cultures, not forsake one.

In Ensign Mendon's case, he discovers a new life form that happens to eat the ship's hull. He discovered it on the Klingon ship when Riker was transferred over. He told no one. Later we learn that this new life form is endangering the Klingon ship. The Enterprise seeks to relocate the Klingon ship to assist, and the misunderstanding almost results in an attack. When Captain Picard questioned Mendon as to why he did not report what he had discovered, he replied, "It is a Benzite regulation. No officer on the deck of one of our ships would report an occurrence like this until he had a full analysis and a resolution. I have simply followed proper procedures." The Captain told him, "It is our procedure, ensign, to notify command of any possibility of danger to the ship. The decision is not yours." While visiting a new culture, Mendon decided to use only *his* culture to drive his decisions.

This is an official officer transfer program and certainly can't be strictly applied to the civilian population. But the philosophy behind the official procedures may offer insight. Regarding immigration and language in America today, it might prove beneficial for the U.S. to better prepare newcomers to our society, e.g. language learning, and, once here, provide as much immersion as possible. Conversely, immigrants to the U.S. might fare better to understand the culture of their new home and seek to immerse themselves in the new culture. It is dangerous to think that opening oneself to a new culture will somehow damage you.

In Riker and Mendon's cases, they were in an exchange program and differences would be brought back to the respective cultures and discussed. They weren't leaving their cultures permanently. They were simply trying to learn how other cultures do things and see what they could apply to their own culture. As a result, full immersion was immediate. That might not be beneficial in terms of immigrants, but it is still something to consider. Immersion is not necessarily bad.

Cultural diversity is combining multiple cultures to improve and enrich the general society. Cultural diversity doesn't mean having many cultures living in separate communities and living day-to-day as if they were back home. True diversity requires interaction between members of the various cultures. This means, people meeting people, sharing experiences and finding common ground.

This kind of diversity comes when people of different cultures can speak to each other. The importance of families is the same around the world. Living in China, I can tell you there is a strong sense of family. I believe any father or any mother would want their child to succeed in life. That is a shared value that becomes apparent only when people meet people, when families meet families. Having a sense of self-worth is important to us all.

Governments cannot legislate cultural diversity. They can support policies that make it easier for citizens to communicate and share with each other. Resisting efforts to have a common language creates a barrier for people. In a sense it traps them. They become comfortable living in "Little China", or "Little Saigon" or whatever community their particular culture has created inside the United States. These minorities are scooped up by special interest groups and told it is their right to be segregated…all in the name of protecting their culture.

When I think of this in terms of my personal experience, it is scary. Remember that little bar I visited in Japan? The one that was full of English-speaking people and made me feel at home? What if the Japanese government had no problem with every city having a place for English speakers. What if all the signs would have been in English? What if everywhere I went there were special people to help me translate my needs, special forms in English and special places to go to get them. What if the whole system was built to make it easy for me to never have to learn the language?

I think I would still have enjoyed the experience. I would still be able to tell stories and show pictures…but I would not feel what I feel for Japan and the Japanese people. I would not have enriched my life, I would have simply lived it in a "Little America." Policies and programs that support barriers to sharing cultures result in fractures. Special interest groups and lobbyists spend billions every year insuring that our culture continues to fracture. It is obviously working.

We could not be further away from our future counterparts in *Star Trek*. They do not believe people lose themselves or their cultures when they broaden their experiences, but rather they enrich themselves. They share a common language and they are all self-actualized, free thinkers who contribute to a culture that shares common values. They see diversity as a means to grow stronger, not a reason to fracture apart.

You will never hear any human's skin color being used to identify someone. What your genitals look like and with whom you share them is of no concern. Groupthink is all but extinct in the future. Individuals are responsible, and accountable for their actions. The common good of improving the human condition is the shared vision. All the little things that we are told are important mean nothing in the future. The best response to anyone who tries to frame what people say into group think is that of Captain Picard when Dr. Crusher suggests his order for allowing the crew to die with dignity was from a male perspective: "Rubbish!" ("The Last Outpost," *Star Trek: TNG*; S1, E5).

A culture in which the people share traditions, values and language will likely outlive a culture that doesn't. We should seek to stop efforts to define us by our color, our genitals, our heritage or our favorite team and in their place initiate efforts to celebrate our common interests. In its simplest terms: Life, Liberty and the Pursuit of Happiness….FOR ALL.

In the first episode of *Star Trek: The Next Generation* ("Encounter at Far point," Part 1 and 2), Captain Picard is put on trial for the crimes against humanity that his species has committed. Although, this is out of context a bit, what he stated about humans having evolved and gotten past their petty squabbles could easily apply here. We need to stop engaging in these petty squabbles and recognize a very simple fact: Without each other we will all fail.

Chapter 9

We The People

There are many issues in our country that stand in the way of our becoming the society portrayed in *Star Trek*. In the future we are self-actualized. We have gotten rid of poverty, want, war, hunger and money. Our culture is one of peace, enlightenment and personal growth. We are free to explore, free to discover, free to be curious. We contribute to our society as an expression of our lives, not because we must "earn a living."

Sounds too good to be true? It isn't. It is very achievable. We have been made to believe that this kind of future is utopian. We have been made to believe we must all "sell" ourselves to someone in order to have a good life. In a sense, a maze has been constructed and, like mice we have been trained to run through it and chase after the piece of cheese at the end, regardless of the obstacles. And, to add insult to injury, the cheese at the end is processed cheese.

In the current political arena we sometimes hear how bad capitalism is, and some people are even suggesting we should move to a different system. I have talked about this earlier in the book. But ANY non-capitalist system that takes the means of production out of the hands of the individual, by definition is a top-down system. Someone at the top will administer government and the economy. All top-down systems require larger bureaucracies to run them. Bureaucracy creates anonymity, which in turn invites corruption. As the bureaucracy becomes larger, the risk of losing transparency and efficiency increases. Creating a system from the top down is not only incongruous with, but could actually stifle the growth of, a self-actualized society.

In a society of self-actualized citizens without poverty, hunger and want, large bureaucracies are not needed. Therefore, a system that accommodates building a society from the bottom up would be more useful. Fundamentally, capitalism caters to the individual. The challenge is that capitalism has been misused. Our current system of capitalism has been manipulated by outside agents—corporations, politicians, special interest groups, etc. As a result capitalism has benefitted only a few. That does not mean that capitalism is bad. Maybe we just need to rethink how we practice capitalism.

In the future portrayed by *Star Trek*, the system is built from the bottom up. They value each new life that comes into the world by providing stability and teaching him or her the skills needed to begin the journey of self-discovery. They understand that developing each citizen to become a self-actualized and independent member of society will benefit everyone. By investing the necessary amount of time and nurturing, individuals will grow into contributing members of a society that does not need a large bureaucracy. Within that context, capitalism would be a natural fit.

In the interest of full disclosure, let me say now that I believe in humanity. I believe each human not only has good in them, but is more good than bad. I believe "badness" is either a learned behavior or a physiological defect. Environment and experiences from birth can interfere with the natural goodness inherent in each child. If the early environment and experiences are not bad, then most people, by nature will be good. And I don't mean just behave well. They will be full of goodness, kindness, generosity and compassion. We are a communal species. Without negative early experiences shaping children to override their inborn goodness, they will grow to become individuals who can live together, solve problems together, grow together and flourish together. Moreover, this would happen naturally because it is how we are built. In this context, distant bureaucracies and central governments mandating how people live are repugnant to me.

I don't know what the motivation of Roddenberry and subsequent writers for *Star Trek* was or is. The possibilities I will lay out in this chapter are mine alone and are influenced by my belief in humanity and my own interpretation of how that might apply in a *Star Trek* universe. However, I will have to work with our current reality. First, we are not a global government, we are a single nation and our culture is still complicated by our use of money.

Some of the underlying principals that drive the suggestions you will hear include transparency, logic, and alignment. Transparency is fairly obvious, but my take on transparency will focus on who decides what is transparent and how transparency is practiced—not the politicians, but the PEOPLE. The logic I will use can best be characterized as the scientific method. Alignment will be determined by the issues that are important to the PEOPLE and how well they are addressed by Congress.

Finally, the Constitution. I believe it is important to support the Constitution as a process of law. That is to say I support the idea that we are a nation of fundamental laws driven by the PEOPLE. Having said that, you have only to look at how the 14th Amendment has been used to understand that lawyers and politicians have constitutionalized many laws without actually amending the Constitution. (That can be said for many Amendments, but the 14th probably represents the biggest example of this practice as the application of due process has been greatly expanded.)

When I refer to the Constitution, it is meant to include the ideals of the authors: A regulated and small central government, supporting liberty, equality and protection of individual rights. Moreover, many of my suggestions would not be legal under our current Constitution. My assumption is that the necessary changes would be made constitutionally to keep the power of that document in place.

Many people stand firmly in support of the Constitution and are willing to fight and die for it. Yet they may have different notions of what the most important part of the Constitution is. For me, the genius of the Constitution is that it was designed to restrict the power of the federal government thus allowing states and individuals more autonomy. The 9th and 10th amendments speak to this. The ninth amendment states: "The enumeration in the Constitution, of certain rights, shall not be construed to deny or disparage others retained by the people." The tenth amendment declares that powers not delegated to the federal government, nor prohibited by the constitution, "are reserved to the states respectively, or to the people." Our founders were making sure that if there were any mistakes in the Constitution, the PEOPLE were the first to be protected, then the states. A strong central government was not the aim.

This is genius to me because even then, when our government was new, had no standing army to speak of, barely agreed on a national currency, even then they knew that someday our nation and its Constitution could represent a powerful country and potentially a powerful government. To prevent it from becoming more powerful than the PEOPLE, they wanted to make sure that individuals and states would not be swallowed up by a strong government. They believed in the individual. They believed local governments needed the autonomy to govern locally. We are not one nation that has divided itself fifty times to make different states. We are fifty states with sovereign power that have come together under the principles of the Constitution. We are a federation of states.

I see a correlation between this notion and that of the Federation of Planets. Federation members govern themselves, but are part of a council, much like the UN is today. In the beginning that is how our government was designed. The simple logic: Centralized power is dangerous. The simple fear: Centralized power corrupts. This is similar to the Federation, as its Prime Directive is to avoid all interference with other cultures. (Granted, states aren't necessarily other cultures, but they could be. Therefore, to the extent that they do not violate a specific right protected by the Constitution, they should have autonomy.)

Of course, this notion that we are a federation of states can be debated and I certainly don't want to pretend my interpretation of it is correct just because I believe it to be so. I point this out because as we talk about our national issues, both in complexity and quantity, ideas for solutions are often limited to the U.S. Congress. If you believe two heads are better than one, as I do, you can quickly see how we are missing a great opportunity to solve problems: Bring in more heads! Politically, there can be some debate about giving states too much power, or not giving them enough, and that debate is beyond the purpose of this book. However, from a problem-solving perspective, it should be a no-brainer.

What if our fifty states were seen as fifty laboratories in which different solutions to the same problem could be tried and tested? (You have probably heard that before, but I am talking about actually putting that notion into practice.) What if we didn't have Congress giving us a one-size-fits all solution to a problem, but rather each of the fifty states looked at the same problem and found the most effective solutions, and then shared them? The answer should be obvious: We might actually solve a problem. As an example, let's look at the issue of the minimum wage.

A current effort is being made to double the national minimum wage to $15.00 an hour. For everyone. One size fits all. (A standard approach for our national government.) I am not an economist, but here are some questions we should ask. Do different states have different types of economies? Different demographics? Different ideas? I believe they do. By extension, municipalities and towns within one state might differ. By further extension, the *people* within a state might differ. Yet, there are those who support this one-size-fits all solution to the minimum wage.

Let us consider two probable recipients of an increased minimum wage: a single mother on her own, and a high school student living with both professional parents. For the single mother, an increase in the minimum wage puts warm food on the table two meals a day instead of one, a second pair of shoes for her kids, a visit to the dentist for the whole family and the leaky faucet is repaired. You get the idea: albeit modest, a general improvement in day-to-day living.

For the student, the increase means more snacks at the movies, a spike in fashion accessory purchases, an extra make-over every month to look really nice for that guy in her chemistry class and so on. For the mother, some needed help, for the student, more fun and accessories. To approach tens of millions of individuals with so many different possible needs with one solution is unfair and ineffective. The results could create even greater economic disparity….the very thing a minimum wage hike is supposed to solve.

Here is the math. Two people earning $7.50 per hour equals $15.00. Doubling that would come to $30.00 and both people would receive $15.00 per hour. What if we take the high school student from $7.50 to $10.00 per hour and the single mother from $7.50 to $20.00 per hour? The total cost is still $30.00 but "needs" are addressed more fairly. And this is just one idea. What if all fifty states were working on the same problem? They can share solutions and, by virtue of being closer to the issue, they can track results more quickly and respond more quickly. States with the best solutions would be highlighted and their results would be shared nationally.

Central governments cannot solve solutions as affectively. Each solution from the central government requires more overhead to monitor, respond and adapt. Bureaucracies grow and bureaucrats get more money, but solutions are inconsistent. Moreover, the unique differences that exist among the states cannot be addressed.

This is the approach I will take in presenting possible solutions for how our government might function more effectively. I will talk about politics, government and business—all of which is predicated on rebuilding our education system. (See chapter 2.)

These are just ideas and some of the numbers are arbitrary. So please do not get hung up on the details.

Politics

The campaign process in an America that applies the solutions of the future would be completely revamped. The purpose of campaigns would be to allow voters to listen to candidates directly, understand their positions and ask for any clarifications. What others thought about a politician's message would not be considered to be important, because each member of society is capable of thinking and making his or her own choices. Media and money would be removed as much as possible. Spin would not be allowed. The focus would be on issues and how each candidate would address those issues. Differences would be part of the discussion, but character attacks would not. To this end, our government would sponsor a new commission.

The National Campaign Commission would have several responsibilities. They would fund all national campaigns. They would have oversight for the following:

- Administration of the Campaign channel and associated media

- Campaign debates

- Candidate travel itineraries and budgets

- Candidate web sites

- Campaign staffing

- Rating all candidates after the election

- Administer and report polls for all candidates

As you can see this change would require some heavy lifting in terms of constitutional change. The concept of free speech would be understood and practiced differently. People would have the ability to speak their minds, but they would also understand the importance, and accept the responsibility of being honest and truthful. They would be held accountable to that standard. A self-actualized society would recognize how lies and deceit are counterproductive in terms of solving problems.

There are no political parties, just candidates for election. Moreover, only the National Campaign Commission will be permitted to administer polls. Polling of candidates on national tickets will not be allowed until after the convention and will be limited to twenty-one day cycles. This will help remove big business and special interests from the process. They would not be allowed to use commercial media to create narratives.

Since campaigns are federally funded. Donations are not accepted from anyone in any amount. The campaign trail has become more digital. It consists of one TV broadcast station, one radio broadcast station, one streaming Internet site and one digital newsletter site. All other outlets may not be used for campaigns. No campaign ads will be allowed on any commercial media outlet. Any commercial outlet that discusses the candidates on any of their programming must conform to the truth in advertising regulation which includes displaying a graphic, as well as an audio version informing the audience who owns the station, and for which presidential candidate they voted for in the past four presidential elections. This must be done before and after any commercial media outlet discusses the candidate: each time for a minimum of ten seconds. Any outlet that does not want to provide this information may freely choose not to discuss candidates. They may cover other issues instead.

Moreover, they must present a graphic displaying the percent of time they have discussed the candidate in a negative light compared to the percent of time they have discussed the candidate in a positive light for any discussion that does not pertain to the National Issues web site. (More about the NI website later.)

The primary season for a campaign is four months long, beginning in January of the current election year. Prior to the primary season there is a "Call for Candidates" process. This process begins in September of the year prior to the current election year and finishes on December 31st of that same year. During each of these periods candidates will be restricted to three months of travel.

During the Call for Candidates period, the National Campaign Commission will schedule all travel, and all candidates will travel together and speak at the same venues. During the primary season the National Campaign Commission will provide the budget for each eligible candidate, but each candidate may select the city and the date. However, all venues will be identical for each speaker. In the event of a scheduling conflict the National Campaign Commission will decide which candidate gets to attend a specific venue and reschedule the other candidate(s).

During Call for Candidates, any eligible American can register as a candidate for President of the United States. During this period, each candidate will be allowed to hire three staff members to assist with the campaign. Each candidate will have four months to qualify to enter the primary. Qualification requires each candidate to:

- Gain approval of the national vetting board of elections commission.

- Gain the signatures of at least 10% of each state's electorate on an electronic petition for candidacy

- Sign a transparency pledge committing to, and providing all documents pertaining to taxes, investments, education (these include all admission and discipline records as well as transcripts—secondary and post-secondary), all court records of which the candidate was a primary party—civil and criminal, all work records (including personnel reviews and performance evaluations) and all voting records from any previously elected or appointed public office. Any document that is knowingly withheld will disqualify the candidate.

- Submit a proposed campaign website that includes all of the information above as well as:

  - Policy statements on each of the issues identified on the National Issues web site as well as link to a blog for each issue.

  - A "National Press" room link for all credentialed press to ask questions at digital "press conferences" as well as individual interviews. Everything will be archived for the voter to access at any time.

  - A talk-show format link that schedules popular TV and radio personalities to talk with the candidate with their audiences. Everything will be archived for the voter to access at any time.

  - A visionary statement

  - A pledge to focus on only the issues that appear on the National Issues web site.

  - A pledge to actively denounce any funded effort by any group to advance the individual's candidacy, or campaign in any way.

  - A pledge to use only the federal campaign outlets during the primary and general elections.

  - A pledge not to attack any other candidate's character or motivations for running for president.

  - A pledge to conform to the "Yes-No" Question policy that states all yes/no questions asked must first be answered with "Yes" or "No" and then any explanation the candidate wishes.

All candidates who meet the requirements listed above will be eligible to be entered in the primary. As such, they will receive equal time on all federal campaign outlets. During the primary all candidates will appear in three debates on each of the five issues identified in the National Issues web site. Each debate will be a minimum of three hours, held in an electronic town-hall fashion.

There will be no moderator. The format will include an opening statement limited to ten minutes.

Questions will be selected randomly from the National Issues web site. All candidates will be given equal time to respond to each question. All questions are restricted to the particular issue for which the debate is being held. All candidates' prior voting records (if they apply) and policy statements relating to the particular issue being debated may be questioned. All debates will be archived electronically and accessible to all citizens to access at their convenience.

The primary election will be held nation-wide during the first week of May of the current year of the election. The top five candidates will qualify for the general election campaign. During the second week of May each of the five candidates will select a vice presidential running mate. Each team will present a new web page to the nation. The web page will be consistent with their primary web page with the following additions:

- All information required for each candidate's primary web site will be included for the vice presidential candidate as well.

- Policy statements will include how both candidates will work in tandem to achieve their stated goals.

After the vice presidential selection process and through the month of June, each team of candidates will establish their strategy. Each team will be allowed an additional five staff members to assist in their campaign. No staff member for any candidate may speak in any way for the candidate. Any and all questions must be directed to, and answered by, the candidate throughout the campaign. The general election campaign will include two phases: state and national. The state phase will begin on July 1st and end September 30th of the current election year. During this period candidates may establish their travel itineraries. Their budgets, however, will be identical.

The final debate series will happen during October of the year in which the election will occur. The debate schedule will be identical to the debate schedule from the primary election campaign. Also, throughout the month of October all candidates will host five electronic "town halls." Each town hall meeting will be at least four hours long. Each town hall's topic will be one of the five issues posted on the National Issues web site. The town halls will include only live questions from the electronic audience.

There will be two general elections. Each election period will be one week. The first will be scheduled to begin on the first Tuesday following the first Monday in November of the election year. The second will be scheduled to begin the first Tuesday following the first Monday in December of that same year. The Electoral College will no longer exist, popular vote will be used. The two candidates who received the most votes in the first election will qualify for the second general election in December. The candidate who receives the most votes in the second election will be declared the winner and become the president elect.

Following the second election, all the candidates' web sites will be closed. All data from the winning candidate's web site will be transferred to her or his presidential, or congressional web site. All campaign promises will be posted and easily accessible to all visitors. They will be tracked and scored throughout that person's tenure. Data from the other candidates' web sites will be cached in the National Campaign Commission's web site and made easily accessible to all visitors.

The National Campaign Commission shall open a blog and invite all citizens to comment on the just-completed campaign. Input will be encouraged. The blog will remain open for six months. After such time, the comments will be collated, summarized and made available on the same web site. Moreover, established criteria will be applied to each candidate's campaign and then scored. The criteria will include integrity, honesty, consistency, originality, and leadership. The data from the campaign blog as well as the scoring of the candidates will be presented at the next State of the Union address.

Data collection and collation will be processed by high school students as their civics class project. The data will be reviewed by the National Campaign Commission and posted for the general public.

Government

The government will run much as it is today in terms of procedures. However, there would be some differences, which will focus on alignment, transparency and accountability. While I don't believe any of these changes would require a constitutional amendment, if that were the case, the assumption is that it would be done. I must also confess my bias here. I am one of those who believe all members of Congress work for the PEOPLE…as employees, not bosses. As a result of my bias I will refer to national politicians in a way intended to remind all of us that they work for us. It is not meant to be disrespectful, although it may sound that way.

Members of the Senate will be referred to as Senate servants. Members of the House will be referred to as House servants. The President and Vice President will be referred to as Executive servants. I will only address the judicial branch to the extent changes in the Executive or Legislative branches might have an impact.

In an effort to align what Congress is doing with the wishes of the PEOPLE, a new web site will be sponsored by the government. The website will be the National Issues web site. This site will serve to document what our voters want their employees to do. There will be a national survey taken every presidential election. This survey will be done on two levels: eligible voters and high school students. Government servants will be held accountable to the eligible voters' survey. The high school student survey results will be posted on the National Issues web site, as well as presented at the next State of the Union.

The survey will ask each eligible voter to identify his or her top ten concerns for the nation. The five issues receiving the most votes will be the priority of our servants. Those issues will be clarified and finalized during the period of time between the election and December 31st. Prior to the State of the Union, the issues will be clarified and reframed as goals. Each issue will have no more than three stated goals, all of which will be quantifiable. Timelines and cost projections will be included in this process. The issues, the goals, how they will be measured, the projected time frame and projected cost will all be presented at the State of the Union.

Senate and House servants will no longer be seated by ideology. Seating will be random and regularly changed throughout each session. Proximity can influence attitudes toward others. To date, proximity has been used to create and maintain a divide. This practice will stop.

A caucus may be formed around any of the five issues identified on the National Issues web page. No caucus may be formed in which the stated goal is to advance a particular group of Americans, such as ideological, ethnic, religious, or geographical groups. Senate and House servants shall focus all attention on the issues we are paying them to address. It is not the role of any Congressional servant to show favoritism toward one specific group, or, by virtue of exclusion, to disenfranchise any specific group.

All servants will be required to wear a body-cam while working. A member of the Inspector General's executive and legislative offices will account for the time for each member. The video auditor will receive all necessary clearances in order to view all conversations by servants. There will be a procedure for any servant to turn off his camera for specific purposes. For example, personal and classified conversations do not require the body camera to be on. However, all offices in the Executive and Legislative branches of government will be fitted with a camera (with audio) that may not be turned off.

When a House servant wishes to turn off the body camera, she or he must state the reason and the estimated duration of time. The body camera will time stamp these events. However, the office camera will continue to run. The video-auditor from the IG's office will audit the body cams and the office cams to verify the periods of time the body cam was off. Time-lines for each servant will be fully accounted for and made public.

Let's use me as an example. When there is a need to turn my body-cam off, if I am in a government office the office camera will record all my actions and my words. The only time I am not watched is during my private time at home with my friends and family. As soon as I begin working, all cameras are on again. For the times I turn my body camera off for sensitive meetings at work, the office cameras record my movement and my discussions.

My body-cam time is viewable by all Americans since they are my employers. The IG verifies all the time periods that my body camera is off. For instance, when I announce I am turning off my camera for a sensitive meeting at the DOD, the office in which the meeting is held will record my activities. At this point the IG has two purposes: verify the time my body-cam is off with other cameras to account completely for my activities, and determine if the content from the meeting can be published to the public. No servant may turn off the body-cam when speaking with a lobbyist or any representative of a special interest group.

This process is designed to make sure all servants are not engaging in meetings or discussions without someone watching. At the same time, the IG acts as an editor in terms of making sure sensitive information is not published. Executive, Senate, and House servants will no longer be allowed to make that call. Violation of this protocol will be met with consequences. The first offense will result in a 10% pay cut for the servant. The second offense will result in a two-year loss of all pension benefits. The third occurrence becomes a felony and will result in a 100% loss of all pension benefits. The message: You are in our employ. Don't hide what you're doing, don't hide what you're saying.

Much like NFL quarterbacks are rated today, all executive and congressional servants will be scored through a rating system that will measure different aspects of their performance. These include voting record, contact with constituents, responsiveness to constituents, consistency of message, ability to work with other servants, bills introduced, committee membership, attendance, body-cam accountability, leadership, clearly answering questions, and achievement of goals. Servant scores will be published for public view. Because there are no political parties, the Speaker of the House will be selected by the full membership of the House of Representatives. The members with the top five ratings from the congressional rating process referenced above will be eligible to run. A simple majority is required. In the event no one receives a simple majority in the first round, then the second round will include the three members receiving the most votes. In the event no one receives a simple majority, then the top two vote getters will be eligible for the third round. If the results of the third round do not produce a member with a simple majority, then the member with the highest servant rating in the House of Representatives will be the Speaker of the House.

Having no political parties will also impact the process for setting the agendas in both chambers as well as committee chairs. The agenda will be determined by the National Issues web site. That site will post the national issues as well as the goals to measure progress on those issues. Items relating to these issues and goals will be given priority on the agenda. All other issues on the agenda will be determined by a process of voting among the servants and ranking the issues by order of support. The greater the support by all members of either chamber, the higher on the agenda. Both agendas will be posted on the government web site as well as the National Issues web site.

Committee Chairs will be selected from a pool of candidates with personal experience relating to the particular committee. For instance, members with a degree in finance would be eligible for the chairmanship on the finance committee. Chairs will be selected by a simple vote of all members of the relevant chamber (House or Senate). Only members in the top 10% of the ratings are eligible. New chairs will be selected for each session of Congress.

The State of the Union will change drastically. Although it will include Article II of the Constitution's requirement for the President to report to Congress, it will be augmented significantly. Moreover, the time period will be locked. The State of the Union will be one week long, beginning on the last Sunday in January. The schedule will be as follows:

Sunday:

The first day of the State of the Union will be for high school students. Winners of national high school competition for essays written concerning new ideas for the solution of the five issues published on the National Issues web site will be recognized. High school students from around each state will summarize the performance of their state's Senate and House servants using the rating system outlined above. Students will also present the data collected on all candidates from the national elections held the previous year if it applies. The ratings of each member of Congress will also be published and presented, and students will present any special recognition to their state's servants.

Monday, Tuesday:

Governors from each state will present the results of their state's performance relating to the state goals established for the five issues published in the National Issues web site. Recommendations for any changes will be made.

Wednesday:

The Congressional House of Representatives will present the results of their performance relating to the national goals established for the five issues published in the National Issues web site.

Recommendations for any changes will be made.

Thursday:

The Senate will present the results of their performance relating to the national goals established for the five issues published in the National Issues web site. Recommendations for any changes will be made.

Friday:

Leaders from the Senate and House will host a town hall style discussion about the process and its effectiveness. Although the issues from the National Issues web site may be discussed, the focus will be on the overall process and how well it is working. Recommendations for changes will be made at the end of the day.

Saturday:

The president will review the information from the States' progress reports and provide a pathway for the future in terms of which state solutions might work on a national, or regional level and how they might be implemented. The president will make a report on the State of the Union.

You may believe there are a million reasons why this could never work, but those reasons have been sold to us in order to allow Congress free reign over our nation. While I believe some of those in government actually want to serve, especially at the beginning of their careers, the majority merely want to advance their careers and make a name for themselves. Our current system of political parties, special interest groups and lobbyists all influenced by media hype and attention has turned Congress into a show. Undoubtedly politicians, lawyers and other experts would attempt to present all kinds of data and testimony to convince us why they cannot function as I have just described. But remember, these are the same people who built the maze and expect us to run through it…how do you expect them to respond?

The biggest argument would be about rights. They would probably attempt to convince us that members of Congress have rights that cannot be violated. However, if the rules for Congress are laid out and agreed upon by the PEOPLE of this nation, anyone not wishing to serve would have the right to refuse to run for office. If they choose to run, they must understand that as employees they will have responsibilities and duties for which they will be held accountable…just like any other job.

All of the suggested reforms in campaigning and government are designed to remove money, ideology and special interest from government. The structure is designed to clearly identify issues that are important to the PEOPLE, and then align all efforts of those who wish to serve into a logical plan that can be measured, to address the issues and solve the problems in a practical way that keeps the focus on the problem until we actually see a solution.

One special note about the change in caucuses: We have become accustomed to having our servants meeting to advance agendas that are personal, not part of their job. In the future, people are not identified by color, religion, ethnic background, etc. Our government should be the first place that strives to stop using language designed to keep us separate. As a nation we should stop talking about color, gender, race, religion, etc. We are all Americans. What is right for one of us is right for all of us. All laws and regulations should only include the term "American citizen" or "American resident," depending on which one applies.

We'll know we're making progress when we hear someone tell a story anecdotally and you don't hear, "This black guy said…" or, "I can't believe those two white guys were…" or, "I don't know for sure, but he looked Mexican…" or, "Can you believe it, a Christian wanting…." All of us need to stop these kinds of references. If we want to be a nation in which all people are treated the same, why do we talk about each other differently? Congress would be a good place for this practice to stop.

In the future congressional and executive servants will be people who truly want to advance our nation as a whole, not any specific group in it. As such, they will be eager to lead the way in dropping all the references that serve to divide us. They will be leaders who are willing to work hard to achieve the goal established by the PEOPLE. Their leadership will be defined by how well they accomplish those goals. Rather than tell the PEOPLE what *they* want, they will listen, learn and then lead.

Business

Business will also need to change to be more responsive to the PEOPLE. Rather than spending billions telling us what our needs are and creating a false urgency to fill those needs, businesses will be held accountable for their impact on the community, the nation and the planet. Truth in advertising and corporate responsibility will not require any regulation because those behaviors will become profitable, it will be the corporate culture. The current paradigm of using government to take money from corporate America, then redistributing that money to help offset the damage done by corporate America will be replaced with a more logical approach.

The new approach will build in incentives for corporations to reduce any damage they may do in the first place. Successful corporations will draw more customers and more investors in a manner that will create solid corporate profits. At the same time, corporations will compete to help their employees, their communities, their country and the planet. Top tier corporations will be profitable as well as popular. Moreover, this new approach will shrink the size of government, reduce taxes and increase private sector opportunity.

In the interest of self-disclosure, let me say that I believe the private sector is the driving force for jobs and growth. But, more importantly, allowing free citizens to chase their dreams develops a society that stretches itself and reaches a little further than societies in which free citizens are told by the government which dreams to chase. By allowing the private sector to take the lead, more opportunities will be opened for more people. Wealth created by these opportunities will certainly help the rich, but under this new paradigm it will greatly reduce poverty.

By using the private sector to attack poverty directly, the government will reduce in size. This model will effectively eliminate the middle man (government) and streamline the whole process. This will result in an increase in funds to effect poverty (money will not be needed to build the bureaucracy) as well as provide for more local, targeted efforts to combat the fundamental causes of poverty: broken families and a lack of access to a quality education.

I will lay out a system that rates companies based on their practices. Companies will be able to choose between two tracks: rated and unrated. The rated track empowers corporations and details corporate behaviors that support the community. (This approach is simply an extension of conscious capitalism. You can do an internet search of this term. It's very exciting.) The unrated track is a simple corporate tax rate with basic regulations on growth.

The details of what follows are not as important as the ideas themselves. My point is to give you an idea of a corporate structure that incentivizes behavior rather than the system we have now in which the government takes money from corporations and attempts to solve the issues that poor corporate behavior create. The fundamental principal is that profit is to corporations what life is to our planet. There are some pretty amazing life forms that can survive any climate. The profit motive, regardless of any pre-conditions, will still be strong enough to create a competitive market.

The rating system is a simple point system. One point is the lowest rating and three points is the highest rating. The table below will give you an idea of how corporations can use profits to help employees, communities and our planet. These benefits would apply to all employees...full or part-time.

BEHAVIOR	ONE POINT	TWO POINTS	THREE POINTS
Employee			
Workforce	75% United States citizens or residents	85% United States citizens or residents	100% United States citizens or residents
Starting Wage	150% of the state minimum wage	175% of the state minimum wage	200% of the state minimum wage
Health insurance	Company pays 80% of cost	Company pays 90% of cost	Company pays 100% of cost Company has fitness centers for employees
Education Reimbursement	80%	90%	100%
Day Care	100% paid by company	100 % paid by company and on site	100% paid by company and on site Parent given 30 minutes per day to visit children
Married Couple Wage		Employee is paid 150% wages if spouse stays at home to raise children	Employee is paid double wages if spouse stays at home to raise children
Retirement (401K type program)	Company funds 60% of retirement	Company funds 75% of retirement	Company funds 90% of retirement

BEHAVIOR	ONE POINT	TWO POINTS	THREE POINTS
Environment			
Product/Service	50% natural materials	60% natural materials	70% natural materials
Packaging	60% recycled materials	75% recycled materials	100% recycled materials
Process, Environmental Impact (emissions, run-off and other waste)	90% of industry standard	80% of industry standard	70% of industry standard
Distribution	60% is local (less than 200 miles)	75% is local (less than 200 miles)	90% is local (less than 200 miles)
Marketing	60% electronic	80% electronic	100% electronic
Community Support			
Corporate Contribution to Public School System	3% of profit before taxes	5% of profit before taxes	8% of profit before taxes
Corporate Contribution to Community Outreach Programs	3% of profit before taxes	5% of profit before taxes	8% of profit before taxes

The listing of corporate performance by each category, as well as an overall rating based on the average of all categories, would be published for all consumers to see. While the behaviors listed may seem to be quite a lot, as I said, the profit motive can be powerful. The incentives for corporations are listed in the table below.

Corporate benefit	One point rating	Two point rating	Three point rating
Corporate tax rate	15%	10%	0
Expansion funding from outside sources (Banks and other investors)	Less than 50%	Less than 75%	100%
Marketing expenses allowed	Less than 2% of annual gross revenues	Less than 4% of annual gross revenues	Less than 6% of annual gross revenues
Consumer tax deductions	Consumers can deduct 50% of goods/services purchased	Consumers can deduct 75% of goods/services purchased	Consumers can deduct 100% of goods/services purchased
Stock holder/Investor capital gains tax rate	75% of current rate	50% of current rate	No capital gains taxes

As you can see there are some sweet incentives for corporations to do the right thing by their employees, communities and the environment. A company with a three-point average gets some great benefits. Moreover, the consumers and investors receive benefits. It motivates buyers and investors to associate with three-point companies. This model creates pathways to paying fewer tax dollars, not more, reducing the size of government, not growing it, and keeping the money in the community.

This model would apply to most of the private sector. Obviously the size of the company would impact how much they can do for each item being measured. Also, there would need to be some kind of probation period for companies wishing to enter this track. Companies that do not wish to enter the rating system will have simple requirements:

- 60% corporate tax rate.

- All expansion must be funded internally.

- Marketing expenses may not exceed 1% of annual gross revenue.

The model I'm suggesting also develops a positive relationship between corporations and the public. Capitalism is used to provide opportunities for individuals and corporations. One particular exception to this model might be finance. There are some basic changes that could be expected to have a positive impact on the size of financial institutions as well as reducing their negative impact on general consumers:

- Interest charged by banks for any loan must not be greater, by a factor of four of the interest rate banks give to depositors with a balance of less than $1,000. (If the standard rate of interest to a depositor with less than $1,000 in their account is 2.75%, then the bank cannot charge more than 11% interest on any loan: Car, credit card, personal, etc. to anyone).

- Credit default swaps should either be banned altogether, or all banks that participate in the market should be required to set aside at least 75% cash for any potential loss.

- Anyone convicted of financial fraud must serve a mandatory minimum of twenty years in a federal maximum security prison.

- Borrowers for home loans must provide a minimum 10%

cash down payment of the purchase price of the home.

- All credit card products must charge the same amount of interest for all customers.

In addition to these changes, banks would be held to the same rating system in the table above as they pertain to employees. It must be noted that while some of these changes would directly impact the finance industry's ability to prey on the "little guy" by charging outrageous interest rates, some of the changes place more financial responsibility on that same little guy. Loans (especially home loans) and credit cards would be more difficult to get. This would require more planning and saving on the part of the little guy.

This rating system would apply to corporations and subsidiaries or partner corporations. I mention this to specifically target sports and entertainment. In these industries the CEO's make billions, major players make millions and the little guy is squashed. Let's consider movie studios as an example.

A movie studio has many subsidiary or partner corporations that are part of the industry. When a movie is made, the studio is the big winner or loser; actors are next. But the little guy is always underpaid. So, the table above would apply to all employees of all the support corporations and companies for movie studios. This means that the girl selling popcorn at a local theater must receive the employee benefits listed above in order for the movie studio to receive a three-star rating. ALL employees of ALL related companies that support major corporations must receive the benefits above.

Why would they do something that may appear to be ridiculous? Because a three-star movie studio will allow all moviegoers to deduct the price of movie tickets, popcorn, and soda from their taxes. Anyone who invests in the movie will not pay a dime on any return of that investment in taxes…that is a powerful incentive. As you can see, the general idea is the PEOPLE benefit as much as any

CEO…not in terms of salary, but in terms of quality of life. In conservative circles this would be a meaningful trickle-down economy.

This model would create a fundamental shift in the relationship of government and business, removing the wrestling that currently goes on. Corporations would take on more responsibility, and government would take on less. The market would be driven by the people and would reward corporations that behaved responsibly. Obviously, getting a job would have greater significance than it does now. This would require an education system designed for the 22nd century: empowering students to achieve. (see chapter 2.)

Because we have the goal of reducing the need for money—until we can eventually get rid of money—the government would need to be strictly accountable for all expenditures. House Bills that require funding would need to include the following:

- A statement of cost (total cost of the bill)

- An explanation of funding (staffing, administration, implementation, program maintenance, etc.)

- A stated goal of what the bill will accomplish

- A stated process for measuring the success of the bill

- A stated "end date" of funding

Before providing a more detailed explanation of how this process of accountability for government spending might be implemented it is important to address the use of statistics. If I speak Japanese to my friends, they will not understand what I am saying unless they also speak Japanese. Fundamentally, a shared language is required to communicate. The same is true with statistics. The first step in solving a problem is for all parties to speak the same statistics. To this end our government will define a universal data collection process to use to establish universal data sets. Like the universal translator, these data sets will "translate" how progress will be measured and will be used by all public servants.

The only statistics that will be used to define and solve an issue will be the data identified through this process. This will insure that everyone involved in addressing the issue, solving the problem and evaluating the results, will speak the same language. As is too common today, politicians can speak about the same issue and provide "data" that supports virtually any point they want to make. To prevent this, only the objective data from the approved process will be used and discussed.

No bill that requires funding will extend beyond a three-year period of time. Reauthorizations and continuations of funding will not be permitted. A new bill that refers to the original bill must be passed. However, before passing the new bill Congress must post the results of the previous bill. The results must include the final cost of the previous bill as compared to the original statement of cost, an explanation of any variance, and all the data used to measure and rate the effectiveness of the bill.

Even with the changes of corporate behavior and federal spending that I am suggesting we need to recognize that virtually everyone agrees that in the next twenty to twenty-five years, somewhere between 20% and 30% of current jobs will no longer exist. Automation and changing demands will erase them. We need to incorporate this reality into our education system as well as the job market. Our government should work hard to encourage economic sharing, individually and within the community as a whole. The concept is fairly simple to explain, but can be difficult to put into practice.

Economic sharing is the concept of renting or borrowing goods and services from other citizens rather than large corporations. There are many examples of this being practiced today, including Airbnb, Zipcar and Uber that encourage individuals to collaborate to provide services to other individuals in need of those services. As the traditional job markets shrink, economic sharing may actually increase in demand. This approach "shares" the economy with more individuals, rather than letting all the money go to large corporations.

Of course this may have a negative impact on unions and we need to be sensitive to that. For instance, if half of the consumers that travel started using Airbnb, the number of jobs in the hospitality and hotel industries would be reduced significantly? These changes, however, should be seen as necessary and the federal government's role should be supportive of this kind of transition and not attempt to regulate the industries involved. For instance, it now costs almost $750,000 for a person to buy a Medallion to drive a cab in New York City. If the federal/state government established similar requirements for Uber drivers, the new opportunities would dry up.

Economic sharing goes well beyond using Uber to get from your office to the theater. If communities work together, we can use it to encourage less consumption as well as more opportunities for community members to participate in the new markets. We could apply the "library principal" to many different markets. We see this happening with cars and bikes already. But the concept could expand to more non-traditional markets: Small appliances, jewelry and even art libraries could be created. Any library would be open to its members. Rather than buy, share! Use an item for when it is needed and then return it.

Groups of as little as two people could set up a "share group." Using friendship, or common interest, or geography to determine membership, these groups could use current technology to post what items they have available for sharing and then schedule their use. For instance, I love *Star Trek*. If I have friends who also love *Star Trek*, we could all buy different DVD's, or books, and share what we have. Private online exchanges could be established for convenience. Set up a share group for laundry facilities. Maybe three or four neighbors share the cost, buy one set of appliances and share the use. Then it would simply be a matter of scheduling and reserving the use of the items. There would be no need for my friends and me to buy the same items.

These "share groups" could also be for services. Using the internet, local groups could post services they can provide: pet care, shoveling snow from driveways, cutting grass, cleaning homes, chauffeuring, tutoring…whatever service. Then members can reserve someone's time to schedule the service. The requirement would be much like on Aldea ("When the Bough Breaks" *Star Trek: TNG*; S1, E17), for any service you use, you must provide a service. This approach creates a broader base of individuals who can share the economy of any industry. Moreover, these kinds of efforts de-emphasize ownership and consumption.

Individuals who participate in economic sharing can earn money and become a self-employed community member, no longer dependent on big business. Community practices that de-emphasize ownership will make it easier for citizens to make ends meet. The distance between the ends will become shorter. Shrinking expenses and needs impact household budgets the same way a pay raise does. We can begin to focus on reducing expenses rather than just increasing revenues. This would not only empower individuals, it would have a positive impact on our environment.

Foreign Policy

One of the first things a fan of *Star Trek* learns about the Federation is the Prime Directive: Do not interfere with other worlds' natural development. If this principle was applied to our foreign policy it would require us to make some serious changes. Perhaps the biggest change would affect weapons manufacturers. We would no longer sell weapons to any nation whose technology and manufacturing capabilities were not advanced enough to produce the weapons in question.

For instance, if Germany wanted to buy military jet fighters from us, we could do that because they have the technology and industry to produce the jets themselves. Perhaps it is just easier for them to buy a particular fighter from us. However, any nation that did not have those capabilities could not purchase the particular weapon. If Grenada cannot produce the jet fighter, they cannot purchase one from us. This would be applied to all weapons and small arms. It would also apply to any group that self-identifies as a group and/or has any particular goals. The "freedom fighters" from the country of "Prettydamnpoor" couldn't buy machine guns and bullets to support their fight for freedom. They would have to gain that on their own. Like the Prime Directive, it would not be the role of the United States to determine the outcomes of other nations' internal struggles.

Rather than spreading our military around the world to generate a sense of being a global cop, we would recall most of them and replace them with the Peace Corps. The Peace Corps and its efforts would influence the perception most people have of the United States. Our government would seek to expand that program dramatically both in size and scope. Certainly, we would have military interests, but they would be managed from sea vessels or through collaboration with individual nations.

Our global interest would be life, liberty and the pursuit of happiness. Our greatest influence on other nations would be our trade. Nations that wanted to trade with us would be scored and held accountable for how they treat their citizens. Beyond the basic human rights of life, liberty and pursuit of happiness, trade with countries would be determined by how any nation adheres to treaties, their support of the Peace Corps program within their nation, their sale of weapons to other countries and respecting sovereignty of other nations. Countries that engage in war would not be eligible for any financial support from the United States while the war is occurring. Nations, regardless of size or "strategic importance," that maintained peace, upheld human rights, and practiced earth-friendly policies would be fast-tracked for American trade deals.

Having spoken my "dove," it is now time to let the "hawk" speak. As it is with the Federation, we would have high tech weaponry and would not tolerate violations of our borders or our people. Nations in which Americans were murdered would be held responsible for justice, and reasonable time frames for said justice would be put in place. If progress was not made, the US would act unilaterally to bring those guilty to justice. This stipulation would be in every treaty we have.

Immigration

Under our current political system, the result of the politics of polarization, politicians today don't really focus on problems. They focus on symptoms of problems. In order to remedy this we should use logic to recognize that before a problem can be solved we need to clearly identify and understand the problem. This would be done through the National Issues web site. We will assume that immigration is one of the top five issues. "Immigration" is a broad category and doesn't really describe the issue. To be more specific, we have many people in our country who are here illegally. This means that immigration per se is not the issue; the issue is people being here illegally. And the fact that they are here isn't actually the problem. They are here because of the problem: weak adherence to visa laws and an insecure border. That is the problem.

The simple test of that would be to use the following hypothetical question: If everyone in our country were here legally, would we be talking about this? The most likely answer is "no." There might be concerns over wait times, or quotas, but as a national issue it would not be on the radar. So, the question put to the PEOPLE would be simple: "Do you wish the United States to have open borders?" If the answer is yes, then the illegal immigration issue would disappear immediately.

Let's assume for this discussion that the PEOPLE don't want open borders. They want to control who and how many can become American citizens. In this case one policy is already established.

We must tighten our border and visa-control programs. The trick-iest part of this process would be to establish what data sets we will use. Once that is established our method of solving it as out-lined above would be put into play. I am going to make up some numbers. Let's say these numbers are from the data set we all have agreed to use.

Let's assume there are 12,000,000 people here illegally. Forty percent of people (4.8 million) here illegally are violating visas they were granted by our government: work, student, visitor, etc. Sixty percent of them (7.2 million) got here by crossing our border illegally (55%, or 6.6 million from Mexico and 5%, or 600,000 from Canada). Using the data set that we all agree on we have established the following: Every year 350,000 people cross the southern border illegally; 30,000 people cross the northern bor-der illegally; 220,000 people over-stay visas. This means we have 600,000 people in our country illegally every year.

Congress would establish three specific goals to fix this prob-lem. The process would need to demonstrate alignment with our issue, include the cost, have a stated outcome, and be measurable. Additionally the time frame for solving the issue would need to conform to the three-year limit for any bills that require funding. The process would be fairly simple once the goals were established.

National Issue: Insecure borders and weak visa monitoring.

Goal number one:

Reduce the number of people that over-stay visas by 80% every year for the next 3 years. This will be done by:

- Increasing the number of visa agents tracking visas by 1000.

- Requiring all sponsoring agents to report to ICE when indi-vidual visas expire.

- Requiring a $2,000 deposit for everyone applying for a

work or study visa. The deposit will be forfeited if the visa is violated.

- Maintaining current quotas for all visa types.

- Requiring all sponsoring agents (schools, business, travel agencies, employment agencies, etc.) to pay an additional $2,000 deposit subject to forfeiture for each application.

- Increasing fines for anyone here prior to the introduction of the $2,000 deposit.

Increased costs, fines and forfeit deposits will be used to help fund the changes. Additionally, it has been determined that an annual budget of $25 million will be required to fund Goal number one. Each year the progress will be reported at the State of the Union.

Goal number two:

Reduce the number of people crossing borders illegally by 80% every year for the next 3 years. This will be done by:

- Increasing the number of border agents by 3,000.

- Increasing electronic surveillance to effectively cover the entire southern border. This may include building additional barriers where necessary.

- Renegotiating all treaties with Western Hemisphere nations to include each nation's responsibility toward border security and directly attach progress in meeting that responsibility to all foreign aide to that country. The renegotiation will include host nations incarcerating their citizens who violate our border and are deported from the United States.

- Renegotiating all business contracts with Western Hemisphere nations to include each nation's responsibility toward border security and directly attach progress regarding that responsibility to all business agreements with that country. The renegotiation will include host nations incarcerating their citizens who violate the border and are deported from the United States.

- Third-time offenders will be ineligible for future entry into the United States. Moreover, any of their relatives will be ineligible for entry into the United States. Relatives of third-time offenders who are currently in the United States illegally will be deported immediately.

- Any foreigner who has relatives currently living in the US, legally or not, may petition for a one-time special visit visa once per year. The visa will be good for thirty days and individuals will be eligible as long as they honor the visa.

It has been determined that an annual budget of $500,000,000 dollars will be required to fund goal number two. Each year the progress will be reported at the State of the Union.

Goal number three:

Establish a national plan addressing all people currently here illegally. This plan will be developed by:

- Asking all Americans the following question, "Should all illegal immigrants be deported?" If the answer is "yes," then Congress should develop a plan to complete all deportations within a three-year period.

- If the answer is "no" then Congress should develop a second survey asking for guidance from the PEOPLE (see below).

This goal might be a bit more difficult to develop because it would require follow-up guidance from the PEOPLE. However, once Congress is instructed, the goal would be simple. I am one of those who believe all illegal immigrants should not be deported. I believe they should be allowed to get on some pathway to citizenship, but it is not the "Constitution of Dave." It is the "Constitution of the United States." So, everyone needs to be involved in the decision.

Let's assume that Americans choose not to deport all illegal immigrants. The second follow-up survey may ask Americans to choose three, four, or five options from a larger list (as well as include an "other" space for Americans to direct Congress on how to proceed). It might look like the survey below:

Place a Y (for yes) or N (for no) in the box to the left of each item

	They should be allowed a pathway to citizenship
	They should be allowed to become legal residents
	They should all be treated the same
	The length of time they have lived here should be taken into account. Please elaborate: Less than ______ years they should be deported More than ______ years they should be allowed to stay
	Their employment history should be taken into account. Please select one: ___If they are currently working they should be allowed to stay ___If they have worked for at least ____ years they should be allowed to stay
	Their tax history should be taken into account. Please elaborate: If they pay taxes they should be allowed to stay If they have ever paid taxes they should be allowed to stay If they paid taxes for at least ____ years they should be allowed to stay

	Their police record should be taken into account. Please elaborate: If they have any record, misdemeanor or felony, they should be deported If they have a felony they should be deported If they have not been convicted of a violent crime they should be allowed to stay If they have been convicted of a DUI they should be allowed to stay
	Their family should be taken into account. Please elaborate: If any member of their family is a legal resident or citizen they should be allowed to stay If they have a family, legally or illegally here, they should be allowed to stay
	Anyone allowed to stay should pay a fine
	Anyone allowed to stay should do community service
	Anyone allowed to stay should pass an English test
	Other

Once the survey above is collated, Congress would be obliged to introduce a bill conforming to the principles of alignment, measurability, cost accountability and the proper time line.

This would be a process driven by the PEOPLE. Elected officials would respond to the PEOPLE's wishes. With technology being what it is today, presenting choices and gathering input would be a fairly quick and simple process.

The National Issues web site would be a "go to" site for Americans. They can express their concerns, engage in issue-related topics, provide guidance, offer suggestions and follow the status of progress on all issues on a national site that is accessible to everyone. Congress would be held responsible for doing as they are directed. I am not sure a process could be any more transparent.

Obviously, some issues and information would have to be addressed behind closed doors. However, even those issues can be decided by the American public. We all understand the importance of national security and can offer guidelines for when that would apply. Politicians would not be able to summarily choose what should be classified. Any "privilege" that allows politicians to keep information from the PEOPLE would be thoroughly scrutinized and agreed upon by the PEOPLE.

In summary, the immigration issue would be more accurately described as an illegal immigration issue, and more specifically a border/visa control problem. Using agreed upon data, the current impact of the problem would be stated, specific goals targeting each of those concerns would be listed, projected costs would be included and all of it would be tied to a timeline. The original issue and the goals would be presented at the State of the Union. Congress would then act on it by allocating funding and reporting back to the PEOPLE at subsequent State of the Union addresses.

The performance of each politician: getting relevant bills passed, aligning solutions to the will of the PEOPLE, staying within budget, timeliness of reporting, voting records as they pertain to the wishes of the PEOPLE, etc. would all be measured and used to determine an overall rating for all congressional and executive servants. This information would also be presented at the State of the Union.

Too good to be true. Right? Wrong. It is not only possible, I would suggest it would be very easy if...our citizens were all self-actualized, independent and shared a common culture and language? If we were like the people we see in the *Star Trek* universe, this would be very simple to do. I would dare say it would be the only way people in the future would think to do it. It is logical, measurable and transparent. It empowers citizens, not politicians. It focuses on issues not ideologies. It emphasizes moving forward, not gridlock.

As with many things I have talked about in this book, we are our own worst enemy. We have either been suckered into believing that the way things are, is the only way they can be. Or, we are part of the group doing the suckering. In either case we are defying a basic law of physics: objects move in the path of least resistance. The process proposed above would feel very natural to all of us, but we don't choose it. We seem to deliberately choose the most difficult path. We continue to run through the maze. We do this because we are told to, not because we have to or want to. It is time to destroy the maze.

Perhaps space is not the final frontier. Perhaps our minds are. It has always fascinated me when I talk to ideologues (most of whom insist they aren't) and it is so clear to them how right they are, and how wrong those with whom they disagree are. As a former member of a religion, I can tell you when I talk to political ideologues I feel as though I am talking to a devout believer. Reality is theirs to define, and everyone else must try to fit into it. In our current condition we go to great lengths to avoid doing what is easy and effective. Maybe it's not about boldly going where we haven't gone before, but rather to boldly stop going where we are going now.

Chapter 10

First Steps

As the last of three different Enterprises is holding on for dear life, the anomaly that is destroying the universe is nearly collapsed. The Enterprise from the past and the Enterprise from the present were destroyed trying to contain it. The Enterprise from the future is the last chance. After Data announces the other two Enterprises have been destroyed, Q appears and says, "Two down, one to go." Data confirms that the anomaly is nearly collapsed, but LaForge reports that the ship is losing containment of the anti-matter.

The ship is about to explode and Picard is out of options. Q smiles and says, "Goodbye, Jean-Luc. I'm going to miss you. You had such potential. But then again, all good things must come to an end." Jordy speaks his final words, "Containment field is at critical. I'm losing it!" There is an explosion, the Enterprise appears to be lost. The scene changes and Picard finds himself in the courtroom he originally appeared in years ago when he was on trial for the crimes of humanity. Picard is with Q who opens the conversation.

"The Continuum didn't think you had it in you, Jean-Luc, but I knew you did." Picard begins to realize that his plan worked and the Enterprise survived. The anomaly that was destroying the whole universe completely collapsed. Jean-Luc, with the help of Q had traveled between three different time periods scrambling to figure out what the anomaly was and how to stop it. He discovered the anomaly got bigger as he went back in time. The paradox was confusing at first and appeared to offer no solution, but Picard finally figured it out.

Unbeknownst to Picard, Q was transporting him back and forth through time. As he kept slipping into different times, Picard enlisted the aid of the Enterprise crews from two other time periods to enter the anomaly and create a static warp shell. Although two of the Enterprises were destroyed by this move, the third survived and collapsed the anomaly. To everyone's extreme relief, and in the words of Q, Picard had, "saved humanity once again." Picard responded by saying he hoped he would not cross paths with Q again. Q told Picard that he just didn't get it. He said, "The trial never ends. We wanted to see if you had the ability to expand your mind and your horizons. And for one brief moment you did."

Picard realizes that it was Q's help that guided him to see the paradox. He thanked Q. Q smiled and said, "For that one fraction of a second, you were open to options you had never considered. That is the exploration that awaits you. Not mapping the stars and studying nebulae, but charting the unknowable possibilities of existence."

In the final scene of this final episode of *Star Trek; The Next Generation* ("All Good Things…" S7; E25 & 26), the senior staff are playing poker like they have on many occasions throughout the series. And for the first time, Picard enters and asks to join the game. He expresses regret that he hadn't done so earlier. Troi tells him he was always welcome as the game of five-card stud begins.

One of the themes that is consistently reinforced throughout all the *Star Trek* franchises is not giving up, doing whatever it takes to overcome any obstacle. Our future counterparts refuse to say "no." They live their daily lives by respecting others and understanding they have purpose. However, it is in times of real need that they really shine. Their training and experience helps them control their fear. They stay focused on the problem and true to their cause. Their ability to trust in each other and work together sees them through many trials. Most of all, they share the vision.

We are a long way from that future, but it is not out of reach. We have been trained to rely on business or government to create our reality, establish our goals and define our future. As our nation has grown, the efforts of big business and big government have become more relentless and more invasive. Our own dreams have been stolen and replaced by corporate dreams. Our personal liberty has eroded, and our actions, our words, even our thoughts, are more restrained. We have allowed this to happen. In some ways it is easier for us. When things go wrong we can blame someone else. If we abdicate responsibility then we don't have to face our own mistakes or our own failures. As a result we, each of us, have learned to identify with certain groups and/or designate other groups that we can readily blame for whatever misfortune befalls us. Group thought and group identity offer anonymity and for some that means safety.

This way of thinking is anathema in the world of *Star Trek*. If *Star Trek* teaches us anything, it is that individuals are the most important variable in any equation. Challenge, change, and disruptions are natural occurrences in life, and are presented to each of us in different ways. If we fail to respond on our own and choose rather to defer action to others, we are in a sense giving up. That is not to say we don't need help, or shouldn't seek it. We will always need help. Indeed, it is in seeking help that individuals come together to form communities. WE THE PEOPLE came into being as the result of individuals seeking help from each other. That is what America is all about. But the help needed should be, must be, determined by the individual. More importantly, the individual needs to participate in that process. We can never learn from our mistakes or meet new challenges if we are not part of the process.

When we presume others will take care of our problems, or when we blame others for our problems, we begin to close doors figuratively and literally. We stop growing. Curiosity, the need to know, is one of the fundamental traits of humanity. There is no need to know, no need to grow, when others will take care of us. Further, as we blame others for our problems and depend on others to solve them, there is no need to seek help. Communities are replaced by residential areas, neighbors are replaced by strangers, and lending a hand is replaced by not wanting to get involved.

As the power and control of big business and big government grow, we fade into the background of life, not really living it, just existing. Certainly this does not apply to everyone, but as each day passes the number of people fading into the background increases. Like Jean-Luc Picard whose paradox was a problem getting bigger as he went back in time, we are faced with our own paradox: The challenges we face today require large collective efforts. However, the more resources we commit to these efforts the worse they become.

I have described these challenges throughout the book and speculated on why they appear to be nonexistent in the future portrayed in *Star Trek*. In the introduction I suggested we could use *Star Trek* as a blueprint for how to move our society to more closely mirror that kind of future. In this chapter I will offer some suggestions.

Although it might sound counterintuitive, the solution for getting us to our goal of a society without war, want, crime and money, a society where everyone lives in harmony with each other and our planet is very simple: Us. Each of us. All of us.

To be sure, in today's very divisive America it will be a challenge, but from this challenge we can grow. What is important to remember is that the individual, especially the self-actualized individual, is the most important variable in any effort. With this in mind, my suggestions will not rely on government or business to lead us. WE will lead them.

The very first step is to acknowledge that we are more alike than different. We must learn to identify as Americans. Identifying ourselves by focusing on our differences only serves to retard our growth. Identity politics does not recognize individuals and can actually strengthen prejudice. In the future we have worked hard to get rid of prejudice. (Although, as Data points out in "Encounter at Farpoint" (*Star Trek: TNG*; S1, E1) prejudice is "very human.") Nonetheless, prejudice seems to have been conquered. In that future identity organizations are gone. We are all the same, and as self-actualized individuals we have come together to build something special.

To the extent each individual contributes to society, that society evolves more quickly. It is the People that make up any culture. Not politicians. Not CEO's. Not government. It is the people that need to establish our society. Therefore, it needs to be the People leading the effort for change. We have spent a couple hundred years building obstacles, painting our current false reality to convince ourselves that what we have today is just the way it has to be. So it will be a long struggle and we need to understand there is no such thing as a single right answer. There will be mistakes and we will rely on small steps. Steps that each of us can take.

Our cultural values define us and help strengthen our society. I will offer ideas in support of a culture consistent with the *Star Trek* universe. These ideas are meant to empower individuals. They are first-steps in becoming self-actualized. This whole approach is built on the notion that we need to step-up and take responsibility for change, not leave it to others; that change can come slowly and still be effective and sustainable; that until *individuals* change their behaviors real change will never occur.

I have grouped ideas by general categories that are in no particular order. The ideas are meant to be something each person can do immediately to start the process of becoming self-actualized. They are all partial lists. However, I have created two spaces to discuss the lists, share new ideas and share experiences. I have created a private group on Facebook called, "Make it So…America." I have also created a blog at www.makeitsoamerica.blogspot.com. You are encouraged to join the groups and the discussion.

Your ideas, your leadership, your participation are important. This effort will require all of us to work together, to find new ways of transforming small changes into big changes.

Social networking

1. We can use social networking to gather ideas and discuss our future, to create a coalition to discuss problems in America with a commitment not to use color or gender in our discussion. We should define problems and solutions without reference to color, gender, religion, creed, or favorite sports team. Those subgroups will distract us.

2. Create your own chat to set up a single day when you will change a behavior. Maybe your passion is recycling. Contact a friend online and make a date to devote your whole day to supporting recycling: What you eat, wear, where you go, how you get there…all of it. And celebrate the day online. Ask friends to "like" or "share" your post. Ask friends to join you the next time. Other ideas include helping a neighbor, giving a homeless person a meal, spending an hour or two at your child's school. A movement starts with one person who is committed to a cause. Social networks can help with this process. Using social networks to share individual change provides a wider audience and increases opportunities for changing others' behaviors.

3. Find a picture that includes people of all races and post it to some close friends. Challenge the group to describe everyone without using color. Talk to each other about the differences and the similarities in the descriptions. Do this often and include more friends each time, until it becomes easier to see beyond color.

4. This is a two-parter.

- Part 1: Record a ten to twenty second excerpt from a favorite poem or passage and post it to some close friends. Have everyone reply with what they heard and how they interpreted it. Talk about the differences and similarities and try to determine the basis for each.

- Part 2: Do the same thing with a ten to twenty second excerpt from a politician's speech. Perhaps we can begin to focus on messages rather than the messenger. Having these types of discussions will broaden our understanding and open our minds to solutions rather than allowing us to remain trapped by our own biases.

5. Facebook has become a dumping ground for memes that disparage others. The political ones are the manifestation of the politics of polarization. We need to combat this. If you're one of those who generally post memes that support your ideology, challenge yourself. Find someone, or something you support from the opposite side of where you sit ideologically. Share that support, post it on Facebook. Conversely, identify someone or something from the same side of the ideological fence as you whom you believe to be wrong, post it on Facebook, share why you disagree. As an alternative, stop sharing these kind of memes.

Personal Behavior

1. Choose a language you hear in your community that is not your mother tongue. Learn how to say, "Hello, how are you?" and "Thank you." Then say it to three different people.

   - One person you know that can speak the language so that it might inspire you to learn more.

   - One person you don't know that can speak the language so that you might make a new friend.

- One person you know that can't speak the language so that they might be inspired to try.

2. Commit to one week (Seven consecutive days) of no TV and no Internet. (There is an international screen-free week every year usually in the April/May time frame.) Find some books, write letters to friends and family, write a short story, work in the yard, volunteer in your community. Do anything but watch TV and go online. Spend two of those days with your neighbors and tell them what you are doing. Share your experience, what you miss most, what you don't miss at all, and encourage your neighbors to try the same "diet."

3. Introduce yourself to a stranger, someone who doesn't look like you. Tell them who you are and what you are doing. Ask if they would be willing to sit down with you over coffee or a beer, just to get to know each other. Share your experience with a friend and encourage her or him to try it. Encourage your new friend to do the same.

4. If you like watching the news on TV, spend five days not watching the news on TV. Instead go to a web search for "unbiased news" and spend four of those days from that week getting your news from four different news sources. On the fifth day search for, and get your news from a non-American web site. Share your experience with your friends. Perhaps post a short review of what you learned online. Encourage others to do the same. Repeat this practice often.

5. Read and learn about economic sharing. Choose a particular industry and try one of their services. For example, when I travel abroad I use Airbnb instead of hotels. I stay at people's homes and get a better feel of the community. I don't have room service and linen service, but this forces me to go to local markets and get things done on my own. It puts money into the hands of regular people, or small businesses,

not corporations. Try it. Share your experiences and encourage others to try it.

6. Learn to prepare a meal from outside your culture…something you don't usually eat. Try it a few times to get it as good as you can; then invite someone you know from that culture to dinner. Breaking bread together is a powerful way to build relationships with others. Sharing a cultural dish can open new doors into that culture. Tell your friend why you did this and encourage them to try it as well. Maybe they can prepare a meal from your culture and have you over for dinner in the future. Share your experience and encourage others to try.

7. Learn about conscious capitalism. Conscious Capitalism, Inc.'s stated purpose is, "Recognizing that every business has a purpose that includes, but is more than, making money." It suggests that business is a form of human social organization: people getting together for a purpose, to do something together, to deliver value to themselves and others. You can read more about it online at www.consciouscapitalism.org. Find companies that support this and try to shift your shopping behaviors to support those companies. Share what you learn and your efforts with your friends.

8. Start a garden…big or small, a garden can offer a great sense of accomplishment as well as providing healthy alternatives to supermarkets. If possible join a community garden or start one. Aurora, Colorado is a great example of how to incorporate community gardens into neighborhoods and city planning. They offer a lot of suggestions and ideas. You can go to www.auroragov.org for more information. Include a neighbor or two. Share your experience and encourage others to try.

9. I'd like to propose a toast, no really, a new toast. Use it whenever you are with friends celebrating an event. Stand up and raise your glass then say, "May you only want what you need, and may you need very little."

Political Behavior

1. Support and spread the word on the "Yes/No" question rule. (I just made this rule up.) All politicians should be required to answer "Yes" or "No" to yes/no questions. When you hear a politician not answer in that way, point it out on Facebook. Have a group dedicated to tracking politicians and collecting data as to which politicians answer with a yes or no, and which politicians try to avoid answering. Invite your friends and share the posts as much as you can.

2. Open a Petition Chat where like-minded people can generate and sign petitions that begin to stop the divide within our government. Some suggestions:

    • Require presidents to nominate only people from the opposite party for federal judge positions. The Supreme Court is no longer following the Constitution, they are "fitting" it into their ideologies. That needs to stop. Ideology does not create unity. If presidents were forced to appoint people from the other party, they would choose more center-based appointees that would be more likely to see the Constitution as the law and not a tool to shape law. Perhaps we could bring the Court back from extreme activism.

    • Require the House and the Senate to alter their seating every session. Do not allow the aisle in the middle to become a barrier that defines each side by ideology. Use members' height, random letters or numbers, alphabetical order, any random means to frequently change seat location. Proximity can assist in getting to know someone. The House and the Senate is no place to establish firm divisions.

- Prohibit Congressional caucuses that are defined by physical and spiritual differences. As our national legislators, the only group Congress should be focused on are Americans… all Americans.

3. Are you a one-party voter? Do you always vote the "ticket"? Here's an idea: Choose one candidate (actually look at the issues) from the other party and vote for that candidate in the next election. Break with the party for one candidate. Step across that line once and, when you realize the world does not come to an end you might try it again. Share your experience and how it made you feel. Encourage others to try it.

4. After the next election, cut out a couple of hours of time. Sit down and write out a list of four or five issues that are important to you. Look at your life to make the choices, not an elected official's speeches! After you list four or five items, write out what you would like to see done about those issues. Try to write how you would approach those issues. Keep this list safe until the next election and then compare it with what candidates are saying. Support the candidate who agrees closest with what you want. There are many websites that can help. Here are a couple: www.isidewith.com and www.ontheissues.org. It takes time and effort, but we should not be voting by party, looks, gender, race or any other meaningless measure. You should vote for a person with whom you agree. DON'T SETTLE for the "least bad" candidate. Share your experience with others. Encourage them to try it.

5. Learn to use the word "some" when talking about groups. "Some liberals say….""Some conservatives believe…,""Some

short people….," "Some Cardinals fans…." Individual behavior should not be ascribed to a whole group. It serves to divide and to remove individual accountability.

6. If you are a Republican or Democrat, quit the Party.

Environment

1. Commit to live totally in harmony with nature for one day a month. Don't drive, eat only organic food, use only packaging that is completely biodegradable, use environmentally friendly candles for lighting. Do whatever you can think of that has little or no impact on our planet. Do some research and learn what you will need to do and how to prepare for it. Then do it. Share your experience with friends and online.

2. Are you a gift giver? Here's an idea. Identify one friend with whom you can experiment with gift-giving. Talk to them first and explain that you are trying to change a behavior. Ask your friend what kinds of tasks they usually do during the week with which you can help. It might be cutting the grass, doing laundry, sweeping out the garage, etc. Then write four or five of the tasks on a piece of paper and give that paper to your friend for his birthday or Christmas. Explain to him that he can choose one task and you will complete if for him one time in lieu of a present. Share your experience with others and encourage others to try. For the next "cycle" of gift giving, choose two friends. This practice is good for the environment and will also enrich your friendship.

3. Do you work out at a gym? Do you use the treadmill? Here's an idea. Choose one day a month that you normally would work on the treadmill and just jog in the park, or around the neighborhood instead. This will reduce the energy we take from our planet. It might result in meeting a new friend as

well. Share your experience with others and encourage them to try it. After a few months, choose two days a month to stop the treadmill from burning energy.

4. Stop using straws unless you have a physical need to do so. Straws are made of plastic and are non-biodegradable. I have no idea how many straws America goes through each year, but they end up in landfills and are now part of a floating island of garbage in the North Pacific sea. If you use a straw simply for convenience, learn to hold a cup, bring it to your face, open your mouth and take a sip when you want one… pretty simple operation actually. And it has great potential if you consider the pollution that is generated by producing billions of straws as well as the amount of garbage created. Encourage your friends to try it.

5. The next time you go shopping for clothes, commit to buying no clothes with logos or writing. Nothing with any branding at all. And select natural fibers only. Share what you did with friends. Encourage them to do the same.

6. Use the carbon footprint rating chart and behavior rubric to analyze your current carbon footprint. Copy the worksheet (Appendix C) to calculate your score, set and track your goal. Share your experience with a friend and encourage others to try it.

Education

1. Whether you have children, or not, volunteer at your school. Contact the front office and ask how you can help. Start with one hour a month and go from there. Share your experience with your friends. Talk about it online.

2. If you have a child in school, develop a homework station

and a schedule for your child/children to follow. Encourage her to do her best and celebrate the completion of assignments as well as achievements. Share your experience with a neighbor and encourage them to do the same.

3. Join your school's PTA or PTO and get involved. Ask any neighbors and friends who have children in the same school to join.

4. Attend school board meetings.

5. Read your child's/children's history texts. Know what is being taught. Discuss it with your children. Let them see your interest and challenge your child by offering an alternative point of view to that in the text if you wish to. Share your experience with others.

6. Invite a teacher to your home for dinner. Don't talk about education or your child. Use it as an opportunity to make a new friend. Encourage your neighbors and friends to do the same.

7. Read to your child every day. Find a neighbor or friend with a child close to the same age and have everyone read the same book. Then you can discuss the book together…perhaps online, but it is better in person. Let your child see your enthusiasm. Share your experience.

As you can see these are partial lists and can be implemented immediately. Start small, and do not try more than one or two in the beginning. The important piece of this is to complete an item, any item and share it. You can go to the online spaces I previously mentioned to share your experience, but it is even better to share it with a friend you see regularly. You can also go to the spaces to add suggestions for the lists above, or add a new list altogether. Self-actualization is a state of being that strives for growth. Small successes in the beginning can produce larger successes, as well as increasing the number of people working together. But, it requires YOU to make changes and, in a sense, become a leader…a leader within a group of one. You can expand your efforts as you gain confidence and comfort with the process.

As promised, there are no magic solutions. You have probably heard some of these ideas. They are not about changing the government, but rather changing us first, to help us self-actualize. They help point us in a direction that builds a common culture based on face-to-face interactions and personal experiences, not government programs. Personal relationships are our best chance to build respect, trust and understanding. These ideas are designed to build a culture of empowerment, to help us remember that we are the most important players on the team and we do not belong on the bench. That is our greatest strength: self-determination. While it can be slow, and may sometimes lead us astray, it also holds the potential for greatness.

If you are one of those who believe America has peaked and can no longer be a benefit to the globe, if you believe our past mistakes cannot be forgiven and certainly will not be forgotten, if you believe America should be fundamentally changed to reflect other countries, then these ideas are not for you…yet. I believe in time they could be.

I believe commitment to this effort will help remind those of us who have forgotten, what America is all about. Those younger Americans who have learned to dislike America, or learned to remember only our mistakes, will have an opportunity to see what made this nation great for the first time. Our mistakes have cost lives and caused suffering. But we have also saved many lives and healed a lot of suffering around the world.

I don't want to sound cliche, but the lives that have been lost and the suffering that resulted from mistakes will have all been in vain if we simply walk away. Mistakes are no reason to quit. In the episode I talked about above, Captain Picard placed three different Enterprises at risk, losing two, to make up for a mistake. Had he simply walked away all would have been lost. Had he dwelled on the mistake, all would have been lost. He recognized the mistake, but moved to correct it.

In a sense, the United States is the very first USS Enterprise. This nation boldly went where no nation had gone before. We began with the basic notion that individuals should have liberty, freedom of choice, and control over their own destiny. That is truly the American dream. Not a house with a white picket fence, but a life that each person can choose, in a nation in which all have the same opportunities, with a government that listens and supports their wishes. Yes, some were left out. But many have struggled to change those mistakes. I believe that is how our efforts should be spent: Stay true to our origins, and make sure that all are included.

Some believe it is too late for America, or that what it was and what it meant no longer have relevance. They believe the proper course for the USS America is to find a nice planet, beam everyone down with a promise to care for them, and leave the ship in a decaying orbit to be destroyed once it enters the atmosphere. They believe exploration and discovery are too dangerous, and not everyone is up to the task. They believe America has done the best it will ever do and it is time to stop searching…sit down, flip on the TV and grab a cold one…let the experts handle things. I could not disagree more. Being a leader is difficult, but necessary. If the choice is letting the bankers, lawyers, and politicians lead, or building a society that inspires individuals to lead, I would choose the latter, mistakes and all.

To those who oppose allowing America to exist as it was created, I would ask patience. It may not happen until season 9, episode 21 of your life, but at some point in the future it will happen. A friend of yours, a distant relative, a relative of a friend, a friend of a relative that was distant but is now close…someone will come to you and say, "I just tried this idea I heard about from a friend. I learned how to say, 'Hello, how are you?' in Chinese and I said it to a clerk at the Chinese market on the corner. I don't think she speaks English. When she heard me, her face kinda lit up, and she smiled and said it back to me. She said something else, but I didn't understand what it was. It was really cool though. I am going to learn a little more and go back there again. You should try it."

When that happens, you will know that all is not lost. America's journey is not about giving up. It is about moving forward. Mistakes are not a reason to quit, but a way to learn. This nation can help earth become a Federation-ready planet, but it needs everyone on board. This journey may span the next two centuries. We'll make more mistakes and more lives will be lost before we figure it all out. But, like Captain Picard above, we will figure it out—we will make things right.

Like the colony on Omicron Ceti III that I talked about in Chapter One, we are being controlled. We believe this is the way it should be. We believe we should let experts make our decisions for us. We believe we need to struggle in life, rather than to thrive. We believe life is supposed to wear us down rather than raise us up. We believe owning great things is more important than doing great things. We believe war is inevitable, and peaceful coexistence is impossible. We believe dreamers are naive and reality is harsh. Just as Captain Kirk struggled to break free of the influence of the spores on Omicron Ceti III, we must break free of our "spore's" influence. Life is not supposed to be like this. Life should be an adventure for everyone. That does not mean challenges will not present themselves, but we should not be creating challenges that would otherwise not exist.

We need to believe we can expand our minds and our horizons. This is what we are here for. Without exploration, without discovery, our species might as well swing from tree branches. Risk and failure will occur; it is only natural. It is not the role of government to create a safe space for all of us. It is the role of government to ensure that each of us has an opportunity to soar, to dream, to choose our tomorrows…and for each of us to be able to handle the failures and challenges that come naturally.

Our future counterparts know this. I have provided many examples and there are many, many more that remind us that when we allow ourselves to be controlled by others, no matter how benign they may seem, we are not fulfilling our destiny as free human beings. Rather than fearing our inborn need to be free, we should celebrate it. To paraphrase Q, we need to recognize that we can, and should, be open to options we have never considered before. We should recognize that beyond any technology and new discoveries, it is the human spirit that will allow us to, "Explore strange, new worlds, to seek out new life and new civilizations, to boldly go where no one has gone before."

APPENDICES

Appendix A

The Food Exchange

The food exchanges are designed to provide food for all their members. (Membership would be determined geographically.) The two primary functions of the food exchange would be to eliminate the chemical and sugar additives commonly put into foods today, as well as to reduce the distance between food production and delivery. By reducing the distance, we can eliminate a lot of the carbon emissions used to transport food—especially processed and refrigerated foods—across the country.

Although credits could be used to get food, working at the food exchange can also earn credits, or a direct swap of food. Much like the principles practiced by the Aldeans, whatever is taken, something is given ("When the Bough Breaks" *Star Trek:TNG*; S1, E17); anyone who worked at the food exchange could use that effort to "purchase" food. However, all credits would be accepted. Individuals wanting other foods not offered through the exchange would have to work out how to get them.

The food exchange would be a system of farms (dairy and produce), fisheries, hatcheries, and small and large game preserves. Food exchanges would be limited in distance from the population served. Each food exchange, for example, might service an area of 2,500 square miles. Each food exchange might have several production sites—farms (gardens), dairies, fisheries, hatcheries and small game preserves—spread throughout its zone. Moreover, anyone living within the particular zone could grow food that could be used individually, or collectively through the exchange.

Food exchange markets (FEM) would be established to balance the delivery distance with the convenience of its members. In this society where working for money is replaced by working for time, people would have more time to shop, prepare and eat meals. People would not do their shopping at one location, nor would they buy groceries "for the week." They might go to the FEM every other day for fresh produce and dairy products. Small granaries would be established and members might go there once a month to buy what they need.

The fisheries and small game preserves would be maintained by the food exchange. However, those wanting fish and meat would be responsible for catching, cleaning and butchering. Obviously, there would need to be limitations for each member to insure the needs of the many get met. Perhaps each adult citizen might be eligible for one or two animals and a few fish a week (The animal here is small: rabbit, squirrel, chicken, etc.).

Using that quota and a family of four (two parents) as an example, the monthly shopping might look like the following. Once a month someone would go to the small game reserve to hunt. Because of their tastes, they kill four chickens and three rabbits and maybe a duck. Once a month someone would go to the granary and get wheat and oats for cereal and baking bread. Four times a week someone would go to the local FEM and pick up fresh produce and dairy products.

Of course, by living in communities in which members help each other, efforts at any of the "shopping" could be combined so that one person might do the hunting for three or four households. They may go on a three-day hunting trip and love it. Someone else who loves to bake bread might do it for a whole block of neighbors. Sharing would be a practice that would have become second nature in this society.

The exception to the 2,500 square mile area of service might be large game and beef. There might be one ranch and one large game preserve to service three or four food exchanges. However, the process would be the same. Individuals who wanted large game or beef would be responsible for going to the ranch or game preserve and killing, cleaning and butchering the animal. Again there would be some quota and, again, one individual might do the work for several neighbors.

I want to digress a bit. In a future with food replicators animals are no longer "enslaved for food purposes" ("Lonely Among Us" *Star Trek: TNG;* S1, E7). However, without food replicators there would be a need to enslave animals. Unlike today, though, we would not ship everything to some grocer's meat cooler, or frozen food section. Requiring individuals to do the hunting, fishing and butchering themselves, would probably reduce meat consumption. Requiring restaurants to do the same would further reduce the amount of meat eaten.

Obviously, there would be some logistical challenges given our current living patterns. Large cities of four, five, seven, million people, or even more could not survive on one food exchange for their city in a 2,500 square mile area. As the economy changes from capitalizing on dollar opportunities, to capitalizing on time opportunities, individuals might not be drawn as much to the big city that has all the jobs.

In addition, large corporations and factories would decentralize their operations to prevent the need to transport products across the country. Decentralizing operations would help draw populations away from high-density areas. As the current model of a standard forty-hour week transitioned, individuals could move where they wanted, rather than be forced to live where the jobs are. In the event many people wanted to stay in a particular city, there might be a need for two food exchanges together, or a particular part of an exchange could be shared. For instance, a single hunting preserve might serve two, or more food exchanges. Whatever the challenge, a solution could be found.

There would be seasonal crops. Consumers would have to adapt to not getting some things all year long. Perhaps cold areas like Minnesota might not be able get the variety of fresh fruits year round that they get today. People would have to re-learn how to preserve foods they liked. This would result in a hybrid society of agriculture/industry in which individuals would participate more in the preparation and storage of food items.

From a birds-eye view as one looked down on a community, one might see solar bicycles, wireless…everything, a maglev rail system, and sophisticated construction methods used for building, mixed in with local fresh produce markets, backyard composting, natural materials for clothing and people hunting.

Citizens would be more central to providing food, and large corporations would no longer be in control. This approach helps communities bond as different individuals might form small groups that share in the hunting, collecting, and preparation of food. Also, the environment would be less damaged because our carbon footprint would shrink. Lastly, our garbage wouldn't become the separate threat as it is today. With far less packaging and more organic food products, most of the waste could be recycled or composted away.

Appendix B

Religion

Religion is a very sensitive issue to talk about, especially if the discussion concerns dismantling it. At first glance there seems to be a bit of a dichotomy in the *Star Trek* universe. God does not exist, yet spirituality is respected and no judgments are made about those who have spiritual beliefs. However, god is not religion. Religion is what occurs when god is given money. In a community of self-actualized citizens where poverty and hunger no longer existed, and without money, organized religion would be much different, if it existed at all. It is more likely that individuals would practice their spirituality in a way that strengthened their personal bond with their deity as opposed to funding international TV networks and megachurches.

I believe individual choice, and respect for that choice would lead not only to a breaking apart of organized religion, but also would prevent an active push to stop or ban religion. Self-actualized citizens are not subject to other people's insecurities. The belief in individual liberty, and respect for each individual's rights would preclude organized efforts to squelch anyone's personal belief. I don't think a government that is based on liberty would be involved in attempting to eliminate religious beliefs.

If you have always been a non-believer, you may not understand the power of faith. Although thresholds of tolerance vary between members of any religion, a strong majority of followers would react in a similar fashion when they reached their threshold…they would fight, die and possibly kill for their god. To many believers right now, religion is god. Asking a believer to get rid of her religion would be like asking a non-believer to remove one arm and one leg voluntarily: not many volunteers could be found.

Any government that pushed hard enough would find itself in a clash that would include violence, and could escalate into something that no one wants. I understand those atheists who see faith and/or god as an enemy to science. However, in reality no scientist can produce proof god doesn't exist. There is proof that stories from the bible are not factual…but there is no proof that god doesn't exist. If we want a society in which everyone respects each other, then we need to recognize that proving who's right is not necessarily a search for truth.

I believe truth always wins out and that in time religion will evolve away. Indeed, that is currently happening. According to a 2012 Pew Research Center survey, the fastest growing religious cohort group in America are the "nones" (those with no religious affiliation) at 20% of adult Americans. This represents forty-eight million Americans over the age of eighteen. Another Pew Research Center survey revealed that between 2007 and 2014 the number of followers of Western religion shrank by more than 7%. As the gap between what believers think and what we know to be true shrinks with new knowledge, more believers will simply walk away from religion. This may take longer than non-believers wish, but with an alternative that includes high levels of emotional stress, psychological trauma, and even possible physical violence, patience is the preferred path.

Furthermore, the science hard-liners who see it as their duty to "expose the lies" and try to stop their influence are taking the first steps in creating their own religion. Liberty is not defined as people all choosing to do what is "right." As long as laws are not violated, liberty is defined and practiced by each individual on his/her own terms. It is not for others to create something new that requires adherence.

I understand that many non-believers think religion and god have resulted in the deaths of many people in war. That is not exactly true. Very few wars were fought for god. Most religious wars were about wealth and expansion…god was just a rallying cry. Religion was used as an excuse to kill, and convincing faithful followers was fairly easy and quick. Most of the grunts in those wars—from 5,000 years ago to today— would have happily walked away from war if they'd had an alternative, but when you are a servant to a king or country, defiance can cost you your life. Greed for money, territory or power is what causes war. Religion can be easily enlisted to hide true motives.

On the other hand, religion can also be used for good. Over the years trillions of dollars has been raised by churches and used to help the poor. Despite a decline in membership in congregations, according to a report sponsored by the Giving USA Foundation, churches received more than $114 billion in 2014 alone. In addition to giving financial assistance, religion has also been used to prevent violence. It was god and religion that stopped violence from occurring in Charleston, SC recently when a racist walked into a church and murdered nine people. Unlike other communities, Charleston immediately turned to god first, then responded peacefully to the tragedy…their god did that, not science!

Issues of religion and god require each of us to make some very personal and powerful choices. I have some close friends who are very religious. I would not want to do them any harm. I would not want to shame them. I certainly would not want to claim I know everything. I only know what I believe. Scientists are free to believe the Big Bang had nothing to do with god and was an entirely random event. (Although some suggest the Big Bang is congruent with western creationist beliefs.) They have no proof of that, only their faith in their science. We should not use their faith to attempt to destroy those who have faith in god.

As I see it, the truth is St. Louis, MO. There are two people going there: one from Portland, the other from Phoenix. They are both half way to the destination. Both of them have seen, and will continue to see, very different things along the way, yet they know they are getting closer to the truth. These two travelers' experiences could be considered their truths of the journey. It is understandable that each person's truth is different now. Let's wait until they both get to St. Louis before we insist that one of them is wrong. Like the Buddhists' belief that there is more than one path to Nirvana, perhaps there is more than one path to truth.

Carbon Footprint Rating

SCALE

RATING	WHITE BELT	ORANGE BELT	GREEN BELT	BROWN BELT	BLACK BELT
POINTS	<12	13-18	19-24	25-29	30

There is a behavior rubric on the next page that you can copy and use as a work-sheet to calculate your current carbon footprint using the rating scale above. Explanations for each measurement are in the work sheet.

Start small and tailor it to your needs. The first two categories, "Shelter and Transportation," should be relatively easy to calculate. For "Home Items," you might begin by choosing one room in your house and only select major items (furniture, wall-hangings, floor coverings, etc). For "Home Energy," maybe choose just yourself to begin with. Include electrical items you use regularly. I would further suggest you disregard the kitchen altogether for now. For the "Food" category, since there is no community food exchange, include the percentage of food that was grown in a garden—by you or a friend. For "Clothing" maybe you can take a random sample of clothes from one drawer in a dresser, or one section of a closet. Again, I recommend that you choose just yourself to begin with.

After you calculate your score, identify one category in which you can set an achievable goal. Develop your goal and track your progress. Share your progress with a friend. You are also welcome to share it on the group's blog (www.makeitsoamerica.com). I will post mine there as well. Once you have achieved your goal, you can either set a new goal for yourself or expand the project to include other permanent residents in your home.

Behavior Rubric

POINT VALUE	1	2	3	4	5
SHELTER (square feet) This number represents the number of square feet per permanent resident in the home.	>2,001	1,501-2,000	1,001-1,500	501-1,000	<501
TRANSPORTATION This number represents the percentage of time you use fossil fuels when you leave home. This does not include using mass-transit.	>60%	50-59%	40-49%	30-39%	<30%
HOME ITEMS This number represents the percentage of items in your home that were produced or manufactured within a fifty mile radius of your home.	<60%	60-69%	70-79%	80-89%	>90%
HOME ENERGY This number represents the ratio of electrical items per permanent resident in the home. This number does not include items for basic meal preparation (refrigerator and stove/oven).	>4:1	3:1-4:1	2:1-3:1	1:1-2:1	<1:1
FOOD This number represents the percentage of food eaten by permanent residents of the home, purchased from the community food exchange.	<60%	60-69%	70-79%	80-89%	>90%
CLOTHING This number represents the percentage of clothing that is completely natural. This includes fabric, coloring and any design. This is measured for each permanent resident of the home.	<60%	60-69%	70-79%	80-89%	>90%

www.ingramcontent.com/pod-product-compliance
Lightning Source LLC
Chambersburg PA
CBHW051434250726
48655CB00001B/56